THE WELLINGTON BOMBER

The Wellington Bomber

CHAZ BOWYER

WILLIAM KIMBER · LONDON

First published in 1986 by
WILLIAM KIMBER & CO. LIMITED
100 Jermyn Street, London SW1Y 6EE

Typeset by Print Co-ordination,
Macclesfield, Cheshire.
Printed in Great Britain by
Redwood Burn Limited, Trowbridge, Wiltshire.

To the men and women of the Wellingtons

'*There be of them, that have left a name behind them, that their praises might be reported. And some there be which have no memorial...*'.

Ecclesiasticus IV, 9

Contents

List of Illustrations

Introduction

The Vickers Wellington – or 'Wimpy' as it was universally and most affectionately dubbed by its myriad air and ground crews – was almost unique in several respects. Its greatest claim to fame in the context of Royal Air Force history is usually considered to be the fact that it was produced in greater quantity than *any* other bomber ever to enter RAF service. Yet the Wellington's outstanding record did not rest simply on statistical prominence. Wellingtons saw active employment in the RAF from 1938 to 1953, including operational service from the first to the last days of the 1939-45 war, and during those years readily assumed many vital and, on occasion, pioneering roles. Although designed originally as a pure bomber, the Wimpy quickly undertook with aplomb such diverse and demanding tasks as submarine hunterkiller, torpedo-strike antishipping weapon, reconnaissance eye, supply and freight workhorse, mercy ambulance, VIP and troop transporter, communications hack, experimental vehicle and test-bed, and – possibly of almost equal importance to its original role – as flying classroom for a vast host of embryo operational bomber air crew men.

In its prime bomber role the Wellington was unquestionably the real backbone of the RAF's bombing offensive against the Axis Powers during the first three years of World War Two. For merely two examples of RAF Bomber Command's dependence on the Wimpy, by the spring of 1942 Wellington squadrons comprised some 40 per cent of UK-based bomber striking strength, while a year later Bomber Command still had 15 complete and two part-equipped Wellington squadrons in its firstline strength i.e. over 20 per cent. In other operational spheres Coastal Command Wellingtons alone claimed more than 50 enemy submarines as sunk or at least severely damaged during 1942-45. In the Middle and Far East theatres of war Wellingtons provided a prime long-range offensive capability until heavier, four-engined bombers joined and/or superseded them in that role.

No matter where it operated the Wimpy hugely deserved its

reputation for rugged reliability and, in particular, physical strength. As virtually the last major 'cloth bomber' – i.e. metal-framed with fabric 'skinning' – to see RAF firstline use, the Wellington's unorthodox (then) geodetic style of airframe enabled it to absorb often frightening battle scars and yet still, in numerous cases, continue to bear its human load back to safety; an asset directly responsible for saving the lives of many hundreds of Wimpy air crew members. While summarising the character of the Wellington, perhaps I may also confirm the authentic origin – and *spelling* – of its universal nickname. The Wellington was named after a confederate of the popular cartoon figure Popeye (of contemporary wartime fame in the *Daily Mirror* newspaper); one J. Wellington Wimpy, a rotund, somnolent devotee of the American savoury hamburger – *not* 'Wimp*ey*' as the name continues to be mis-spelt even among some present-day writers.

Patently, no single volume can possibly hope to include *every* facet of such a widely diversified aircraft as the Wellington. Hence, while I have attempted at least to provide here the more significant aspects of its long and doughty career, I prefer to regard what follows in these pages primarily as a sincere tribute, rather than any form of 'academic' history; particularly because excellent examples of the latter already exist as detailed in my list of associated literature at the rear of this volume. Accordingly, I have leaned heavily upon the first-hand experiences and views of those men best qualified to judge the Wimpy – its myriad former air and ground crews. In this respect therefore I might well claim like Montaigne (1533-92): *'It could be said of me in this book I have only made up a bunch of other men's flowers, providing of my own only the string that ties them together.'* I offer the reader no apology for adopting such a form of description – in my personal opinion history is made by humans, not inanimate ironmongery, however much the latter may be necessarily involved, or nostalgia dictates. Nevertheless, it should be added that throughout lengthy correspondence and/or interviews with several hundreds of ex-Wellington crews, one common factor has emerged. With only *very* rare exception, all were unanimous in their praise and sincere affection for the 'good old Wimpy'. I can but hope that they, at least, will approve.

CHAZ BOWYER Norwich, 1986

Acknowledgements

Without the aid and goodwill of very many individuals this book could not have been written. Accordingly, and with deep gratitude, I wish to record my debt to the following. Foremost must be the many ex-Wellington air and ground crews who voluntarily provided me with documents, photographs, and accounts of their service with 'Wimpys', listed here in no significant order. Group Captain P.H. Stembridge, DFC,AFC; Wing Commander A. Ashworth, DSO,DFC,AFC; C. Clark, DFC; E.C. Smith, DFC; C.J. Woodrow; F.R. Cork; A.R. Tettenborn; J. Wright; G. Pearson; J.H. Wade; N. Leonard; T.T. Edwards; P. Healey; R. Thackeray, DFM; T.C. Peters, MBE; the Reverend R.J. Pope, MA,BD; H. Yeoman; D. Bruce; W. Gaul; J.L. Pickersgill, AFC; E.A.J. Evans; J.R. Barnes; J.E. Checketts; R. Silson; J.L. Bulmer; L.J. Gore; T.H. Dean; T.H. Claridge; C.L. Jones; J. Edwards; W. Taylor; E. Roberts, AE; H.D. Rogers; C. Pearce; C.L. Hughes, DFC; L. Butler; R. Pearce; R.D. Rees; W.H. Martin; E.E. Woodhouse; G.A. Stalker, MBE; Squadron Leader B.P. Baker, DFM; F. Hill, E. Richardson; C.F. Hughesden, AFC,FRAeS; J.L. Whitworth, DFC; J.A. Atkins, H.R.W. Kidney; P. Brewster; A.E. Billson, DFC,AE; J. Rees; G. Cole; S.G. Stevens; J.H. Cattee; J. Arthurson; N.V. Jones; E.H. Laithwaite; R. Corlett; A. Rippengale, DFC,DFM; Squadron Leader D. Guthrie; J. Patterson; A.E. Rock; P.S.F. Walmsley, DFC; L.W. Perkins; J. Overton; K. Ketley; P. Seville; J. Dermody; Squadron Leader G. Gray, DFC,AFC; F. Oldfield; D. Francis; B.J. Warren; F. Jenkinson; A.J. Payne; W.D. Spence; W. Williams; J. Fontaine, DFC,CD; J. Rounce, DFC; W.D. Moore; K. Moore; G.F. Osborne; T. Brown; G.G. Lindsay; J.R. Sutton, DFC; J. Murray; Squadron Leader L. Curtis; T.L. Shield; D. Humphries; Captain F.J. Tricklebank; Squadron Leader E.A. Woodhouse; D.R. Emms; R.G. McCadden, DFC; N. Nava; G.L. Gunter; M.W. Griffin; R. Oliver; Wing Commander G.E. Willis, DFC,AFC; H.E. Fryer, DFC,AFC; G.S.W. Challen; Group Captain A. Montagu-Smith; F.H. Cannings; the late AM Sir John Baldwin, KBE,CB,DSO; R. Williams; Group Captain M.J.A. Shaw. DSO; N.E. McIntyre; B.J. Todd; D. Fraser;

W.R. Stevenson. DFM; S.D. Simpson; C. Williams; D. Pinches; L.H. Jordan; A.E. Hands; J. Taylor; W.E. Wilkinson; Squadron Leader J.H.F. Murphy.

In addition to those exWimpy men, many friends, acquaintances, and other aviation history knuts offered their customary unselfish help in a variety of ways. First must be mentioned W.R. Chorley – 'Bill' – who spent untold hours of voluntary unpaid labour on my behalf amongst the official archives to produce invaluable data and statistics for this book. Equally selfless assistance was afforded freely by Norman L.R. Franks; Jerzy B. Cynk; Zdenek Hurt; Bart Rijnhout; Richard L. Ward; Professor David Gunby; David Collyer; Bruce Robertson; Squadron Leader R.C.B. – 'Chris' – Ashworth; Flight Lieutenant 'Andy' Thomas, RAF; Squadron Leader Ray Leach, BA,MBIM,RAF; Bryan Philpott; G.R. – 'Tim' – Wrixon; SAC G. Burston, RAF; Ray C. Sturtivant; Roy Bonser; Ron Wilson of *British Airways News*; David Dorrell, Editor of *Air Pictorial*; David Mason, Editor of *Flight International*; 'Bill' Berry of the RAFA's quarterly *Air Mail*; Mrs P. Bergel; Reg Mack of the RAF Museum; Danny Boon of the Aircrew Association; and the staffs of the RAF Museum, RCAF Archives, and Imperial War Museum Photo Library. My thanks too to the Controller of Her Majesty's Stationery Office. Last, but *never* least, Dave Gray and Jane Richardson of Walkers Studios, Scarborough for their customary skills in producing splendid prints from yellowing and faded private snapshots for my use in illustration of this volume.

CHAPTER ONE

Birth of a Bomber

In October 1932 the Air Ministry put out to tender its official Specification B.9/32, the prime theme of which was a requirement for a twin-engined, medium (*sic*) day bomber possessing a good performance 'envelope', capable of carrying a 'useful' load over a good distance at reasonably high speed. Paradoxically, within such vague terms the specification also detailed the need for a minimum range of merely 720 miles carrying a 1,000lb bomb load, and significantly stipulated that the empty, all-up weight of the aircraft was *not* to exceed 6,300lb. This latter restriction – a direct result of the very recent Geneva Disarmament Conference postulations – immediately limited the type of power plants which could be fitted; while among the possible engines designated for the projected bomber was the steam-cooled Rolls-Royce Goshawk which was optimistically held in high hopes by certain Air Ministry officials at that period.

Such cramping restrictions on all-up weight and power plant dismayed many contemporary British aircraft manufacturers' design teams, but with the existing financial depression both nationwide and indeed worldwide, several manufacturers decided to prepare possible tenders. On 29 May 1933 an official tender conference eventually accepted two contenders for the original B.9/32 Specification; one from the Handley Page firm for its HP52 design – later to emerge as the Hampden bomber – and one from the Vickers firm for its Vickers Type 271, a prototype one-off design which would ultimately 'father' the Vickers Wellington.

Although both firms had produced tenders within the strict parameters of B.9/32, both were also vociferous in their representations to the Air Ministry that the restriction on all-up weight, allied to the inferred official preference for the Goshawk engine, could only result in a far less effective aircraft than might – indeed *could* – be produced if such limitations were discarded. In particular, Reginald – 'Rex' – Pierson, Vickers' Chief Designer, was adamant that the projected bomber must be fitted with the most powerful engines available, whatever the effect on all-up weight *et al*. Pierson's view was fully shared by members of his design team which at that time included men like George Edwards (later, Sir George, CBE) and a restless, uncommon genius Barnes Neville Wallis.

Having joined Vickers initially in September 1931 as an assistant to the firm's Chief Draughtsman (Airships), H. B. Pratt, Barnes Wallis was a devotee of rigid airships for the next 17 years, being responsible within those years for such successful airship designs as the R.80 and the R.100. By 1930, however, Wallis was reluctantly coming to the pragmatic view that the future of the airship was, logically, about to be superseded by that of the aeroplane, and notwithstanding his lingering deep affection for the 'silver queens of the air', he readily accepted an appointment as Chief Designer (Structures) with Vickers on 1 January 1930, and began channelling his legacy of long, ingrained experience and personal invention into the field of heavier-than-air craft; a decision dramatically reinforced with the disastrous demise of the airship R.101 at Beauvais, France in October 1930. Though Wallis had played no part in the design of the R.101, its crash emphasised to him the prosaic wisdom of his decision.

Part of Wallis's legacy of experience with airship design had been his conviction of the efficacy of using the new light alloy metals introduced by industry in general for airship and, now, aeroplane structures; primarily for their huge savings in weight of overall structure, but also as the basis for another avenue of personal research, geodesics*. Put at its simplest definition, geodesics are the shortest distance between two points on any curved surface – derived from the 'great-circle' principle of mathematics utilised in trans-oceanic navigation. The basic application of geodesic principles to aircraft structural design was by no means new in 1930 when Wallis commenced serious investigation into the subject; a similar fuselage construction for a French aircraft had been on public display at the Paris Salon in 1921, for merely one example of earlier application. Nevertheless, Barnes Wallis's eventual introduction of *overall* geodetic construction in airframes was undoubtedly a watershed in British construction methods. His aims were not only to provide substantial savings in overall weight, but also to eliminate unnecessary traditional bulkheads, bracers, *et al*, thus, in effect, offering a self-

* Geodesy: Definition: the mathematical survey and measurement of the earth's surface, involving allowance for curvature. (From Greek: *ge* – the earth, & *daiein* – to divide).

Sir Barnes Wallis – father of the Wellington.

stressing, hollow structure, having a loadbearing safety factor figure virtually twice that of contemporary, traditional structural designs.

Wallis's first venture into complete aeroplane design was with the Vickers M.1/30 project, a fairly conventional single engined, tractor biplane two-seater built in response to a March 1930 official specification for a shipborne torpedo-bomber. Wallis incorporated plentiful light alloy, duralumin, in its construction, though no geodetics, and the completed aircraft proved greatly lighter in overall weight than was usual for the period. In the event, the M.1/30 (it was never given a name) was first test-flown on 11 January 1933 by John – 'Mutt' – Summers, Vickers' chief test pilot, but was eventually destroyed when it broke up in mid-air while under test on 23 November 1933; its crew of Summers and John Radcliffe managed to to evacuate their respective cockpits by parachute safely. In the interim Wallis became involved in designs of new projects to meet the requirements of Air Ministry Specification G.4/31 for a 'general purpose bombing and torpedo aeroplane' (*sic*). To meet this requirement, the Vickers' design team prepared three alternative possible designs, for two monoplanes and a biplane. In the event the Air Ministry opted for the trusted, traditional biplane configuration and accordingly gave Vickers an order for 150 biplanes. Wallis proceeded with the 'acceptable' biplane design, despite his personal preference for a monoplane, and incorporated geodetic structure in the G.4/31 biplane's fuselage, though having to employ standard-constructed wing assemblies in deference to Air Ministry preference.

Meantime Wallis persuaded his Vickers 'masters' to go ahead with the monoplane project as a private venture, and into this he incorporated a complete geodetic construction throughout the airframe. In his own words:

> The Wellesley [as this monoplane venture was ultimately named] is metal constructed on an entirely new principle – the Vickers-Wallis 'Geodetic' system....... all parts of the structure are formed as geodetics in the streamline shape of the fuselage, and also in the curved profile of the wings... this method of aeroplane construction is the most important contribution to aircraft engineering since the completion of the first successful metal aircraft. For example, it permits each wing to be hollow and entirely free from any kind of obstruction – the additional space thus can be utilised for extra tankage or other loads, and the complete structure is one of extreme lightness combined with great strength and rigidity, thus

making possible a range and load-carrying capacity that has hitherto been considered unattainable*.

In the event the G.4/31 biplane was completed, then first flown by Mutt Summers on 16 August 1934, with the official serial K2771. Ten months later, on 19 June 1935, Summers also undertook the first test-flight of Wallis's private venture monoplane project. The consequent comparison of both aircraft's performances came as something of an embarrassing jolt to Air Ministry officialdom, for the monoplane had proved far superior in every respect, including a maximum speed of at least 100 mph faster than the biplane. The chairman of Vickers, Sir Robert McLean, armed with the respective performance figures as 'ammunition', immediately pressed the Air Ministry for permission to abandon further development of the G.4/31 biplane to concentrate on the private 'G.4/31' monoplane venture. Accordingly, the biplane order was cancelled, and an official contract for 96 machines placed with Vickers for their new monoplane, with the name Wellesley, to a revised Specification, 22/35, with the role now amended to 'medium bomber'.

The first production Wellesley, K7713, was first flown on 30 January 1937, and the type entered RAF service when No 76 Squadron commenced re-equipment starting on 22 March 1937, when a Vickers test pilot, Flying Officer Jeffrey Quill, delivered Wellesley K7715, the third production aircraft to the squadron at Finningley for service trials†.

Although the Wellesley ultimately equipped a total of ten RAF firstline squadrons, apart from various other secondline units, and remained on active service – albeit in dwindling numbers – until early 1943; its general effectiveness and concept were virtually obsolete by the outbreak of the European war in 1939. However, it had represented almost a giant step forward in the context of progressive aircraft designs for RAF use, and had certainly fully justified Barnes Wallis's (and Vickers') faith in geodetic stucturing. The extant method, in general use, of various forms of monocoque airframe designs was now clearly superseded; while stressed-skin construction was as yet in virtually experimental stage only and would not overtake Wallis's 'basket-work' ideas for several years after the first

*Paper entitled 'Vickers Wellesley Long-Range Medium Bomber (Pegasus Engine) – Vickers-Wallis Geodetic construction'. Undated but circa 1936-37.
†No 76 Squadron was *officially* reformed on 12 April 1937 from B Flight, No 7 Squadron, and was fully equipped with Wellesleys by 30 July 1937.

appearance of the Wellesley. Thus, the Wellesley's patent success had set the scene for Wallis's next – and many would say, greatest – venture into geodetic structure design, the prototype B.9/32 aircraft, which in turn would 'father' the vast family of Vickers Wellingtons.

In its original terms Air Ministry Specification B.9/32 contained a host of restrictive limitations. Foremost of these was the imposed maximum all-up empty (tare) weight figure of three metric tons (roughly 6,300lb). Such a figure automatically restricted all potential designs to medium power engines, with resulting performance figures well below those possible if more powerful engines were permitted to be fitted. Although this weight figure was cautiously raised to 6,500lb in December 1932 – a paper ploy of redefining some items as parts of the military load – the upper limit was to remain in force until 7 June 1934 when the Chief of the Air Staff, MRAF Sir Edward Ellington, authorised its removal from the specification, and transmitted this decision to Vickers in a letter dated 13 June*.

The prompt reaction from Vickers was a formal request in August 1934 to be allowed to fit either Bristol Pegasus X or Bristol Perseus engines to the B.9/32 prototype; a request quickly agreed by the Air Ministry on 21 August. In its original design concept the prototype B.9/32 was to have been a high-wing monoplane, though this layout was soon revised to become a mid-wing design before the end of 1933, thereby not only improving the general aerodynamics, but incidentally giving the pilot a better field of vision.

By 1936 the B.9/32 prototype aircraft (officially serialled K4049) incorporated numerous improvements and modifications to its initial design, most of which offered increased performance, fuel and military load capacities, and more efficient aerodynamics. At the time of its first test flight, by Mutt Summers (with Barnes Wallis aboard) from Brooklands on 15 June 1936, the aircraft's tare weight had reached 11,508lb, while its overall weight was now 21,000lb. Powered on that maiden flight by twin Bristol Pegasus X engines, it offered a speed of 250 mph at 8,000ft, with a range approaching 3,000 miles and a bomb-carrying capacity in excess of 4,000lb. Significantly, provision had been made for defensive gun locations in its nose, tail, and mid-upper dorsal positions, although all three were single, manually-operated Lewis machine guns†.

*The tare weight restriction of 6,500lb was removed from the specification formally on 21 June 1934.
†How any potential air gunner would have coped with operating a manual Lewis gun in a 200 mph-plus slipsteam is, to say the least, a moot question! – Author.

Wellington prototype, K4049, in its original form, June 1936, fitted with Pegasus X (915hp) engines; the B.9/32.

Side-view of K4049. Note use of Supermarine Stranraer fin and rudder (to save design hours), and perspex cupola nose and tail fittings.

Wellington L4212, the Mk I prototype taking off from Brooklands, 23 December 1937, on its initial test-flight, piloted by 'Mutt' Summers.

Wellington I fuselages under assembly, Weybridge, 1939, displaying their geodetic construction to advantage.

The life of the prototype, K4049 was destined to be brief. On 19 April 1937, during one of its final trials at Martlesham Heath, a high-speed dive caused the aircraft to break up – due to elevator overbalance producing sudden negative 'G' forces – and its pilot, Flight Lieutenant Maurice Hare, was forced to take to his parachute. Tragically, his flight observer for this particular test, AC1 G.P. Smurthwaite, failed to evacuate the machine and thus died in the subsequent crash near Waldringfield. Although this accident completely destroyed K4049, it had served its purpose admirably.

Just eight weeks after the B.9/32's 'maiden' flight on 15 June 1936, the Vickers firm received official recognition of the aircraft's obvious potential – a contract, No.549268/36 dated 15 August 1936, for an initial production batch of 180 machines, to be built to a revised Air Ministry Specification, B.29/36. Even before that maiden flight the B.9/32 had been given the name *Crecy* on 5 June 1936, thereby following the contemporary Air Ministry custom of naming certain types of service aircraft after towns and cities having outstanding historical military connections.

However, on 8 September 1936 this title was changed to *Wellington* for all future production aircraft, in accordance with Vickers' wishes. This change of nomenclature thus perpetuated the memory of the first Duke of Wellington (1769-1852) – the 'Iron Duke' – whose family name had already been honoured with the name of the Wellesley bomber. This alliterative use of the initial 'W' for the various Vickers' geodetic-constructed aircraft also complimented their designer, Barnes Wallis, and was continued with the Wellington's stablemate design, the Vickers Warwick and, later, Vickers Windsor.

The award of the initial production contract in August 1936 secured the Wellington's immediate future, and the Vickers' design team immediately tackled the various aspects of pure production. The Wellington I (as this first batch was to be titled) differed in many ways from the B.9/32, being in effect a redesign. Foremost was the need to convince other aircraft manufacturers planned to be contracted makers of Wellingtons that geodetic airframes were relatively simple to produce – a form of construction virtually unknown to most British contemporaries. This particular problem was quickly resolved by Wallis and the rest of the Vickers' Weybridge production team, headed by Trevor Westbrook, who between them devised all vital tools, jigs, and production procedures. The success of their efforts may be judged by the fact that ultimately, of the gross total Wellington production figure of 11,460 aircraft, almost exactly 9,000 were built in factories other than the Weybridge parent works.

In the event production of all Wellingtons was shared among three major factories i.e. Weybridge, Chester, and Blackpool. The Chester works was sited on the south side of Hawarden airfield, and work commenced on building the factory in November 1937. Originally intended to be a Vickers-Armstrong factory, it became a government-owned shadow factory, managed by Vickers, in 1938, solely for production of Wellingtons. Unlike Weybridge and the Squires Gate factory outside Blackpool, both of which built Wellingtons literally from scratch, the Hawarden works* was designed from the outset as a mass production assembly plant, not a manufacturing works. The adjacent land to the Hawarden factory was converted steadily to become an RAF airfield eventually. At Blackpool the nearby existing airfield of Squires Gate was selected as the site of a shadow factory for the production of Wellingtons, being designed as virtually a duplicate of the parent Weybridge factory and situated on the perimeter of the airfield.

The production Wellington I was intended to have twin Bristol Pegasus XVIII engines of 1050hp apiece, thereby offering a maximum speed of 245 mph at a gross weight of 24,850lb, able to carry a load of 4,500lb at most. Defensive armament initially comprised a single 0.303-inch calibre Browning machine gun in a cramped Vickers-designed nose turret, with two more Brownings in another similar Vickers turret in the tail-end of the fuselage. A fourth machine gun, manually-operated only, was located in an open hatch in the top fuselage a few feet behind the pilot's cockpit; this hatchway having a sliding cover-panel which could be hinged upwards to provide a windshield for the gunner. The first Wellington I ever to emerge from the Weybridge factory was L4212, temporarily powered by Bristol Pegasus XX engines, and this Wellington I (regarded as the production prototype) made its initial test-flight in the very capable hands of Mutt Summers from Brooklands on 23 December 1937. In the following months flight-testing produced a need for a number of minor modifications, while by mid-April 1938 the originally intended Bristol Pegasus XVIIIs became available on completion of their own acceptance trials and were fitted to L4212 to complete the aircraft's test schedule. After further minor modifications resulting from further tests, the Wellington I finally received

*Often titled Broughton, from a nearby village.

Wellington P9249 on pre-delivery test. Served as 'T', 38 Squadron and crashed at Marham on 16 June 1940.

L4250, the prototype Mk II (Merlin Xs) at Brooklands. Later utilised for 40mm cannon turret experimental installations. Became Instructional Airframe 3477M in December 1942.

its service clearance, and on 10 October 1938 the first Wellington to be issued to an RAF firstline unit, L4215, was collected by a crew from 99 Squadron and duly flown to the squadron's base airfield at Mildenhall, Suffolk – and, incidentally, being landed there in darkness. Further production Wellingtons reached 99 Squadron during the following weeks and by 12 January 1939 the squadron was up to its full establishment of the new bombers. (See Chapter 'Into Service' for further details of initial RAF issues).

Within weeks of the first flight of L4212, the Mk I production prototype, in December 1937, the Vickers' designers were engaged in future developments of the basic Wellington design. In particular, the need for possible alternative engines was given deep consideration, resulting in the projected Mk II and Mk III Wellington variants being planned to have Rolls-Royce Merlin Xs and Bristol Hercules IIIs respectively. Since neither of these powerplants was as yet available in production form, Vickers decided to at least produce some interim Wellingon variants which could include other improvements in design and equipment eventually intended to be incorporated in Mk II and Mk III versions. Accordingly, a Mk IA variant was first produced which had many differences to the basic Mk I – though it should be remembered that the Mk IA was really based on the (as yet unproduced) Mk II, and was therefore not, as might at first be thought, simply an 'improved' Mk I.

The most obvious differences between the Mk I and IA concerned the defensive armament installations. The Mk I's Vickers gun turrets and upper-fuselage manual gun hatch had soon proved to be inadequate for their purpose and difficult to operate. At the Air Ministry's insistence (and despite protest from Vickers) these initial turrets were replaced in the Mk IA by three Frazer-Nash power-operated gun turrets; an FN5 in the nose location armed with two 0.303-inch Brownings, an FN10 in the tail, also with twin Brownings, and an FN9 ventral 'dustbin' gun turret with two Brownings, this latter being retractable into the fuselage belly.

To accommodate these turrets, Vickers necessarily redesigned the nose and tail sections, stressed the airframe at an all-up weight of 28,000lb, strengthened the undercarriage assemblies to carry the increase in weight, plus necessary 'adjustments' to the aircraft's hydraulics and oxygen systems to take the new gun turrets into account. Additional defensive armament in the shape of hand-operated Vickers VGO ('K') 0.303-inch calibre machine guns were fitted in beam positions in a Mk IA, P9211, later, mainly for trial purposes.

Following the Mk IA came the Mk IC, a variant destined to be built in large quantity, which incorporated the wealth of experience already gained by the Vickers' designers. Of various new features to be included was a completely redesigned hydraulics system (thereby introducing VSG pumps), a 24-volt electrical system, and the deletion of the unsatisfactory ventral 'dustbin' FN9 gun turret; the latter defence being 'replaced' by mid-fuselage beam guns. Powered by 1050hp Bristol Pegasus XVIIIs, the Mk IC proved to be a firm foundation for most future Wellington variant designs, apart from a host of individual 'specialist' modifications, experiments, and trial installations; while in RAF operational service it was to become the backbone of Bomber Command's aerial offensive against Germany in 1939-1940.

Design of the projected Mk II and Mk III Wellingtons, which had begun at the start of 1938, proceeded reasonably quickly, but both

P9238, the prototype Mk III (Hercules IIIs). Served with 25 OTU, then became Instructional Airframe 3410M in October 1942.

projects depended on the availability of production quantities of their respectively intended Rolls-Royce and Bristol engines. Two Mk I machines were set aside to act as prototypes for these new variants; L4250 for the Mk II, and L4251 for the Mk III. The Mk II prototype, L4250, was first flown on 3 March 1939, while the equivalent Mk III 'first', L4251, made its initial flight on 19 May 1939.

The Rolls-Royce Merlin engines of the Mk II soon produced some general aircraft stability problems requiring fairly extensive compensating modifications and eventually delaying full production of further Mk IIs – which had originally been scheduled to begin in June 1939 – until early 1940, by which time all the teething troubles of the first Merlin-Wellington had been satisfactorily resolved. The Mk II finally entered RAF service in late 1940. Meanwhile progress with the Mk III was delayed by its intended Bristol Hercules engines, and the first production aircraft, P9238, first flew in January 1941 and entered RAF squadron service five months later.

CHAPTER TWO

Developments

Apart from the fact that the Wellington was produced in greater quantity than any other bomber *ever* to enter RAF service, the basic design was also subject to myriad modifications to provide a more extensive range of variants for specific, differing roles than any other RAF bomber – in itself a worthy tribute to its design team's sound original concept. No less than 19 distinct marks of Wellington eventually emerged, while records of Vickers aircraft Type Numbers show a total of 56 such numbers, albeit some of these being merely 'one-off' experimental vehicles or even paper projects which never materialised in physical forms. The early Mk Is, IIs, and IIIs have been described in the preceding chapter, while the several variants modified and produced for Coastal Command operations etc are detailed in later chapters in their context; but of the lesser-known marks probably the most ambitious projects were the Mk V and Mk VI 'high altitude' Wimpys.

The possibilities of producing bombers capable of operating at altitudes in excess of 35,000 feet began in the mid-1930s at a period when normal RAF firstline bombers, such as the Harrow and Whitley about to enter RAF service, had service ceilings of little more than 20,000 feet at best. Initial thoughts were for designs of four-engined aircraft carrying heavy armament and warloads, with 'special' bomb-sights – indeed, the projected Short Stirling and Handley Page Halifax were considered as possible vehicles in this form – but in the autumn of 1938 the Air Ministry asked the Vickers firm to investigate a possible adaptation of the Wellington design for a bomber able to operate between 35,000 and 40,000 feet, carrying a crew of three in a pressurised 'cabin', a bomb load of 1,000lb, with an endurance of at least 9½ hours, at an all-up weight of 30,000lb. For defensive armament, a single gun turret was to be installed in the tail location only. An official specification, B.23/39 was then issued to cover two prototypes, serialled R3298 and R3299 – two converted Mk Ics – which were intended to be powered by Bristol Hercules VIII engines, fitted with exhaust-driven superchargers.

The overall concept of a pressurised aircraft meant breaking new ground for Barnes Wallis and the rest of the Vickers' design team, but they soon produced a cylindrical pressure cabin, not unlike a steel boiler, measuring 18'3" in length and 5'5" in diameter. This steel cocoon was 'attached' to the inside of a drastically revised Wellington nose section by means of integral 'feet' fixed to nodal points of the geodetics – thereby allowing for cabin expansion and contraction without endangering the main airframe structure. This cabin was to maintain a pressure of 7lb sq/in – the equivalent of an apparent altitude of 11,000 feet – and incorporated a 3½ ft circular pressure-tight door at the rear end for crew access and exit.

To provide the necessary outside vision for the pilot, a small circular hole was cut in the cabin top and a non-jettisonable, hemi-spherical dome of double-skinned perspex sealed over the opening. This highly restrictive cockpit left the pilot blind in forward vision to some 15 degrees either side of dead ahead, making taxying and take-off 'adventurous'... Bomb-aiming was provided for by an optically-flat window in the underside of the forward end.

The first two prototype Wellington Mk Vs – as these were to be titled – were intended to be powered by Bristol Hercules VIII engines, but delay in production of these specific powerplants led to the temporary installation of Hercules IIIs. An order for 30 Mk Vs was given on 1 March 1940 (serials W5795-W5824), though in the event only one production Mk V (W5796) was built *per se*; nine being cancelled (W5816-W5824), and the remainder being 'converted' to Mk VI versions. Despite fitting Hercules VIII engines to R3299 in November 1940, it became apparent that the Mk V was well below its expected power/performance; this being anticipated even before the first Mk V flying trials, by developing a Merlin 60 variant of the Mk V to be entitled Mk VI. Accordingly, W5795 of the Mk V production order became the prototype Mk VI (Type 431) and a production order for 100 Mk VIs was placed in 1941. Of these only 44 were actually completed (DR471-DR528), the rest being cancelled in July 1942. The only major difference between the Mk V and Mk VI was the change from Hercules to Rolls-Royce Merlin engines, and Mk VI versions underwent a long series of trials and minor modifications during 1942. At least four Mk VIs were issued to No 109 Squadron – W5801, W5802, DR481, & DR485 – as the projected vehicles for testing the secret *Oboe* radar equipment then under trial by that unit.

One of 109 Squadron's *Oboe* pioneering pilots was Flight

R3298, the first prototype Mk V, 1940. Eventually SOC 5 March 1943.

W5798, a Mk V converted to Mk VI. SOC 29 March 1943.

Lieutenant H. E. 'Hal' Bufton (later, Group Captain, DSO,OBE, DFC,AFC) who recalled:*

By early 1942 *Oboe* was becoming practicable and it was decided that the only suitable aeroplane for it was the Wellington VI. This was one of the really tremendous aircraft of the war, but unfortunately it never had the chance to prove itself in anger. It had a seven-pound pressure cabin and a cruising speed of 280 mph at 35,000-plus feet; its 4,000lb bomb load was felt acceptable because *Oboe* would put it in the right place. We had tried hard to persuade ourselves that the Lancaster could do the job, but with its relatively low ceiling we could not count on it operating higher than 24,000 feet, which would have been useless. We had also thought of using the Mosquito early in 1942 but its – then – small 2,000lb bomb load precluded it.

From memory, out of some 150-plus practice bombs dropped blind from 10,000 feet, we got an average error of 108 yards. In the Wellington VI we used to fly in shirtsleeves with no oxygen at 30,000 feet in perfect comfort, apart from the fear that the pressure cabin was going to burst at any minute! Having settled our choice of the Wellington VI, we took delivery of three or four of them and a modification programme was undertaken by the Ministry of Aircraft Production (MAP) to fit 60 of them with *Oboe*, and modify them in certain ways – in particular to fit an emergency exit! The only method of getting out of a standard production model was to unscrew the pressure cabin floor, which took half a minute, and then walk 40 feet down the fuselage to the rear exit...about mid-1942 there came available all the bits for a target-finding force – Dr Coxen's target indicator, Reeve's *Oboe*, and the Mosquito – and it was 109 Squadron's commanding officer, Wing Commander C.C. Mullen, who produced the last gleam of genius to put those bits together. One week before the final decision to begin installation of the Wellington VI on a production basis, he got hold of a Mosquito and installed all our bits in it, just in time for the conference. The Wellington VI was rejected in favour of the Mosquito.

Indeed, by late 1942 the need for the pressurised Mk VI Wellington had been nullified by the latest Marks of the De Havilland Mosquito which, with adequate oxygen equipment and a bomb load up to

*Correspondence with author, 1971-72.

4,000lb, could reach high altitudes without the need for pressurised cockpit. Thus in late 1942 and 1943 the remaining Mk VIs were used primarily for experimentation, thereby providing invaluable data which assisted production of other high-flying aircraft designs, such as photo-reconnaissance Spitfires, and in the post war years other more advanced civil and military aircraft requiring pressurised cabins etc. By December 1943 virtually all Wellington Mk Vs and VIs had been struck off RAF charge.

In 1940 the crucial requirement of Rolls-Royce Merlin engines for Spitfires and Hurricanes took high priority, and one result was the decision to use an American engine for further development of the Wellington, this engine being the Pratt & Whitney Twin Wasp R-1830-S3C4-G of 1050hp with Hamilton Standard propellers; power plants originally ordered for the French air services but never delivered due to France's collapse in mid 1940. Accordingly a Mk Ic, R1220, was converted to accept Pratt & Whitney Twin Wasps as the prototype Mk IV Wellington, which first flew in December 1940.*

Initial test flights revealed excessive noise levels from the Hamilton propellers and these were later replaced by Curtiss electric propellers which gave more acceptable decibel figures. Deliveries of Mk IVs to Bomber Command squadrons commenced in August 1941 where the all-round improvement in engine performance, particularly higher speeds (up to 300mph at normal operating altitudes) was welcomed. The major differences between the Twin Wasps and previous Pegasus or Merlin engines created a host of minor (?) problems for the maintenance crews on squadrons operating Mk IVs (see chapter, 'Ubendum, Wemendum'), but air and ground crews were generally in agreement in praising the American powerplants once the initial 'bugs' had been ironed out. A total of 220 Mk IVs was eventually produced.

Apart from the various Wellington variants employed by Coastal Command (detailed in chapter 'Webfoot Warriors') the next significant Mark was the Mk X. By increasing the all-up weight maximum figure, through use of new light alloys for structures, and fitting higher-performance Hercules VI or XVI engines offering 1675hp, the basic Mk III could be 'converted' to the new Mk X standard, and a Mk III, X3374,became the first Mk X prototype in early 1942. The Mk X was to become the most-produced version of

---

*Decisions to utilise American engines for Wellingtons dated back to late 1939, but the Mk IV really became a fact after a meeting held on 27 July 1940 at Weybridge.

R1220, the Mk IV prototype.

RP589, a T.Mk X, January 1949.

MF628, a Mk T.X, the sole surviving complete Wellington, now in the RAF Museum, Hendon, seen here at Abingdon, 1968 during HM Queen's Review of the RAF.

the Wellington – a total of 3,803 – and in its basic bomber role, probably the most efficient variant. Although superseded as a bomber generally by late 1943 in the UK, Mk X Wellingtons continued in firstline operational bombing roles in the Mediterranean zones and Far East theatre until the end of the war. Almost equally important in the Mk X's long career was its T.X training role; this being a simple conversion by dint of removing both gun turrets and fairing over their previous nose and tail locations, and installing internally all necessary specialised radio and navigational equipment when needed. Wellington T.Xs were destined to remain in RAF service until the spring of 1953 before being honourably 'demobilised'.

Today (1986) only one complete Wellington survives in the world, a T.X, MF628, resident in the Royal Air Force Museum at Hendon, London, albeit now having its gun turrets reinstalled to represent the Mk X bomber role. MF628 was built at Squires Gate and delivered to the RAF initially on 11 May 1944. It saw no war service, but was later issued to No 1 ANS, Hullavington in April 1949, being coded there as FFK-B. After an accident in December 1951 it was sent for repair and restored to flying condition again, but on 24 January 1955 it was sold to Vickers. On that date J.L. Pickersgill, AFC and Flight Sergeant 'Herbie' Marshall were lumbered with the task of 'delivering' the last 'Wimpy'. Pickersgill takes up the story:

On 24 January 1955, while stationed at 20 MU, Aston Down, Flight Sergeant Marshall (pilot) and myself (Flight Engineer) found ourselves at St Athan MU, with the job of flying Wellington MF628 to Wisley. Also in attendance were a camera crew from the Air Ministry and their Airspeed Oxford, who were to formate after take-off for a few air-shots – though we weren't aware of this at the time. The Station Commander was in the near background whilst I was perusing the travelling copy of the Form 700 and he asked me what I was doing. On receiving the reply that I was somewhat curious about the fuel contents, he told me that it was 'adequate for the flight'. He then approached 'Herbie' and asked him if he had flown Wellingtons before and, tongue in cheek, Herbie assured him that he was conversant with the aircraft.

On approaching MF628 we had to pose for the camera wallah and I said to Herbie that 'with this brevet of mine this snap will go down like a lead brick with the old Wimpy mob!' We clambered in and started to wend our way through the check list – with remarks like 'The what?' and 'Where the hell's that?' – until all was complete, engines running fine, no drastic mag drop, and therefore taxied out and took off. The next snag was trying to find the Oxford, get close, and get the snaps taken – which didn't help my map-reading style of navigation as we were whizzing all over south Wales. We had no R/T contact, hence all was visual and handsigns, until at last Herbie got fed up and I gave him a course to steer. We next decided to check the fuel state, the four relevant gauges being behind the 2nd pilot's head with a pushbutton in between. The gauges all read zero! – a frantic grab for the Crew Notes was immediate action from which it transpired that there were two nacelle fuel tanks, one behind each engine, so I quickly selected these 'ON'.

With that minor panic over, Herbie became visibly relaxed and remarked that as this was the 'Last Wellington', we'd undoubtedly receive a good meal at Wisley, even possibly a replica as a presentation. We landed at Wisley, taxied to the hangars and found these firmly closed. One wee door then opened, an overalled figure beckoned us forward, stop, switch off, then said, 'Chuck me the 700', caught it – and beat a rapid retreat back inside the warm hangar, closing, the door behind him. So much for my pilot's dream of a slap-up meal or presentation! While talking to another pilot, who had flown Wimpys, in the bar much later. he said, 'You were lucky. Those nacelle tanks didn't usually work!'

Eventually presented to the RAF in 1964, Wellington MF628 ultimately moved to the RAF Museum on 26 October 1971.

The prolific production of Wellingtons, particularly during 1940-42, led inevitably to a host of individual aircraft being used as test vehicles for numerous minor and major experimental installations and modifications, not all of which had a direct bearing on Wellington basic development. To detail each and every one such one-off Wimpys would necessitate a separate volume, but selected examples of some of the more significant may suffice to illustrate the versatility – and patience – of the basic Wellington as a willing workhorse in this context. Among the earliest demonstrations of the aircraft's inherent strength were various decisions to use Mk II Wellingtons for ultra-heavy armament tests and trials. First suggestions concerned the feasibility of installing a 40mm cannon turret, designed by Vickers-Armstrong Ltd and, later, in liaison with the Vickers' Weybridge team, commencing in 1938 and developed

L4250 fitted with 40mm cannon dorsal turret, displaying the two different tail assemblies fitted respectively.

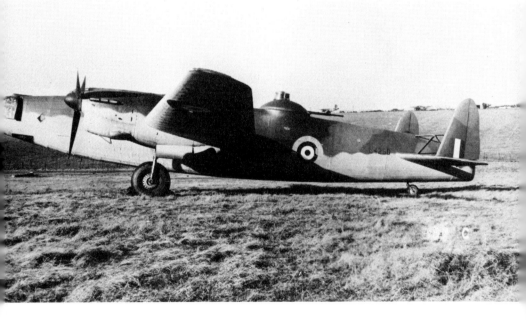

over the following two years.

By the spring of 1940, the prototype Wellington Mk II, L4250, having passed its normal trials' programme, was allocated for installation of the 40mm cannon turret as a mid-upper fitment, complete with its own predictor sight system – in effect a self-contained weapons system in miniature whereby the cannon was automatically linked in traverse and elevation by the actions of its gunner when merely aligning the sight on any target.

Initial testing revealed a tendency for this mid-upper turret to create severe vibration on the aircraft's normal single tail unit*, and as a result L4250's tail was re-shaped to a twin-tail configuration to bring the two fin/rudders in line with the engines' slipstreams. In this guise further tests were undertaken on 8 March 1942 albeit with only partial success. A second Mk II, Z8416, featured an alternative 40mm cannon turret installation as nose armament, though beyond basic functioning testing this form of modification was not further progressed. L4250 was also a test-bed for an experimental mid-upper gun turret having four 0.50-inch Browning machine guns, but again this experiment was not developed.

In the same context of increased or experimental armament used or tested by Wellingtons, one significant development was a major modification enabling the Wimpy to carry a 4,000lb bomb. Resulting from a proposal by Barnes Wallis in mid-1940, the first actual conversion was made on a Mk II, W5389 in October 1940, followed by W5399 and W5400. To carry the bomb involved removal of existing standard bomb beams and the inner bomb bay doors, then installing a specified bomb beam and necessary fitments for support, release, and general accommodation of the 'Cookie'. Flying trials of the modified 'block-buster bomb' Wimpys were carried out in January–March 1941 and led to approval of the modification for conversion of other Wellingtons; this conversion being officially referred to as 'Type 423' to cover any Mark of Wellington subjected to the modification.

Another Mk II, BJ895, became the test vehicle for another armament installation, Barnes Wallis's famed 'Dam-busting' bouncing bomb which was ultimately used to such good effect by

*Bringing to mind the parallel problems encountered when the mid-upper gun turret of the Avro Manchester caused slipstream problems to its tail units. This experimental 40mm cannon turret was intended as sole armament of the projected Boulton Paul P.92 single-seat, twin-engined fighter of 1938-40 which was cancelled in May 1940.

Wing Commander Guy Gibson, VC and his 617 squadron against the German Möhne and Eder dams on the night of 16/17 May 1943. Piloted by Mutt Summers, BJ895 flew a series of drop-tests of this weapon off Chesil Beach in December 1942, albeit in prototype forms of the eventual weapon actually used by Gibson and his men.

The Merlin-engined Mk II Wellington, with its greatly improved take-off power, higher speed, and greater all-up weight capabilities was quickly exploited as a basis for many other developments. In particular, the basic Mk II played a vital part in the practical airborne progression of early jet engine development, specifically the powerplants designed by Air Commodore Frank Whittle, OM,KBE,CB, FRS,LLD (as he became). Three Wellingtons, Z8570, W5389, W5518, were eventually modified – the latter pair ostensibly Mk IIs but fitted with Mk VI-standard wings and more powerful Rolls-Royce Merlin 62 engines with a view to high altitude trials of the various jet engines installed. In each case a Whittle jet was mounted in the aircraft tail section, and tests of these extended from July 1942 until 1945, providing a wealth of data for future jet engine and aircraft designs. Individual Wellingtons had, naturally, been used for progressive development of a wide variety of radial and in-line engines during the early years of Wellington production, but even in postwar years the Wimpy continued to be a flying test-bed for more advanced powerplants; a case in point being Wellington X, LN175, which had twin Rolls-Royce Dart turbo-prop engines fitted for airborne trials in 1948 – engines which soon became standard on such successful civil air liners as the stablemate Vickers Viscount.

The relative roominess of a Wellington's internal fuselage, along with its long-range potential – exemplified by the near-direct ferrying flights by Wimpys from the UK to the Middle East – led to consideration of the design as a possible civil transport and general service freighter, though the onset of war in 1939 shelved any immediate 'off-shoot' forms in order to increase pure bomber-version production for the RAF. In mid-1941, however, Vickers were requested urgently to convert an unspecified number of early Marks of Wellington for troop and equipment transportation, particularly for use in the North African campaigns. Since such a conversion involved relatively straightforward removal of all forms of armament and ancilliary equipment, plus oxygen system, etc., this work became mainly a 'local' matter initially on units where the need was felt.

The variety of 'transport' Wellingtons thereafter converted covered a wide spectrum of duties and occurred in most theatres of

Hybrid. Test-bed for a Whittle jet engine, tail-mounted, at Bruntingthorpe, 1944.

LN715, flying test-bed for Rolls-Royce Dart engines at Wisley.

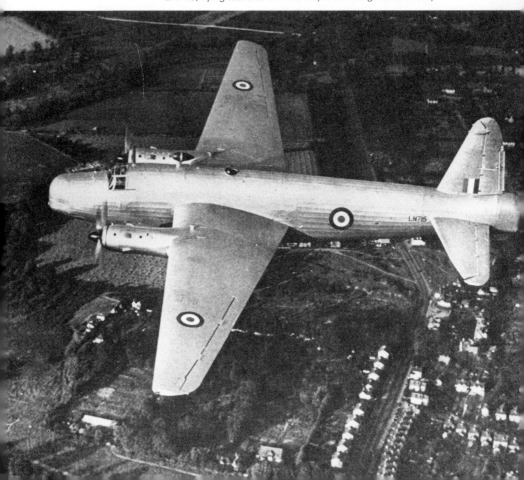

operations. For example, in India Squadron Leader John Sutton, DFC, an operational Wimpy captain with Nos 99 and 215 Squadrons, was for a short time attached to Rawalpindi for training paratroops in Wellingtons:

> The paratroop dropping in which I was engaged in Rawalpindi was training only of Indian and Gurkha paratroops. Their initial training at Rawalpindi was in Vickers Valentias and they then moved on to Wellington Ics for their operational training. We normally carried eight paratroops and these were dropped in 'sticks' of four men. The paratroops were 'aimed' on to the dropping site by the navigator using the bomb sight to assess drift. As a signal for the troops to drop he pressed a button linked to a light system back in the fuselage by the dropping position – this being a wooden trapdoor positioned over the hole in the geodetics which had originally been left to accommodate an under-turret – and the men were despatched by the wireless operator who stationed himself at this point to act as 'jump master'. We trained both Indian and Gurkha troops, and sometimes an Indian would refuse. If this happened then invariably the succeeding men would also refuse – yet I never knew a Gurkha to refuse on these training sorties. I should add that, certainly up until I left India in the spring of 1944 – no Wellingtons had actually been used *operationally* in this role.

Wellington 'VIP' transports were used occasionally in the United Kingdom, the chief unit being No 24 Squadron, based at Hendon (site of the present RAF Museum), which employed unarmed Wellingtons from mid-1940 until early 1944, apart from several other types of aircraft. They were by no means the only 'VIP' Wimpys, however, as ex-Warrant Officer J. H. Wade recalls:

> In July 1945 Wellington X, LP201 was allocated to Air Vice-Marshal Cuckney* for his personal use when making tours of inspection in his capacity of Director of Maintenance & Supply, Middle East & Central Mediterranean Forces. The crew posted to MAAF Rear Comm as his personal crew were Flying Officer Chapman (pilot), Warrant Officers Ludlow (nav) and Wade (myself, wireless operator), Corporal Eggerton (rigger) and LAC

*AVM E.J. Cuckney, CE, CBE, DSC retired from the RAF in May 1950.

215 Squadron Wellingtons on training drops of 10th Gurkha Paratroop Battn, near Rawalpindi, India.

N2990, coded NQ-D, of 24 Squadron, Hendon, 1943. Nose & tail 'gun turrets' were in fact painted on fabric fairings. Had previously served as 'P', 115 Squadron, and with 11 OTU. SOC 19 March 1943.

'Raymond (engine fitter); the fitter and rigger being part of the air crew and responsible for *all* servicing when away from base at Maison Blanche, Algiers.

LP201's conversion to passenger work was interesting in as much as the airframe was divided into three sections. Aft of the faired-over nose turret position along to the nav's table was normal Wimpy layout, then came a plywood 'bulkhead' with an access door to a small compartment containing three seats for the fitter, rigger, and batman/driver, Corporal Lynch. Then came a further 'bulkhead' and door leading to the main passenger section where 'The Old Man' held court with his staff, including a Flight Lieutenant Walker, his personal aide. The crew could enter through the nose hatch as normal, but the AVM and his staff made a more dignified arrival through a door about three-quarters down the starboard side. The bomb doors were sealed apart from a small section under the crew compartment where a luggage stowage section had been constructed.

When not required for inspection tours the Wimpy, nicknamed 'Sister Anna', was considered to be available for normal scheduled services in the Med area. However, ATC Passenger Services seemed reluctant to get too involved with a VIP aircraft, a circumstance which I'm afraid our crew exploited to the limit! 'Cuckney's Private Airline' – a name gained from the AVM's flag doped on the nose – acquired a reputation that postwar travel operators would have envied! Any scheduled flight from Algiers to Cairo would usually mean one or, at most, two nightstops before delivering its passengers – not so 'Cuckney's Enterprises Ltd' . . . You left Algiers for a few days in Malta with the swimming, good food, and a trip round the harbour laid on, then across to Sicily (especially if among the passengers were conniving air crews) for a few days at the Hotel Timeo at the Taormina aircrew rest centre. A quick nip across the Adriatic for a few more days of culture in Athens, and then on to the fleshpots of Cairo, where worn-out but happy passengers said a tearful farewell. We preferred to select our own passengers and the key question was not 'Where do you want to go?', but 'Do you mind how long it takes to get there?' Oddly enough, no matter to which Service they belonged, or how senior in rank, our passengers seemed to be as corruptible as the crew! Certainly, no one ever complained. Whether the 'Old Man' ever knew or not we never dared try to find out. Of course, it couldn't last. The AVM was eventually posted home to the UK for a further appointment and we had to rejoin the *proper* Air Force.

One incident concerned a Company Quartermaster-Sergeant, RASC – 'Jimmy' – whose duties involved flying on inspections of ENSA cinema units around the Med. CQMS Jimmy was a great friend of our crew, but had a phobia about flying. Since keeping his cushy number depended on his ability to endure travelling by air, we made a quiet arrangement with ATC Passengers whereby Jimmy would arrive at the airport suitably 'tranquillised', had a few more nips, and before the wheels were up he was fast asleep; arriving at the other end slightly ruffled in appearance but with all nerves intact. You just don't get that sort of service on British Airways or B-Cal nowadays! The last I heard of Sister Anna was in an accident survey report stating she had (apparently) pranged on landing at Heliopolis and burned out; yet true to herself, the old girl caused no casualties and everyone aboard got out unhurt.

A majority of 'official' and unofficial (i.e. *ad hoc* local) conversions of standard Wellingtons to trooper, passenger, and/or freight carriers were originally Mk Is, IIs, and, occasionally, Mk Xs. In the troop-

VIP Wimpy. AVM Cuckney's 'private' Wellington.

carriage role it was found possible to transport up to 18 fully-equipped Servicemen, or an equivalent military load, over ranges up to some 2,000 miles. Eventually all such conversions were ratified with official titling as either Mk XVs or XVIs – referring to ex-Mk Ias or Mk Ics respectively, although the actual overall total of conversions to the passenger/freight roles is now impossible to confirm. Among the very first Wellingtons to be converted to any form of pure transport role was a Mk I, L4255. Issued originally to 149 Squadron on 24 January 1939, by 1940 it was in the hands of the Air Transport Auxiliary (ATA) at White Waltham, locally modified for use as an air ambulance, and continued in service until being struck off charge on 19 November 1944.

In 1942 a Mk III, X3286, was actually modified for towing an Airspeed Horsa glider, but the effect on its geodetic fuselage structure was 'not encouraging' (*sic*); while another Mk III, X3479, after service with No 75 Squadron and as 'Y', No 156 Squadron, was used experimentally as transporter of a Smith gun and its crew with the thought of parachuting both gun and crew into battle situations. In the event, X3479 was returned to mundane training duties with No 30 OTU, and remained in RAF use until 31 May 1947. Another 'one-off' conversion was to Mk Ia, P2522, as a so-termed 'Mk IX' troop-carrier, serving with 214 Squadron eventually but struck off RAF charge on 10 March 1943.

Only one Wellington actually received a British civil registration, a T.Mk X, RP468, powered by twin Hercules XVIs, which in 1949 was fitted with a tail boom radar device experimentally and civil-registered as G-ALUH simply to cover some test flights off the Norwegian coast. It was then returned to the RAF as RP468 again in October 1949. However, 'civil' Wimpys were employed during the war by the British Overseas Airways Corporation (BOAC) as passenger/freight 'airliners'. In view of a lack of civil airliners in the Mediterranean and Indian theatres of war, the RAF was ordered to provide (initially) four Wellingtons in mid-1942 from RAF squadrons for BOAC use. These four included T2609 (ex-37, 70, & 28 Squadrons); X9692 (ex-70 Squadron & 28 Squadron SAAF); and Z8783 (ex-38 Squadron), and in the event all four aircraft were handed back to the RAF between 14 and 18 July 1943.

One pilot involved in the 'Wimpy Airline' was Frank Tricklebank, who had operated on Wellington Ics with Bomber Command, ferried one to the Middle East and then continued operations over the desert and from Malta before a spell with British Overseas Airways

(Left) BOAC Wellington BAW3. Note 'BRITISH AIRWAYS' logo, with 'Speedbird'.
(Right) BOAC Wellington BAW1 with ENSA party at El Adem.

Corporation, followed eventually by a tour as an instructor on 'civilised' (*sic*) Mk Xs with Transport Command:

In 1942 the BOAC landplane fleet in the Middle East consisted of a number of Lockheed 18 Lodestars, one Lockheed 14 which had flown Neville Chamberlain to Munich, a few Armstrong Whitworth Ensigns, and about nine De Havilland Flamingos. They were not enough to meet the commitment of the 'Tedder Routes' and no further civil aircraft were available, so the bomber squadrons in Egypt were directed to transfer four Wellingtons. One can imagine the joy with which engineering officers got rid of their Jonahs – I remember 'Q' of 38 Squadron which became, I believe, BAW2! The aircraft were modified by the removal of front and rear turrets and the fitting of primitive seating for some 16 passengers. Entry was by ladder through the hole in the floor alongside the pilot's station. The logo was interesting – the Speedbird motif with the words BRITISH AIRWAYS, not BOAC; anticipating some 30 years perhaps!

The Wimpy was not a bad aircraft for its day, though with Pegasus engines the Mk Ics were always underpowered, and the hotter and more humid the climate the more underpowered they were. Take-off always seemed to be 95% of the available distance, 'whilst single-engine performance was downhill. With the boost and rpm advised by BOAC for cruise – which, of course, had to be different from RAF thinking – the cruise speed out of Cairo was of the order of 125 mph. By the time we reached the Gulf the fabric would be stretching until the wings resembled eiderdowns, and the speed would be barely three figures. A few cases of torn fabric in these conditions resulted in very unorthodox handling. The early flying was done by contract captains, but there were legal problems since the aircraft were not civil-registered and lacked details such as C. of A. (*Certificate of Airworthiness*). So, they were handed over to a dozen or so ex-Wellington seconded pilots, and we got commands within a year of joining – which must be a record? We operated a scheduled service from September 1942; Cairo-Lydda-Habbaniya-Shaibah-Bahrein-Sharjah-Karachi, and back. Supposed to be six days, and once or twice it was, though I think I may have held the record at three weeks. After Alamein the Wellingtons were also used up the desert to Matruh, El Adem, Marble Arch, etc.

The 'fleet' was in being for about nine months. Something of a 'private air force' atmosphere developed as many of those who remembered the glories of Imperial Airways did not care to be associated with such a Fred Karno outfit. Although rough and slow, the Wimpy was robust and viceless, so though there were many incidents and damn close-run things, we managed not to break anything – so its BOAC safety record was 100%. One or two 'funnies' – at the time the airfield on Masira Island was under construction by a gang of Arabs supervised by one RAF officer and one NCO, under the command of RAF Sharjah. One night Sharjah received a garbled radio message which was understood to say 'a demonstration of force was desirable'. Our aircraft were commandeered to take a force of soldiery down to sort out the Arabs. We had no radio contact with Masira but on arrival overhead everything seemed to be calm, so we landed and deployed the Army, ready for war. The resident RAF were greatly entertained by all this and told us the real story. They had been a bit upset to realise that all the (Arab) workers carried knives and muskets, whilst all the RAF had was one 0.38in revolver. So one Friday they told them, 'Hand over your arms or you don't get paid', and to their surprise the locals gave up their armoury. So to clear the position the CO had signalled Sharjah that he had 'carried out a desirable demonstration of force . . .'. We flew a red-faced and disappointed 'task-force' back to the boredom of Sharjah . . .

I had one occasion to tick off my First Officer when the bottom hatch blew open on take-off and we were subjected to a sandstorm. He got a bit excited, but as he pointed out, the cause was that my suitcase had dropped out and vanished into the Western Desert! I remember too, watching a Wellington which had been grossly misloaded trying to get into Almaza. After some half-dozen hairy efforts, including hitting the boundary wall and various bounces, it eventually made it – just. The captain got out, very white and trembling, to be surprised by one of his passengers coming along and saying, 'Thank you, Captain, for a delightful flight' . . . Then there was the day we landed at El Adem with an ENSA party which included four young females – to be surrounded by about 1,000 sex-starved Erks . . . there were times when one wondered how far one *could* be responsible for the safety of one's passengers! Most of the pilots involved stayed on in BOAC or BEA to fly evermore efficient and sophisticated equipment, but I suspect that they remember the Wellington Flight as one of the most interesting – and in a perverse way, amusing – episodes of their career.*

The RAF was not the only air service to fly Wellingtons. Between 1942 and 1946 the Fleet Air Arm used a handful of Wellingtons for various purposes, albeit mainly in training roles, and at least six FAA squadrons had Wellingtons on unit strength at some period; examples being L4244; W5357; HZ361; HZ470; MP524; MP547; NB863. By the end of the war, apart from continuing RAF and FAA use as trainers, the Wellington was regarded as obsolete for firstline use. Even so, two foreign countries considered the design worthy enough to order small numbers for their own air forces. In April 1946 eight Wellingtons were delivered to the Greek air service, these being: ME890; ME907; ME940; MF190; MF466; MF643; NC418; NC433. In the same year the French government, anxious to rebuild its firstline air strength, purchased at least 39 Wellingtons, mostly maritime conversions for torpedo-strike and aerial reconnaissance roles with its *Aéronvale*. There were MP623; MP741; MP756; MP771; MP774; MP818; MP825; NB796; NB812; NB826; NB876; NB913; NB919; NB927; NB942; NB943; NB945; NB947; NB971; NB975; NB977; NB980; NB983; NB998; NC122; NC123; NC124; NC942;

The Log (BALPA Journal), 1980

HZ470, 'B' of 765 Squadron, Fleet Air Arm, 1946.

LN374, a B.X, serving with the French air services. It had previously served as 'F', 76 OTU.

NC647; NC922; PF837; PF996; PF997; PG181; PG183; PG230; PG290; PG291; PG316.

The ultimate Wellington to emerge from a factory production line was a Mk X, RP590,* which was delivered to the RAF on 25 October 1945. Nevertheless, Wellingtons were to continue in RAF service, primarily as flying classrooms/trainers for another seven and a half years until finally being withdrawn in March 1953. Reactions to the Wellington in the postwar years varied (naturally) according to an individual's previous flying experience. Les Bulmer, an ex-No 2 Group Mosquito navigator who served in the RAF from 1942-53, had his first flight in a Wimpy in 1947:

My first encounter was at No 228 OCU, Leeming (May 1947 to January 1948) where we were training Mosquito crews for the squadrons in Germany. The Wellingtons we had were used for *Gee* instruction, and at the OCU I flew in them just twice (ND115 and ND119). Then, in January 1948, I was sent in a hurry to the Middle East because a Nav/W was 'urgently' required there. Typically, on arrival no one knew why I'd been sent for, so I finished up in Aden for two years on the Communications Unit. When I joined this unit it had an Anson XIX Flight and a Wimpy Flight. The Wimpys were used mainly for supplying the three satellite airstrips at Riyan, Salalah, and Masira with mail, fresh food, stores, and personnel. They were all pretty clapped out and were replaced in March 1948 by Dakotas. I flew in only one, NC593, on 26 February 1948 en route to Masira – but we didn't make it. We had engine trouble at Salalah, waited for it to be fixed, then returned to Khormaksar on the 28th. The aircraft was fitted with a few wicker 'armchairs' in line astern to accommodate passengers who had to be briefed not to step off the gangway in case they put a foot through the fuselage. On that occasion we had only one passenger, an Army officer who was going to Riyan to take charge of the Sultan of Mukalla's private army. I've never forgotten the sight of that gentleman sitting in splendid isolation in his 'armchair' halfway down the fuselage.

Navigation aids on our Wellington were almost non-existent, apart from a radio compass, so I think everyone was delighted when the Dakotas came along. With *Rebecca* and a radio altimeter in addition to the radio compass, a more civilised form of approach

*Later, coded 'FDBG' with No 1 Refresher Training Unit, Finningley, 1949

to Salalah – a difficult place to get into during the so-termed monsoon period (April-October) because of low cloud down to sea level and mountains just to the north – although these didn't stop our Flight commander ploughing into a 1000-feet cliff-top, killing all twelve people on board . . .! I never had much affection for the Wellington. After the warmth and cosiness of a Mosquito VI cockpit, it seemed a cold, draughty, lumbering brute. But I imagine that those who flew it on operations had just as much love for it as we had for our Mozzies. It was certainly a good old workhorse.

David Guthrie, a pilot, first made acquaintance with Wellingtons during his embryo training at No.201 AFS, Swinderby between August and November 1949:

My training up to this stage had been on Tiger Moths and Harvards, so it was a big step to begin flying with a crew, and to have the luxury of a navigator, backed by the accuracy of *Gee*, and a signaller pounding away at his Morse key. The Wellington was very pleasant to fly, with well harmonised controls and the sort of stick forces one would associate with an aircraft of that size. The only real control problem lay in holding on rudder at high power settings and low speeds on one engine. My most vivid memory is of

T.X, PG262 of No. 1 Air Navigation School

my penultimate trip, on 1 November 1949, which could easily have been my last! It was a night dual check with the 'A' Squadron commander, Squadron Leader J.J. 'Timber' Woods. In those days it was customary to feather engines when carrying out practice engine failures. (This is no longer done, I believe, and many lives and much damage to aircraft have undoubtedly been saved as a result!) The procedure was for the instructor to stop an engine without the student pilot's knowledge by turning off a fuel cock situated behind the first pilot's seat. On the downwind leg at 1000 feet, Timber duly did this, and with eager skill I carried out a feathering drill – on the live engine! With even greater skill and rapidity Timber carried out unfeathering drill, but what has always impressed me was the stream of invective that flowed unceasingly from his lips as his hands flashed around the cockpit!

The T.Mk X training versions of the Wellington, which provided so many embryo RAF air crews in the immediate postwar years with a solid introduction to operating a semi-heavy aircraft, varied in modification according to the specific type of instruction envisaged; while other marks of Wimpy, initially built as operational bombers or maritime strike aircraft, also underwent modification to specialised training variants, involving an official change in mark number reference in RAF records. Examples illustrating such conversions included MP530, originally built as a Mk XI, but converted to a Mk XVIII radar trainer having Mosquito nightfighter nose for SCR720 radar, with the tail turret removed; while NC869, originally a Mk XIV was similarly converted to Mk XVIII standard. In all a total of 80 Mk XVIIIs were produced by the Blackpool factory. The ultimate mark of Wellington was the Mk XIX. This was, in effect, a postwar updating of the basic Mk T.X trainer, incorporating the very latest training equipment available then.

Despite the diversity of operational and non-operational roles calmly taken on board throughout its career, the Wellington, of whichever mark or variant, remained unmistakably a Wimpy in essence. The towering single tail, porcine fuselage with its thrusting, aggressive snout, gently flexing airframe and 'waving' wingtips – all were common to virtually every version built or converted. A gross total of 14,182 Wellingtons was originally ordered for production, but in the event 11,460 were actually produced (plus the first prototype); a figure which placed Barnes Wallis's creation far ahead numerically than *any* other bomber ever to enter RAF service.

CHAPTER THREE

Into Service

The first Wellington to reach a firstline RAF squadron as the start of unit re-equipment was L4215, which arrived at Mildenhall after dusk on 10 October 1938 to join No 99 Squadron. By 3 January 1939 this unit had received a further 14 Wellingtons. These being (in order of receipt) L4216 (11 October); L4217 (15 October); L4219 (22 October); L4220 (24 October); L4222 (4 November); L4224 (8 November); L4218 & L4225 (9 November); L4227 (17 November); L4228 (25 November); L4232 (29 November); L4233 (7 December); and L4244 on 3 January 1939. Prior to the arrival of the Wellingtons 99 Squadron had been flying Handley Page Heyford biplanes, and the conversion to the new monoplanes from their well-used, open-cockpit, biplane 'Clothbombers' produced a number of fresh items and procedures to be learned by the squadron's air and ground crews.

From a pilot's viewpoint the changeover was both exciting and slightly bewildering until inbred flying instincts and familiarity mastered the new 'beastie'. The experience of 99 Squadron's contemporary adjutant, Flying Officer (later Group Captain) A. Montagu-Smith, probably mirrored the thoughts of his fellow skippers:

> As one of the first officers to fly a squadron Wellington, L4220 on 8 November 1938, I found it to be an exhilarating occasion, albeit somewhat claustrophobic due to the unfamiliar enclosed cockpit. Handling the aircraft required a very different technique from that of the Heyford. For the first time one had to operate a retractable undercarriage, which could easily be forgotten; flaps had to be used; whilst the instrument panel was a source of wonderment. Until then one had relied upon the elementary turn-and-bank indicator; now an artificial horizon had to be got used to. In the Heyford the pilot sat high on a level with the upper mainplane, but in the Wellington, with its short undercarriage, one seemed very near the ground.*

*Wellington at War by C. Bowyer; Ian Allan, 1982

Montagu-Smith's reactions to the Wellington were also shared by many bomber pilots of that period in the context of coping with the transition from long- established biplane aircraft flying techniques to the intricacies of handling far more powerful and (then) sophisticated monoplane bombers. By late 1938, when 99 Squadron commenced re-equipment, RAF Bomber Command had already begun a steady metamorphosis to modernity in firstline aircraft designs newly entering service. From 1937 six different monoplane bomber types had begun replacing the Command's well-worn biplanes; namely Handley Page Harrow (five squadrons), Handley Page Hampden (two squadrons), Fairey Hendon (one squadron), Bristol Blenheim (17 squadrons), Armstrong Whitworth Whitley (six squadrons), and the Wellington's predecessor Vickers Wellesley (six squadrons), while other squadrons were also about to convert to monoplanes.

Of these, No 38 Squadron based at Marham, Norfolk – the sole Fairey Hendon unit – became the second to re-equip with Wellingtons. Its first example, L4230, arrived on the squadron on 24 November 1938, to be followed in sequence by L4231 (28 November); L4218 (transferred from 99 Squadron on 2 December); L4234 (6 December); L4235 (6 December); L4236, L4237, and L4238 – all on 14 December; L4239, L4240, L4241 on 30 December; L4242 and L4243 on 5 January 1939; L4245 (10 January); and L4248 on 13 January.

Within a week, on 20 January 1939, a third unit commenced re-equipment when 149 Squadron, based at Mildenhall, started conversion from Heyfords to new Wellingtons. On that date three Wellingtons, L4252, L4253, and L4254, duly arrived; to be followed by 13 more Wellingtons by 9 March 1939 i.e. four on 24 January (L4255, L4256, L4257, L4258); two (L4249, L4259) on 6 February; two more (L4263, L4264) on 7 February; another pair (L4265, L4266) on 10 February; L4271 and L4272 both on 17 February; and L4270 on 9 March.

Fourth to receive Wellingtons was No 9 Squadron at Stradishall, Suffolk, another Heyford unit. In fact, No 9 had originally been told that it was intended to be the very first Wellington squadron, even having specific Wellingtons earmarked for issue to the unit in the autumn of 1938, but in the event its first Wellingtons, L4260 (KA-H) and L4261 (KA-B) were both received on 31 January 1939. These were soon followed by L4262 (KA-P) on 7 February; L4268 and L4269 (13 February); L4273 and L4274 (KA-K) on 20 February;

(above) No. 9 Squadron
...ngtons, early 1939.

(...) Wing Commander Hugh
...d, OC 9 Squadron, 1939

L4304 of 148 Squadron with pre-war coding. It later served with 75 Squadron, Nos. 11 & 15 OTUs, and was eventually SOC on 19 November 1944.

115 Squadron Wellingtons at Marham, early 1939.

L4275 (KA-H), L4276 (KA-M), L4277, L4278 (KA-Z/A) all on 27 February; L4279 (KA-D) on 4 March; L4286 and L4287 on 13 March; and L4288 (KA-A) on 15 March 1939, with three more examples arriving by 24 April. The air and ground crews of 9 Squadron were more fortunate than most in having No 148 Squadron sharing their airfield at Stradishall.

Another ex-Heyford unit, 148 Squadron had begun receiving Wellingtons on 4 March 1939 when three examples (L4280, L4281, L4282) arrived, followed by L4283 and L4293 on 11 March; L4289 and L4290 on 18 March; L4291, L4292, L4293 on 20 March, L4294 on 24 March; and L4267 on 5 April. 148 Squadron was immediately redesignated for training duties as a Group Pool unit, and could thus help in conversion training of 9 Squadron's crews; while nearby Mildenhall's recently installed blind landing aids helped in training 9 Squadron's air crews in Wellington night-flying practice. In March 1939, 9 Squadron's commander, Wing Commander Hugh P. Lloyd,* inadvertently demonstrated the strength of a Wellington when, on take-off, he ran head-on into a flock of starlings – nine well-roasted birds having to be dug out of the engine cowlings later, apart from salvaging the bodies of a further 178 starlings from the runway! †

At Marham No 115 Squadron began replacing its obsolete Harrows with Wellingtons on 3 March 1939 when it received L4299, followed by L4300 and L4301 (4 April); L4305, L4306 (12 April); L4307 (19 April); L4295 (23 April); L4317, L4318 (24 April); L4319 (25 April); L4321, L4323, L4324, and L4325 (2 May); L4333 (12 May); L4221 (15 May); and L4334 on 16 May. Two other Harrow units, both resident then at Feltwell, Norfolk, were Nos 37 and 214 Squadrons, who were next in line to receive Wellingtons. First of these to re-equip was 37 Squadron, commencing on 6 May with L4326 and L4327, then adding L4328 and L4329 (8 May); L4332 (18 May); L4331 (19 May); L4336, L4337, L4339 all on 23 May 1939. The other Feltwell unit, 214 Squadron, received its first three Wellingtons (L4341, L4342, L4343) on 26 May 1939, then took on charge L4344 and L4345 on 2 June; L4346 (5 June); L4354 (15 June); L4356 (16 June); L4357, L4358 (19 June); L4361, L4362, L4363, L4364 (26 June); and L4365 (28 June) and L4359 on 28 August.

Just two more units were to receive Wellingtons before the outbreak of war with Germany on 3 September 1939, these being Nos 75 and

*Later, Air Chief Marshal Sir Hugh, GBE,KCB,MC,DFC,LLD.
†For further details of 9 Squadron's pre-war activities, see *9 Squadron* by T. Mason; Beaumont, 1965.

215 Squadrons, both based at Honington, Suffolk. No 75 Squadron, flying Harrows, had been reformed on 15 March 1937 as a heavy (*sic*) bomber unit, but on 1 March 1939 was redesignated as a Group Pool squadron i.e. the equivalent of what would later be termed an Operational Training Unit (OTU). The subsequent history of 75 Squadron has tended to be slightly confusing in some accounts, and should be clarified at this point. As No 75 Squadron RAF, the unit received its first Wellington, L4366, on 29 June 1939, followed by L4367 (30 June); L4368 (1 July); L4369 and L4370 (3 July); L4371 (6 July); L4372 (7 July); and L4373 on 11 July. In July 1939 the squadron moved base to Stradishall then in September 1939 moved again, to Harwell, still with its training role. Finally, on 4 April 1940, the squadron was merged with No 148 Squadron and SHQ, Harwell to create No 15 OTU. On that same date its 'numberplate' was officially transferred to an embryo unit of the Royal New Zealand Air Force (RNZAF) based at Feltwell; this fresh unit becoming titled No 75 (NZ) Squadron, RAF.

The origins of No 75 (NZ) Squadron traced back to early 1937 when, resulting from a report by Wing Commander Ralph Cochrane, RAF* – on loan to the RNZAF then – regarding future requirements for the RNZAF, the New Zealand government placed orders for a total of 30 Wellingtons and subsequently sent a number of RNZAF personnel to England who, after suitable training, would eventually ferry the Wellingtons by stages back to New Zealand; this ferrying operation being tentatively planned to commence (i.e. the first batch of six aircraft) in the late summer of 1939.

On 1 June 1939 the New Zealand personnel already in England for this task were collectively established as No 1 New Zealand Flight, under the command of Squadron Leader W. Buckley, RNZAF (later, Air Commodore, CBE) and based at Marham. By the end of the next month this Flight comprised just 12 officers – all pilots – and six non-commissioned airmen, though further personnel soon bolstered manning during August 1939; either from New Zealand itself or by voluntary transfers by New Zealanders already serving in the RAF. The outbreak of war on 3 September immediately caused the ferrying operations plan to be postponed. Moreover, since all the New Zealanders due to participate in the operation now expressed their wishes to remain in England and join in the war, the New Zealand government very promptly waived its legal claim to the 30 ordered

*Later, Air Chief Marshal Sir Ralph, GBE,KCB,AFC.

Wellingtons and placed the NZ Flight personnel at the disposal of the RAF – a generous gesture immediately and gratefully accepted by the Air Ministry.

At first it was expected that the NZ Flight personnel would be posted individually to various RAF squadrons, but the commander of Bomber Command agreed to retain the Flight intact as a New Zealand unit within his aegis. While higher authority proceeded to sort out details for eventually raising the Flight to full squadron status in personnel and equipment, the NZ Flight moved base to Harwell in September 1939, then on to Stradishall in January 1940, finally settling in at Feltwell in February 1940.

Soon after Air Ministry issued an instruction dated 1 April 1940 that 'No 75 (NZ) Squadron should be formed round the existing New Zealand Flight at Feltwell', and three days later No 75 (NZ) Squadron came into existence *per se* officially. It should be added that the eager 'Kiwis' had already anticipated officialdom by despatching three Wellingtons to drop propaganda leaflets – *Nickels* – on Brunswick, Ulzen, and Luneberg on 27 March 1940 – all three aircraft returning safely after some ten hours' flying from what was officially recorded as a 'training sortie' – in fact, a euphemism for the Kiwis' initial operational sorties.*

The original 75 Squadron's sister unit at Honington in early 1939 was No 215 Squadron, another Harrow unit, which converted to Wellingtons, starting with L4375 on 12 July 1939, then receiving in sequence L4376 (13 July); L4377 (14 July); L4378 (15 July); L4379, L4380, L4381 (17 July); L4382 (20 July); L4383 (21 July); L4384, L4385, L4386 (24 July); and four more (L4387, L4388, L4389, L4390) all on 1 August 1939. Though 215 became in effect a full-strength Wellington squadron by the latter date, it was to retain and fly a few Harrows during the first weeks of the war.

The first eight months of 1939 kept all Wellington units busy with – for peacetime – fairly intensive training and flying programmes, including in the summer a rather surprising order from 'higher authority' for Wellington crews (among others) to begin practising daylight *low*-level flying – an injunction readily and by no means reluctantly obeyed by Wimpy crews who promptly indulged themselves with 'contour-chasing' sorties, hugging the countryside around south-eastern England in a hitherto forbidden treat! With the near-certainty of a war with Hitler's Nazi regime in Germany

*For details, see *The Restless Sky* by AVM C.E. Kay; Harrap, 1964.

looming largely, the RAF not only practised for its *raison d'être* with tactical exercises, but also became a vehicle for semi-propaganda roles by mounting 'show the flag' exhibition flights to various European countries of ostensibly allied governments.

For their prime role, the squadrons undertook a number of 'war' exercises at the start of the year, with brief detachments to armament camps to train air gunners and bomb-aimers; while 38 Squadron, for example, carried out a three-day exercise in March in which the entire squadron moved to West Raynham and lived 'rough' in tents while flying practice bombing sorties. Then, on 11 April, nine of 38 Squadron's Wellingtons under the command of Squadron Leader J.R. Whitley (later, Air Marshal Sir John, KBE,CB,DSO,AFC) were detached to Northolt for three months specifically for co-operation with army defence units based near Aldershot. This involved both day and night flights and tested anti-aircraft batteries, searchlights, and indeed a few 'night fighters'.

On 15 May, however, 38 Squadron lost its first Wellington when L4243 caught fire in the air and crashed – due to faulty flexible unions on its fuel piping; a defect experienced by several other crews though without serious results. At the end of May a total force of 27 Wellingtons combined in a practice (and ostensibly very success-ful...) bombing attack on ships of the Royal Navy – thereby unwittingly providing a harbinger of a vital future role for the Wimpy – although certain RN senior officers remained unconvinced of the destructive power of 'a few aircraft' (*sic*) against capital vessels of the RN!

In the interim all sections of the RAF practised diligently for the last Empire Air Day, due to take place on 20 May – the annual 'tax-payers' benefit', as this occasion was dubbed in Service circles. On that day the RAF 'opened' a total of 63 Royal Air Force stations to the general public, while a further 15 civil aerodromes also opened their gates. At each airfield a host of attractions both on the ground, and, especially, in the air were laid on for the benefit of the public – although the bureaucratic obsession with so-termed security was manifested by a general prohibition of photographing *any* aspect of RAF life and, especially, equipment; a frustrating restriction for the near-million visitors.

Only three days later the RAF was again 'on parade', this time for an exhibition of its latest aircraft types at Northolt for the benefit of a large party of members of both Houses of Parliament during which a perfect formation of 24 Wellingtons flew over at 1,000 feet. Another facet of the RAF's 'liaison' with the British public was a scheme for affiliating certain squadrons with local towns and cities; a case in point being No 9 Squadron which had been officially affiliated to the town of Ipswich in early 1939, having moved base from Stradishall to Honington on 15 July.

During July and August 1939 several 'long-distance' (*sic*) flights were undertaken to European countries. One of the first such flag-waving occasions involved No 9 Squadron which despatched nine Wellingtons to Evere airfield (Brussels airport) to help the Belgians celebrate the 25th anniversary of the foundation of their *Aéronautique Militaire*. At Evere the Wellingtons proved a slight problem in the context of accommodation overnight – their wings were wider than the available hangar doors! However, the actual display on 9 July proved a huge success. Two days later a total of 12 RAF squadrons flew the first of a series of so-termed long-distance flights over areas of France as part of a reciprocal agreement with the French government and French air services; each air force regarding these flights as pure navigational training practice. On 14 July a total of 52 RAF aircraft took part in the celebrations of France's Bastille Day, based at Paris's Le Bourget aerodrome, with No 149 Squadron's Wellingtons well to the fore. Four days later all serviceable aircraft within the aegis of No 3 Group, Bomber Command were detailed for another flight over France – which very nearly proved disastrous. The occasion is well recalled by A. Montagu-Smith, by then Flight Lieutenant, who led a section of B Flight, No 99 Squadron:

Bad weather south of London forced a change of plan, which was communicated to each aircraft by wireless – we did not have R/T. The result of this last-minute change of plan was chaotic. The new orders cancelled the French trip and substituted a tour along the south coast of England instead.

As we flew west the weather got steadily worse, with low cloud and poor visibility, until it was difficult to even see the nearest aircraft ahead. Eventually I received a 'Return to Base' signal from my wireless operator. At the same time, to my alarm, out of the gloom came a number of Wellingtons on a reciprocal course! These belonged to the leading squadrons returning home, having jumped the gun by following the leader before the signal had reached all aircraft. With Wellingtons gaily passing on either side of me, the scene can well be imagined – I can still remember the look of horror on the face of my second pilot-cum-navigator, Flying

L4265 of 149 Squadron, LY–L, pre-war, which later served on 15 OTU and crashed on take-off at Mount Farm on 18 March 1942.

Crew of 149 Squadron 'Eastland' Wellington climbing aboard at Stradishall during the August 1939 war exercises.

Officer Hetherington, a New Zealander.* However, we were able to extricate ourselves from this shambles, and miraculously there were no collisions.†

Useful as such jaunts were in flying and navigation practice, more intensive (if somewhat unrealistic...) testing of the RAF's firstline potential took place in August 1939 when the annual 'Air Exercise', or colloquially 'War Games' took place between 2000 hrs on 8 August and 1900 hrs on 11 August. For this yearly event a total of slightly more than 1,300 RAF aircraft of every type was involved, split nominally into 'Westland' and 'Eastland' forces – Westland being deemed 'friendly' and Eastland the 'enemy'. The prime purpose of this particular exercise was to provide not only practice for UK-based fighters in interception – though incoming 'enemy' bombers were given routes which would have invited disaster in any genuine war situation – but mainly to provide all forms of ground defences with an opportunity to test their efficiency and organisation.

One novelty of this August 1939 exercise was the first-ever experiment in having metropolitan London – the main target for most 'enemy' bombers – blacked out after midnight. One of many journalists permitted to accompany RAF crews was H.F. King from *Flight* magazine, whose subsequent report read in part:

> On Thursday we motored through the sunny afternoon to Honington, not far from Bury St Edmunds. It was from here that we were to take off in a raiding 'Eastland' Wellington to do some dirty work London way . . . Newbury Racecourse, our target, should be well and truly plastered, even should one be obliged to get out and look for it, for the lights of London were soon to be extinguished.
>
> The cabin of the 'blacked-out' Wellington was like the dim nave of a Gothic cathedral. One installed oneself beside the pilot and the big Vickers was soon charging down the flarepath and sailing seawards. Lowestoft passed below as we nosed up through ice to 18,000 feet, where we stayed for an asthmatic half-hour, turning south to get into position for the raid. Observation of incidental instruments was done by flashlight, though the navigator occasionally switched on the cabin light. The blowers were now set

*Later, Flight Lieutenant E.J. Hetherington, killed in crash on return from an operational sortie, 14 December 1939.
†*Wellington at War* by C. Bowyer; Ian Allan, 1982.

in high gear. As we nosed in north of Southend we were somewhat shaken to see the familiar London glow, though it was, admittedly, subdued. The Estuary water showed up clearly near the lighted buoys, and we saw distinct red lights which we assumed to mark Dagenham pylons. We were unmistakably over London, though it was difficult to get exact bearings, the lights being in broken masses. We set a slightly southerly course and the searchlights started to grope round us in dozens, so very near and yet so far. The Flight Lieutenant (*pilot*) steered straight for any beam which erected itself ahead, and every time it moved just as we were about to pass into it. But a rising chuckle was squashed by a sudden brilliant illumination of the front turret in which we were now installed, and by the sight of another great black Wellington formating a few feet above. We groped meditatively for a Brazil (*nut*) but were soon grasping the gun 'handlebars' as the Flight Lieutenant started ducking our ponderous craft through a field of beams, periodically changing the pitch of one Pegasus to 'fox' the sound locators. One or two pairs of navigation lights slipped by below us. Fighters were on the prowl and they could not see us . . .

And so we droned on with stars above and wavering pillars of light below on course for Newbury. One more light caught us fairly and squarely, but we dodged behind a cloud. Of the actual üccess of our attack we know nothing, but we indicated our [bombing] run on our recognition lights and set off our Sashalites before turning for Bury and the North Sea. As we went we watched those groping beams criss-crossing the night sky. It seemed like a Hollywood first night and, somehow, like the Fifth of November.*

The 'unreal' sentiment expressed by King was also felt by a number of participating air crews, one of whom, destined to complete two operational tours in Wellingtons during the war, summed up his personal opinions of this exercise as:

Useful for totting up a few more hours of nightflying in my log book, but otherwise chiefly a waste of petrol. Much later, flying ops over Germany, I often thought back to that cosy 'exercise' and marvelled at the sheer *innocence* of it all. Had I attempted to repeat those 'tactics' over the Ruhr, I'd *not* be talking to you today . . .

Nevertheless, that ultimate peacetime 'war game' was not without

Flight, dated 17 August 1939

human cost among the air crews. A Wellington from 149 Squadron, L4258, failed to return from a sortie on 9 August and was later recorded as 'Missing over the North Sea', with its crew* officially presumed killed; while on 11 August, L4240 of 38 Squadron crashed at Debden while overshooting, clipping the tail of a parked 87 Squadron Hurricane in the process, and ending up in a nearby wood.

Near the end of August 1939 further Wellington casualties occurred, with the Mildenhall-based units suffering primarily, losing two aircraft completely apart from other minor mishaps. F.H. Cannings – 'Eric' – was a wireless operator/air gunner serving with 99 Squadron then and recalled his own 'adventure':†

> August 28‡ was a bad day for Mildenhall. I was detailed to fly in L4217, 'M', with Flight Sergeant Healy who had recently come from a Handley Page Harrow squadron. Pilot Officer Hillier was navigator, Sergeant Knowles air observer-front gunner, AC Hooker rear gunner, and myself on the wireless. Our detail was low-level attacks on our own airfield. With the wind from the north, our take-off was over Beck Row. Engines were checked and we began our take-off run but as we got part-way an engine faltered, and although it immediately picked up it faltered again, so take-off was aborted and we taxied back to the hangar area. Engines were again run up and since they now showed no hesitation we again started to roll. As we were about to get airborne the port engine back-fired and caught fire. We had gone past the point of no return and could not get airborne. I don't know whether we bounced over the boundary fence or found a hole in it, but we were soon outside the airfield heading for a barn which normally housed seats etc used on sports days.
>
> The port wing struck the barn but we continued on, heading for the main road in line with the wooden Beck Row Chapel. I believe the wing hit another building before the aircraft slewed sideways against the stone wall with our starboard wing across the Mildenhall road. The nose turret was removed when it demolished some outhouses of a couple of cottages. Pilot Officer Hillier and myself, when we saw a crash was inevitable, braced ourselves behind the rear spar, feet against it and holding onto it with both hands. When we came to rest the port wing was blazing furiously.

*Flying Officer T.A. Darling, Pilot Officer F.E. Board, Sergeant A. Linkley, AC1s R.C.B. Collins and J.W. Sadler.
†Letter to author
‡L4217's Record Card states August 29

Wellington Is, L4367 and L4369 of 75 Squadron during August 1939 'war games' and marked with the white crosses of the 'Westland' (i.e. 'friendly') forces.

We first tried sliding the astro hatch open but this was jammed. Hillier grabbed the escape axe with a view to breaking off the rear cupola. It was difficult to see because of the dust, and the fabric on the fuselage was now burning and seeming to follow us down to the tail. The cupola had already gone with the impact against the wall and AC Hooker had been thrown out into a nettle patch.

We then climbed out, ran from the vicinity, and found that Flight Sergeant Healey and Sergeant Knowles were already out having escaped via the broken front end. The pilot was convinced that six men should have been on board, so Hillier and I ran back and looked into the tail section. We climbed back in to where we could see a dark shape but found only engine covers. The first of the petrol tank explosions quickly drove us out (not that we needed any encouragement because the fabric was already burning around us) and ran a respectable distance away. Even so spent bullets were dropping all around us which added to the explosions of petrol tanks and oxygen bottles. Flight Sergeant Healey broke a little finger, Sergeant Knowles needed several stitches in his arms, while the rest of us had minor cuts and bruises – plus nettle-rash for AC Hooker!

The following morning when we viewed the cold wreckage almost everything forward of the main spar had melted except the two engines. The cause was later established as fuel starvation because the fuel cock was not fully open to 100-octane fuel used for take-off. Another Wellington meantime lost six feet from its mainplane when it hit the top of an air-raid shelter in a low-level attack – yet the pilot knew nothing about it until after he'd landed! 149 Squadron had an aircraft down in the North Sea, and one of the search aircraft came down in a tree plantation near the Brandon road.*

The 149 Squadron Wellington referred to by Cannings as lost over the North Sea was L4257, which was seen to dive into the sea south-east of the Happisburgh Light Vessel – the loss being later attributed to poor visibility confusing the pilot as to his altitude over the sea.

A Wellington of 115 Squadron was inadvertently responsible for the death of one more officer in the same month. On 28 August the squadron was engaged in live bombing practice at Larkhill, and one of its aircraft being bombed up at Boscombe Down for a sortie had a live bomb fall off its carrier. Watching was Air Commodore A.A.B. Thomson who instinctively stepped back when the bomb fell – and was killed by a revolving propeller just behind him.

By the close of August 1939 the European political tinderbox which had smouldered for many months finally erupted in flame, and on Sunday, 3 September the British population heard the melancholy tones of its Prime Minister, Neville Chamberlain, declare '. . . that this country is now at war with Germany'. Full anticipatory mobilisation of the RAF had already been effected before this date. On 1 September, for example, No 38 Squadron left its base at Marham to 'disperse' to a satellite airfield at Barton Bendish, then next day moved to South Cerny, finally returning to Marham on 6 September. Apart from such highly temporary detachments by most units, on 3 September 1939 the existing Wellington squadrons were *based* as follows:

9 Squadron	Honington
37 Squadron	Feltwell
38 Squadron	Marham
75 Squadron	Stradishall
99 Squadron	Newmarket†
115 Squadron	Marham
148 Squadron	Stradishall
149 Squadron	Mildenhall
214 Squadron	Feltwell
215 Squadron	Honington

†but still controlled by Mildenhall

*Flying Officer F.W.S. Turner (captain), Pilot Officer T. Watson (second pilot, severely injured), Sergeants A.F.A. Freeman (killed) and H.J. Weller, AC2s J.G. Hoey and C.G. Barker. Accident on August 29.

Of these units, Nos 75 and 148 Squadrons were already classified as Group Pool (i.e. training) squadrons, while Nos 214 and 215 were now titled reserve squadrons – the latter having been reclassified *per se* on 2 September, and eventually transferred to No 6 (Training) Group with effect from 27 October 1939. Between them the ten squadrons had an overall strength of 160 Wellingtons – all Mk Is apart from two Mk IAs on charge to 149 Squadron – while a further 15 Wellingtons were on RAF charge, disposed among various non-operational units or 'in store' awaiting unit issue. For comparison, the equivalent totals for the RAF's only other two 'heavy' (*sic*) bomber types on that date were 169 Hampdens actually on squadrons with 43 more on second/thirdline units, and 140 Whitleys (all Mks) on squadrons with a further 56 'in reserve'. Thus, merely six Wellington squadrons – Nos 9, 37, 38, 99, 115, and 149 – all under the aegis of No 3 Group, Bomber Command (AOC, AVM J.E.A. Baldwin) were available to undertake active operations immediately at the outbreak of hostilities; less than a third of their Command's full striking force.

As full-scale war with Germany commenced No 3 Group's Wellington crews – along with the rest of Bomber Command – were immediately heavily restricted by higher policy as to where, what, even how they might prosecute any form of bombing offensive against German targets. In simple summary, the bomber crews were forbidden to bomb *any* kind of target actually on German soil – though the dropping of propaganda leaflets (*Nickels* as these were code-named by the RAF) on German towns and cities was permissible; while enemy ships – considered then to be prime objects for attack – could *only* be bombed if anchored out in open harbour waters or at sea.

Higher policy (initially) also directed that only Whitleys would be used for night operations – Wellingtons, Hampdens, Blenheims, etc were to be despatched in daylight, without any form of fighter escort, relying on tight formation-keeping to provide necessary concentration of defensive gunfire in the event of attack by German fighters. The myth of the 'self-defending' bomber – born in Hugh Trenchard's 1918 Independent Force, RAF – had yet to be discarded by the air policy-makers . . .

CHAPTER FOUR

Disaster by Day

With the official declaration of war by Britain on 3 September 1939, RAF Bomber Command lost no time in mounting sorties against German objectives. The first aircraft to take off on an operational sortie was Blenheim IV, N6215 of 139 Squadron from Wyton to carry out a reconnaissance over Wilhelmshaven – taking off precisely one minute after 11am on 3 September and landing back at Wyton at 1650 hours.

In the early evening of that same Sunday formations totalling 18 Hampdens from Nos 44, 49 and 83 Squadrons; and nine Wellingtons – six from 37 Squadron and three from 149 Squadron – were all despatched on armed reconnaissances (i.e. with bomb loads) to seek out the German navy in the Schillig Roads area. No ships were sighted and all aircraft returned safely, albeit with most crews jettisoning their bomb loads into the North Sea rather than risk landing with full 'live' explosive bomb loads (which most crews had never practised to date . . .).

Later the same evening a total of ten Whitleys, drawn from Nos 51 and 58 Squadrons, carried six million (approx 13 tons) of propaganda leaflets to Hamburg, Bremen, and the Ruhr area – a type of operation code-named *Nickel* by the RAF – resulting in two Whitleys force-landing in France and a third crashlanding on return, though without injury to its crew.

As a demonstration of Bomber Command's ability to reach German cities, this latter 'bum-fodder' raid may well have given the German citizens of the targets some uncomfortable moments, but was also an example of the Command's necessarily restricted range of action at the start of hostilities. Weak in numerical strength, the Command could not afford to risk more than a small percentage of its firstline aircraft on any individual operation.

The first actual bombing raids carried out by Bomber Command came next day, 4 September. Two separate operations were mounted, the first of these comprising 15 Blenheim IVs – five each from Nos 107, 110, and 139 Squadrons – which left their Wyton and

Wattisham bases to attack some German warships at Wilhelms-haven and the Schillig Roads. 139 Squadron's five Blenheims failed to find the targets and returned to base, but the remaining ten attacked the *Admiral Scheer* – and lost five to a massive flak-gun defence.

The second raid comprised 14 Wellingtons – six from 9 Squadron and the rest from 149 Squadron – making a simultaneous attack on the capital ships *Scharnhorst* and *Gneisenau* lying off Brunsbüttel. The 9 Squadron sextet flew in two sections of three aircraft, the first led by Squadron Leader L.S. Lamb* with Flight Sergeants I.E.M. Borley and A.J. Turner skippering his companion Wellingtons; while the second section were piloted by Flight Lieutenant Grant (leader) and Sergeants Purdie and Bowen. Lamb's leading Vic of three on reaching their objectives ran head-on into a veritable wall of flak and were also attacked by nine Messerschmitt Bf109s from the Nordholz-based II/JG77. Lamb's wingmen, Borley and Turner, in Wellingtons L4268 and L4275, 'H' respectively, were both lost – one to flak, and the other a victim of Sergeant Alfred Held of II/JG77, thus becoming the first RAF bomber to be shot down by a German fighter in World War Two.

Two days later No 9 Squadron received its first Mk IA Wellington with FN turrets in place of the old Vickers' turrets, and was withdrawn to Boscombe Down for training with the new armament. By late December the squadron had 18 Mk IAs on strength, having resumed operations on 9 November with armed reconnaissances over the North Sea, carrying bomb loads of three 500lb high explosive bombs per Wellington.

These sorties apart, Wellingtons were not to mount any further bombing sorties until early December 1939, and in the interim had to be content with fruitless so-termed 'armed reconnaissance' around the North Sea, still seeking the elusive Germany navy and/or enemy shipping. Indeed, these types of sorties were to 'blood' the remaining Wellington units in the context of commencing operations. No 99 Squadron – the first unit to receive and fly Wellingtons – commenced operations on the night of 8/9 September by despatching three aircraft on a *Nickel* trip to the Hannover area, although one aircraft aborted the sortie due to technical difficulties.

*Killed in Wellington L4288, 'A' in air collision with L4363 on 30 October 1939. Also killed were: L4288 – Flying Officer P.E. Torkington-Leech, Sergeant C.A. Bryant and LAC S. Hawkins; L4363 – Flying Officer J.F. Chandler, Pilot Officer C.C. Cameron, ACs E. Grant, W.J. Chapman, G. Dicks.

On 8 October No 115 Squadron's crews made their initial operational sorties – an armed search by six Wellingtons for German shipping reported off the Norwegian coast – while No 38 Squadron's 'initiation' came on 17 November when six aircraft undertook an armed reconnaissance over the North Sea's eastern waters. The resumption of actual bombing operations by Wellingtons came on 3 December when a force of 24 attacked some German warships off Heligoland – the force comprising Wellingtons from Nos 38, 115, and 149 Squadrons.

The attack was made from 10,000 feet, with claims for hits on a cruiser and a trawler. Despite flak and fighter opposition, no losses were incurred, but one 115 Squadron Wellington had one of its bombs hung-up and this was accidentally jettisoned on Heligoland Island – the first RAF bomb to drop on German soil during World War Two.

During this same raid a 38 Squadron Wellington, skippered by Pilot Officer E.F.J. Odoire,* strayed from the main formation and was promptly jumped by enemy fighters and liberally riddled with bullets and cannon shells, perforating the port fuel tanks and top cylinders of the port engine, and (unbeknown to the crew) slashing the port undercarriage wheel. In the Wellington's rear turret Leading Aircraftman (LAC) John J. Copley was injured during a close stern attack by one fighter but returned fire at 200 yards and saw the fighter climb sharply, stall, then fall away out of control. On landing back at base Odoire's aircraft ground-looped due to the punctured port wheel, while Copley on evacuating his turret found a German bullet lodged in the quick release box of his parachute harness!

For his courage and endurance Copley, born in Brierley, Barnsley in 1912 and a former colliery engine-man who had joined the RAF in 1935, was awarded a Distinguished Flying Medal (DFM),† while his pilot, Odoire received a 'Mentioned in Despatches'. The enemy fighter was thereafter claimed by 38 Squadron as its first combat victory of World War Two.

The difficulty of operating the fixed Vickers gun turrets of Mk I Wellingtons had long been recognised, and although no 'new' Wellington squadrons appeared in the remaining months of 1939, the existing Wimpy units began replacing their ill-armed Mk Is with Mk

*Later, Group Captain, DFC,AFC; Wellington, N2879, 'Z'.
†*London Gazette* dated 1 January 1940.

IAs and ICs, with a consequent all-round improvement in defensive armament and general performance. The raid on 3 December had incurred no losses of aircraft despite the Luftwaffe fighter opposition and this appeared, to RAF higher authorities, to confirm their policy of sending unescorted, 'self-defending' bomber formations into enemy skies in broad daylight – despite the fact that on 29 September 1939, when 11 Hampdens from 144 Squadron had been despatched to bomb in the Heligoland Bight area, five Hampdens, including the squadron commander, had all been shot down by German fighters.

Still convinced that a tightly-formated bomber force could ward off any air opposition, HQ Bomber Command issued orders for another daylight foray by Wellingtons on 14 December 1939. At 0600 hrs on that date 12 Wellingtons of 99 Squadron were already fully prepared for this operation, with crews standing by at one hour's notice, and at 1100 hrs the operation order was received – an 'armed reconnaissance' of the Heligoland Bight area to seek out any 'battle-cruisers or cruisers' (*sic*). Each Wellington was armed with three 500lb Semi-Armour Piercing (SAP) bombs, and at 1143 hrs they began taking off, then forming into four sections with the leading section led by Wellington N2958, skippered by Squadron Leader Andrew 'Square' McKee* who had with him as 'passenger' Wing Commander J.F. Griffiths.

Weather conditions were far from ideal and as the Wellington force crossed the coastline at Yarmouth it immediately nosed into thick haze which reduced visibility to no better than 1000 yards. By 1300 hrs the bombers had reached Terschelling but by then were flying through steady rain at a mere 600 feet height above the sea. Setting course for Heligoland the Wellingtons, still in good formation, ran into deteriorating weather conditions of rain and snow-sleet, forcing them further down to 200 feet altitude, then wheeling eastwards on nearing Wangerooge Isle and flying over some trawlers and a submarine.

At 1425 hrs a battle-cruiser and a small cruiser were sighted steaming southwards, and minutes later as the bombers swung onto a northerly course they ran into an intense flak barrage from three destroyers also steaming south; a barrage supplemented minutes later by the flak guns of the two cruisers first sighted – the larger of which was the *Nürnberg*† – and which caused the bomber formation to begin turning away onto a westwards course. While still wheeling on

*Later, Air Marshal Sir Andrew McKee, KCB,CBE,DSO,DFC,AFC.
†The *Nürnberg* had been torpedoed at sea by the RN submarine *Salmon* – along with the *Leipzig* on the previous day, and was being escorted to harbour for repairs.

that turn three Messerschmitt Bf 109s from II/JG77, based on Wangerooge, suddenly appeared and attacked, shooting down Wellington N2986 (Sergeant R.H.J. Brace) in No 4 Section in flames.

Passing over the bombers, the Bf 109s quickly turned and commenced line-astern attacks, riddling N2936 (Flying Officer J.A.H. Cooper) which jerked drunkenly out of formation with its undercarriage flopped down, heading hopefully towards the German coast but falling into the sea within minutes. As Cooper's stricken bomber plunged into the North Sea, three more German twin-engined Messerschmitt Bf110 fighters joined the fight by attacking the bomber formation from the port beam, then turning in behind the force to deliver stern onslaughts. A further six German fighters now appeared and commenced line-astern 'pattern' attacks on the rear of Nos 1, 2, and 4 Sections of the Wellington formation.

As this latest Luftwaffe reinforcement arrived three more Wellingtons were hacked out of the bomber formation, with N2870 (Pilot Officer H.L. Lewis) falling in flames and colliding with N2991 (Flight Sergeant W.H. Downey) which also fell away into the sea, to be followed by N2886 (Flight Sergeant J.E.K. Healey), mortally hit, seconds later. By then some 20 minutes of furious activity had passed and the German fighters had not escaped battle damage. One Bf110 attempting to stern-attack 'Square' McKee's Wellington was met with an accurate pointblank burst from McKee's tail gunner, Corporal Alex Bickerstaff and was seen to spin down issuing smoke and thin flames; while another Bf110, trying to destroy Wellington N2912, 'H' (Squadron Leader R.G.E. Catt) of No 3 Section, was claimed by Corporal Cedric Pettitt of that aircraft. A third Bf110 was claimed later as 'crashed into the sea on fire'. At 1501 hrs the last fighter attack was made without result and then the Germans withdrew, short of fuel and/or bereft of ammunition, leaving seven well-damaged Wellingtons – each *still* with its full bomb load aboard – to set course back to Yarmouth.

Arriving eventually over their Newmarket base airfield, six Wellingtons landed safely with their bomb loads intact, but the seventh, N2957, piloted by the New Zealander Flight Lieutenant E.J. Hetherington, which had been badly damaged in the fight and had attempted to jettison its bombs on the return flight, still had one bomb 'hung-up' in its bomb bay, and crashed on landing in a field near the Newmarket Racecourse at 1730 hrs, killing Hetherington and two of his crew (Corporal A. Sharp, air gunner, and AC1 R. Entwistle, the wireless operator), and injuring Sergeant L.W. Parton, the air observer. As a result of this disastrous operation, DFMs were awarded to three air gunners, Corporals Bickerstaff, Pettitt, and Colin Knight, a New Zealander, while Wing Commander Griffiths received a DFC.

Higher command's reaction to this loss of half a bomber force was to place the blame on bad weather, flak damage, perforated fuel tanks, and a need for crews to maintain a tight formation – apparently being reluctant to credit losses to the German fighters. This blinkered and somewhat complacent view was manifested just four days later, when a force of 24 Wellingtons, drawn from Nos 9, 37, and 149 Squadrons were despatched in daylight to the same objective. Though two aircraft aborted the sortie early with technical problems, the remaining 22, in perfect formation, flying in the glittering sunlight of a cloud-free blue sky, were met over Wilhemshaven by a succession of Luftwaffe fighters from various units of *Jagdgeschwader Nr.1*, and within 30 minutes of unrelenting combats lost 12 Wellingtons, while three more Wellingtons crashed and were wrecked on return to England.*

Yet again Bomber Command staff officers refused to acknowledge openly the sheer folly of sending unescorted bombers into enemy skies in day operations. The AOC-in-C, Bomber Command then, Air Chief Marshal Sir Edgar Ludlow-Hewitt, blamed this latest fiasco on the bomber crews' failure to maintain a tight formation for cohesive defence; while on 29 December his Senior Staff Officer, Air Commodore Norman Bottomley, wrote a tactical memorandum in which he spoke of, 'inviolability of a tight bomber formation', and termed the losses as 'straggling aircraft'.

Statements have commonly been made in both official and other more recent histories that the 18 December 'Battle of Heligoland' – as the contemporary media dubbed the operation – was responsible for a distinct change of policy in the context of RAF daylight bombing operations. In fact, daylight sorties by Bomber Command's heavies' continued until mid-1940, and even thereafter became the accepted mode for such formations as No 2 Group's Blenheim squadrons – with concomitant appalling casualty rates. The intensity (relatively) of night bombing operations certainly increased steadily during the winter of 1939-40, when the prevailing atrocious weather conditions permitted, but any switch from day to night bombing immediately

*For fuller details of this operation, the reader is commended to *Tales from the Bombers* by C. Bowyer; William Kimber, 1985.

No. 9 Squadron Wellingtons, near Honington, early 1940. Note lowered 'dustbin' gun turret on nearest aircraft.

(Left) LAC C.R. Driver, DFM of 9 Squadron, 1939. *(Right)* Squadron Leader S.S. Murray (L) and Pilot Officer A.B. Thompson as prisoners of war at Itzhoe, nr Hamburg after attacking Wilhelmshaven, 1939.

exacerbated the prime problems for all bombing at that time i.e. the poor state of contemporary air navigation, and the crews' apparent inability in far too many cases to even *find* a specified target, let alone bomb it accurately. This state of affairs was really not the fault of the bomber crews, very few of whom (then) had any extensive experience of even flying by night, particularly over unfamiliar territories. Navigational aids and procedures then were merely modified versions of near-obsolete instruments and methods; thus bombing policies naturally veered towards a preference for daylight sorties as the only pragmatic solution. Accordingly, the clinging to the long-held 'sacred-cow' theory of the 'self-defending' bomber was in effect a sop to unavoidable circumstance. And it should be remembered that no RAF fighter in 1939-40 was capable of providing the necessary escort range to protect any bomber force operating against targets in Germany.

Notwithstanding the various 'excuses' propounded by certain RAF commanders for the tragic losses in December, lessons had been learned, and a variety of urgently-requested modifications and other improvements to Wellingtons were quickly recommended. In a note accompanying his official report on the 18 December raid, No 3 Group's commander, Air Vice-Marshal Baldwin, emphasised the vulnerability of the aircraft's unprotected wing fuel tanks and suggested urgent provision of self-sealing and/or armour-protected tanks; while in view of Luftwaffe fighter tactics he also recommended incorporation of an additional defensive gun sited centrally in the top astro hatch. Yet his report also expressed a view that a tightly-formated bomber force was still probably the best form of defence against air opposition – clearly, adherence to daylight bombing still lingered strongly in many minds at 'higher' level. Indeed, it was not until April 1940 that the C-in-C, Bomber Command – by then Air Marshal C.F.A. Portal – received an Air Staff Directive (dated 13 April) in which he was firmly 'directed' that 'the operation of our heavy bombers are to be confined mainly to night action'.

Despite the particularly heavy snow and ice conditions of the 1939-40 winter – the worst European winter for many decades – which nullified areial activities for several weeks in early 1940, daylight sorties continued whenever possible. These were primarily a continuation of the armed reconnaissances and so-termed sweeps of the North Sea zones close to Europe seeking German shipping. These were supplemented from the beginning of January 1940 with night *Nickel* sorties over Germany, with Wellingtons making their first night 'paper attack' on Hamburg on 11/12 January. These types of operation were to continue spasmodically until early April 1940, but on the night of 20/21 February a gaggle of 20 Wellingtons was despatched by night to attempt a *bombing* raid on German warships. In the event dense fog resulted in a recall signal being sent and the Wellingtons came back, losing one Wellington, N2951 of 38 Squadron at sea, and a second which crashed on landing.

By the beginning of April 1940 Allied Intelligence had given ample warning of the strong possibility of a German invasion of Norway, indicated in part by the significant increase in warships and other vessels gathering in northern German ports and harbours. Bomber Command's response was to increase its reconnaissances of the appropriate sea areas, and in the course of one such sortie on 17 April two Wellingtons from 115 Squadron – P2524, 'F' (Pilot Officer E.A. Wickenkamp, MBE) and N2949, 'H', (Pilot Officer R.A. Gayford) – were shot down by Messerschmitt Bf110s off Sylt; yet more victims of the 'daylight' policy.

Then, at the first glimmer of dawn on 9 April, German forces simultaneously invaded Denmark and Norway. Only days before these invasions another Wellington unit had joined Bomber Command's firstline strength when, on 4 April, No 75 (NZ) Squadron officially came into being. In point of fact, the Kiwi squadron had already anticipated its legal formation, having despatched three Wellingtons, skippered by Squadron Leader C.E. Kay* and Pilot Officers J. Adams and I. Collins, by night on 27 March to drop leaflets – *Nickels* – on the German towns of Brunswick, Ulzen, and Luneberg. All three returned safely, despite Kay's aircraft being struck by lightning which ruined the wireless set on the outward trip.

The German invasion of southern Norway posed a major problem to Bomber Command due to the extreme range required for any attempted RAF opposition. Partly in anticipation, in the previous week two Wellington units had been temporarily attached to Coastal Command stations in North Scotland, when 115 Squadron moved to Kinloss on 30 March, and No 9 Squadron moved to nearby Lossiemouth a few days later.† On 9 April, as the Norwegian invasion commenced, No 9 Squadron mounted a series of single-Wellington

*Later, Air Vice-Marshal, CB,CBE,DFC.
†No 99 Squadron had been 'loaned' to Coastal Command already in November-December 1939, but was back at Newmarket by January 1940.

reconnaissances of the Bergen-Stavanger area at hourly intervals, and lost one Wellington, P2520,'U'; while 115 Squadron carried out an attack on the cruisers *Köln* and *Königsberg* at Bergen, claiming damage to one vessel.

Two days later a relatively large operation was mounted by Bomber Command to attack the Sola airfield, near Stavanger. For this 115 Squadron provided six aircraft while 9 Squadron despatched five more Wellingtons. The 115 Squadron crews bombed the airfield from merely 1000 feet and promptly lost P9284,'J' (Pilot Officer F.E. Barber) shot down in flames onto the target, while a second Wellington skippered by Flight Sergeant Gordon A. Powell received three direct hits from the intense groundfire, wounding Powell in his shoulder and left side. Despite the pain of his wounds, Powell dived away to sea level and brought his crew back for a successful belly-landing at base. Powell, who had joined the RAF in 1928, was awarded a DFM – No 115 Squadron's first gallantry decoration of the war.

On 12 April 1940 a total of 83 bombers, including 36 Wellingtons, set out in daylight to attack shipping – the largest bombing force to be despatched by the RAF to date – and these encountered fierce flak and fighter opposition which accounted for the losses of nine bombers. Three of the losses were Wellingtons, including two, P9266 and P9246, belonging to 149 Squadron. Two days later No 9 Squadron returned to its Honington base, and on 18 April No 115 Squadron moved south to its base at Marham. That 12 Äril operation might correctly be termed the last *major* day bombing raid undertaken by the 'heavy' bombers of the RAF in 1940, although daytime operations in general by no means ceased. Thereafter, Wellingtons (in particular) were despatched spasmodically and in small numbers by night. On 21/22 April, for example, 12 Wellingtons set out to bomb German-occupied airfields at Stavanger (Sola) and Aalborg, and lost one, P9218,'O', of 149 Squadron, over Aalborg to flak, although its crew survived to become prisoners of war. Norwegian objectives remained a priority throughout April 1940 for Bomber Command, particularly the various airfields now occupied by the Luftwaffe, interspersed with a series of night mine-laying – *'Gardening'* – sorties in Norwegian coastal waters.

On the last night of April a force of 50 bombers, including 16 Wellingtons, attacked airfields at Sola, Fornebu, and Aalborg again. Three of the Wellingtons were lost – P9276 of 99 Squadron, and P9213 and P9215 from 37 Squadron – while others crashed on return to bases due to flak damage. That same night saw the first true nightfighter interception sorties by the Luftwaffe, when three Messerschmitt Bf110s from I/ZG1, commanded by Hauptmann Wolfgang Falck, managed to catch up with some RAF bombers as these began their return flights after bombing, though no bomber was lost to the fighters.*

Thus, on the eve of the massive *blitzkrieg* advance by German forces against France and the Low Countries on 10 May 1940, Bomber Command was finally convinced of the efficacy of night rather than day bombing by the Command's 'heavies'. The minimal casualties incurred by night operations, due mainly to the lack of adequate German nightfighter defences, radar, or other devices at that stage of the war, seemed to confirm the need for pursuing any future strategic aerial offensive under the cloak of darkness. Moreover, at that period the vital importance of *accurate* navigation to any given target had yet to be given the overall operational priority it deserved.

Optimistic reports by many bomber pilots and crews as to their locating and bombing specified objectives were believed by higher authorities with few reservations (as yet), while photographic confirmation of such reports was mainly lacking in early 1940. The common method of navigation by Wellington crews then was to fly to the Dutch coast by dead reckoning, make a pinpoint there in order to calculate a wind for the run to a recognisable landmark near to the actual target, then rely on map-reading, aided by occasional illumination from dropped 4-5-inch parachute flares, and the traditional navigator's prime aid, the 'Eyeball Mk 1' . . . By May 1940, though with several cautious doubters, the bomber policy-makers were by and large optimistic about night-bombing claimed achievements and were, in the main, to remain so until the inauguration of accurate photographic reconnaissance from late 1940 eventually shattered this chimera.

*German propaganda had *claimed* nightfighter *victories* on April 21 and 25 by Bf109Ds of IV(N)/JG2, but no evidence exists to confirm these claims. See *History of the German Night Fighter Force* by G. Aders; Jane's, 1979.

CHAPTER FIVE

Target Germany: 1940

The German *blitzkrieg* offensive against France and the Low Countries which commenced on 10 May 1940 and ended with the capitulation of France on 25 June 1940 – a mere six weeks of unprecedented Allied disaster – had been foreseen by both British and French hierarchy, albeit not in its eventual speed and sheer strength. Yet RAF Bomber Command had made no specific moves to hinder the preparations for that offensive, being still hampered by sheer lack of aircraft strength and, initially, by political orders to attack only targets west of the Rhine. The latter restriction was removed promptly on 15 May, and that night a force of 99 bombers – 39 of these being Wellingtons – flew to a total of 16 *different* designated targets in the overall Ruhr area; an operation now regarded officially as the first true *strategic* bombing operation against German industrial objectives by the RAF in World War Two.

This 'series' of raids cost the RAF Wellington P9299, 'S' of No 115 Squadron, which crashed into a hillside at Burney, near Rouen, killing Flight Lieutenant A.E. Pringle, DFC and his four-man crew. The following night saw six Wellingtons, plus six Hampdens, despatched to bomb 'oil targets' in Ruhr, and Wellington N3015 from No 9 Squadron failed to return. On the night of 17/18 May a total of 46 Wellingtons were sent out to attack enemy troop centres and communications in Belgium, while Hampdens and Whitleys concentrated on oil refineries at Hamburg and Bremen, and six other Wellingtons bombed Cologne's railway yards; all accomplished without RAF loss.

By 20 May the German advance into France necessitated most bombing efforts to be concentrated on tactical targets in the hope of – at least – delaying German progress, and that evening 32 Wellingtons were part of the 92 aircraft force sent to bomb a variety of targets. Three Wellingtons failed to return; P9298, 'H' (Flight Sergeant L.G. Moores) and R3152, 'J' (Pilot Officer D.W. Morris), both from 115 Squadron, and L7803 of 99 Squadron.* Their targets that night had

*With regard to the loss of L7803, ambiguity in official records gives this loss-date as both 20/21 May and 21/22 May.

been mainly road and rail lines of communication, and these objectives remained the primary targets over the following three weeks; concentrating on communications and troop centres immediately behind the so-termed 'battle fronts' in France and Belgium as the Allied armies steadily retreated towards Dunkirk.

In contrast to the massive casualty rates of the Fairey Battle and Bristol Blenheim units operating by day at this desperate period, the night bombers suffered very light losses to enemy action, but the wintry weather conditions occasionally caused problems; an example being the night of 29/30 May when four of 15 Wellingtons despatched to attack road targets ran into dangerous weather on return over England, causing all four pilots to order their crews to bale out, then achieve safe landings. With the Dunkirk *'Operation Dynamo'* in effect – evacuating trapped Allied personnel from the besieged port – 33 Wellingtons flew night raids on German positions outside the Dunkirk area, losing L7791 and P9288 of No 37 Squadron in the process; but suffered no further losses until 5/6 June when 34 Wellingtons were among a force bombing railway communications and Squadron Leader G.E. Peacock, DFC of 9 Squadron failed to return in P9232, 'M'.

The entry of Italy into the war on the Axis side on 10 June 1940 brought a fresh commitment for Bomber Command, but the first raid on an Italian target from the Command came on the night of 15/16 June when a small detachment of Wimpys based at Salon, near Toulon, sent eight aircraft to bomb Genoa. In the event only one of these actually bombed the target, but on the following night 14 of 22 Wellingtons despatched to Genoa and Milan reported bombing their primary objectives. Moreover, there were no losses on either operation. The main effort for the moment, however, remained targets in Germany, and on 18/19 June 26 Wellingtons were among a force of 69 bombers sent off to raid various oil and communications centres in the Ruhr.

Among those Wimpys were six from 99 Squadron, based at Newmarket, one of which, R3200, '0', was skippered by a pilot destined to become a virtual legend in RAF bomber circles, Percy Charles Pickard (later, Group Captain, DSO, DFC). Pickard's target was a factory on the east side of the Ruhr area, which was duly bombed despite fierce flak opposition, but as he turned for the return leg his starboard engine was hit and ground to a stop. Pressing on, Pickard reached the North Sea but with steady loss of oil pressure in

(Above) 99 Squadron scene at Newmarket, 1940–41 winter.

(Bottom left) Interior of Wellington T2888, 'R' of B Flt, 99 Squadron at Newmarket, late 1940 – taken with a box 'Brownie' camera!

(Top right) R1333, the so-termed 'Broughton Bomber', which was issued to 99 Squadron but crashed on take-off for its first operation on 18 December 1940, killing its rear gunner in the resulting burn-out.

(Bottom right) Kriegie. T2501 of 99 Squadron (Fg Off R.H. Vivian) in German hands after a sortie on 4/5 December 1940. Just below cockpit is an insigne of a tennis racquet with three tennis balls.

No. 311 (Czech) Squadron officers. 2nd from rt is P.C. Pickard, while far left is Wing Commander Toman-Mares, with Flt Lt Tommy Kirby-Green standing next to him.

L7788, KX–E, of 311 Squadron shot down at Leidschendam, Holland on 24/Sept 1940

the port motor, until unavoidably he prepared his crew for ditching, then set the crippled aircraft down on the waves.

All the crew promptly evacuated the sinking Wimpy and scrambled into their sole dinghy. Then, using a tiny compass concealed in the top button of his tunic, Pickard gave his navigator, Alan Broadley (later, Flight Lieutenant, DSO, DFC, DFM), instructions to 'Get us home, old boy'. Unbeknown to any of the crew as they paddled towards (hopefully) the Norfolk coast, the dinghy was in the middle of a mined area! Eventually, some 14 hours after ditching, the crew were retrieved *outside* the mined area by an ASR launch, and they returned to Newmarket.

If German flak was regarded by all Wellington operational crews as something which 'went with the job', casualties due to faulty aircraft identification caused by 'friendly' guns also occurred throughout the war, with few RAF aircraft types escaping such mistaken attentions. On 24 March 1940, for example, P9225 of 149 Squadron was shot down in the early morning by French anti-aircraft gunners; while nearer home, on 24 October 1940 the same squadron's T2740 was coolly fired on by British ack-ack guns near Clacton and was wrecked in its subsequent forced landing, having been returning from a sortie to Berlin. Indeed, by the end of the European war, and in that theatre alone, no less than 33 Wellington air crew members were killed and a further seven seriously injured due to attacks by 'friendly' guns and RAF fighters; the last known example happening as late as 24 February 1945, on which date a Mk XIII, NC604, of 69 Squadron was first attacked by Allied fighters but managed to evade these, only then to be shot down by Allied anti-aircraft guns. The totals of actual crew casualties mentioned do not include an unnumbered, far greater number of crews who, though suffering such attacks by Allied guns, survived in spite of damage to their Wimpys.

By July 1940 the debacle of the French collapse was history and RAF Bomber Command now faced the prospect of targets as far afield as Norway, Italy, and Germany itself, apart from the more immediate dangers of French-based Luftwaffe forces. The obvious necessity of strengthening and up-dating the firstline bomber strength was well recognised, but from July to October 1940 top priority in aircraft production had to be in the context of fighters to sustain Fighter Command's epic struggle to defeat the Luftwaffe – and thereby nullify German plans to invade England – in the so-termed Battle of Britain.

Thus, only one fresh Wellington unit came into being during the height of the battle when No 311 Squadron was officially formed on 29 July 1940 at Honington, composed mainly (though as yet not exclusively) of Czechoslovakian expatriates. On that date an English CO arrived, Wing Commander P.C. Pickard, and on 2 August the unit received its first pair of 'operational' Wellingtons, L7776 and N2880. By the end of August eight more Wimpys had been received, followed by ten more by 11 September. By then the eager Czech crews were more than ready to 'go to war', and the squadron's first operational sorties – five crews to bomb marshalling yards at Brussels – were despatched from Honington on the night of 10/11 September 1940. However, that sortie was regarded as merely a 'blooding', and the squadron moved from Honington to its satellite at East Wretham a week later, and after further training re-commenced operations; the start of some 21 months of continuing sorties under the aegis of Bomber Command – the ultimate operations in this context being on 25/26 April 1942 – before being transferred to Coastal Command for the rest of the war.

Three more units began receiving Wellingtons in October 1940. These were all existing Fairey Battle squadrons, Nos 103, 150, and 301, based respectively at Newton (103 & 150) and Swinderby (301) at the start of that month. No 103 Squadron received its first Wellingtons, R3275 & T2610, on 2 October, with eight more arriving by 24 October; 150 Squadron received its first example, L7870, on 2 October, with nine more by the 9th; while 301 (*'Pomeranian'*) Squadron, comprised mainly of expatriate Polish personnel, took on charge P9214 on 20 October and a further 11 Wimpys by 16 November 1940. By the close of 1940 a further 12 squadrons had received Wellingtons; three of these being fresh units and the remainder exchanging their former Battles or Blenheims. In summary, these were:

Squadron	Base	Remarks
304	Bramcote	Polish (*'Silesian'*) Sqn. 1st a/c received, N2899 & N2989 on 1/11/40.
305	Bramcote	Polish (*'Ziemia Wielkopolska'*) Sqn. 1st a/c received, P2531 on 5/11/40.
40	Wyton	1st a/c received, N3000, T2514, T2515, & T2718, all on 5/11/40.
218	Marham	1st a/c received, R1008, R1009, R1025, all on 6/11/40.

Wellington OJ–W of 149 Squadron at Mildenhall, winter 1940–41.

Wimpy crew of Wellington Ic, R3297, 'S', 75(NZ) Squadron, Feltwell, Sept 1940. L–R: Sgt Henderson; Plt Off C.K. Saxelby; Plt Off D.J. Harkness (Capt); Sgts. D. Humphries, McCrum, & Gosden. Squadron Leader Harkness, DFC was to be killed in action, 31 May 1942, while Squadron Leader Saxelby, DFC became a PoW on 7 Sept. 1942. Note Winston Churchill insigne.

57	Feltwell	1st a/c received, T2804 on 7/11/40.
15	Wyton	1st a/c received, N2871 on 7/11/40.
142	Binbrook	1st a/c received, W5356 on 8/11/40/
12	Binbrook	1st a/c received, W5353 & W5354, on 10/11/40.
221	Bircham Newton	Sqn formed 21/11/40. 1st a/c received, N2910 & R2700 on 29/11/40. Coastal Command ASV ops.
93*	Middle Wallop	Formed as 93 Sqn from No 420 Flt, 7/12/40. For *Pandora* (aerial mines defence role).
109*	Boscombe Down	Reformed 10/12/40 as WIDU initially.
300	Swinderby	Polish ('*Masovian*') Sqn. 1st a/c actually received, L7789 on 7/10/40, but not fully equipped until December 1940.

In addition in 1940 No 24 Squadron, based at Hendon, began operating a few converted Wellingtons as passenger/freight/VIP transports; these aircraft having all armament removed and gun turret locations, bomb bays, etc faired over or sealed.

Until November 1940 Bomber Command's main efforts continued to be aimed at preventing a German invasion force assembling and sailing from the Channel ports, and sorties concentrated on such French ports and harbours, but it also paid attention to the road and rail lines leading to such assembly areas of troops, barges, and the like. These operations were flown mainly by night – to have attacked in broad daylight would have invited disaster from French-based Luftwaffe fighters – and were to well-known targets within easy range, involving little if any penetration of enemy-occupied territories. From November, however, the operational pace slackened considerably, due partially to the onset of winter weather but also to a change in bombing policy directives from the Air Staff which required Bomber Command to make 'oil targets' its prime consideration. The same directives also calmly listed a host of other types of objective classified as 'important' – industrial centres, cities, rail centres, Luftwaffe airfields, and others as far away as Italy.

To Air Marshal Sir Richard Peirse, who had assumed command of

---

*Nos 93 and 109 Squadrons received only a few Wellingtons.

Wellingtons of 149 Squadron, Mildenhall. Nearest aircraft has a kangaroo insigne below its cockpit, probably denoting an Australian skipper.

'Popeye', Wellington 'Z' of 75(NZ) Squadron at Marham, October 1940.

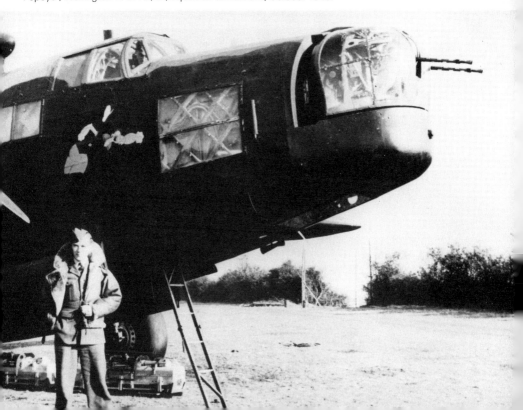

(Above) Mr. W.J. Jordan, High Commissioner for New Zealand, visiting No. 75(NZ) Squadron. Note contemporary style of aircrew flying clothing, including 'Parasuits' (or 'Goon Suits' as these were dubbed).

(Left) Arse-End Charlie's Office in a Wellington.

the bomber force on 5 October 1940, such a diverse (and lengthy) list of 'priority' targets was the stuff of Air Ministry dreams – his *total* bomber force at that moment was, on paper only, 532 aircraft. Of these, 85 were Fairey Battles now totally obsolete, while 217 were Blenheims which were unsuitable for long-range, night operations. Thus he was left with 130 Hampden and Whitley bombers plus 100 Wellingtons capable of carrying out any form of night 'strategic' operations; although normal day to day strengths of actual *serviceable* bombers for such sorties could hardly be expected to be more than 150-160.* Moreover, the Hampdens and Whitleys were planned to be replaced by new 'heavies' such as the Avro Manchester, Short Stirling, and Handley Page Halifax, which would patently reduce any operational efforts during the 'conversion' periods for each unit involved.† Thus, only the Wellington could be relied upon to maintain Bomber Command's offensive for many months to come until the new 'heavies' could supplement them.

One Wellington crew member of those days was Paul S.F. Walmsley, DFC who recalled‡:

The Vickers Wellington and I met almost casually in the late spring of 1940 at RAF Bircham Newton. I'd joined the RAFVR soon after the Munich business and, being over 26 at that time, I was over the age limit for pilot training and therefore opted for air observer. At that time I was living in Hull and when war broke out some 30-odd observers from the Hull area joined a similar number of Derby VRs and were posted to Prestwick to spend three months learning to be navigators, being taught by ex-Merchant Navy navigators (these latter being none too sure what the difference was between an air position and a fix sign!). We were next posted to No 9 Bombing & Gunnery School, Penrhos to learn how to *aim* bombs (not, you may note, to *drop* bombs . . .) and then for reasons known only to themselves the Powers-that-Be thought fit to post five of us – all of our names beginning with the letter W – to Bircham Newton; our names being Walker, Williams, Waddington, myself, and a fifth whose name I'm afraid I've forgotten.

Arriving in April 1940 as shiny-new Sergeants, we reported to

*Figures from PRO Files AIR 22/31-to-/49.
†In the event these designs made their initial operational sorties on 10/11 March 1941 (Halifax); 24/25 Feb 1941 (Manchester); 10/11 Feb 1941 (Stirling), but only in very small numbers.
‡Correspondence with author.

W5359,QT–B of 142 Squadron at Binbrook, Dec. 1940. Later served with 305 Squadron; 1443 Flt; 104 Squadron and crashed at Kabrit on 23 Oct. 1942.

'Pinocchio' of 38 Squadron at Marham, 1940.

'the Station Orderly Room – who promptly stated that they knew nothing about us, but would we go along to the Sergeants' Mess and make ourselves comfortable. By then summer was beginning and I remember sitting around for hours, just watching Ansons of 48 Squadron coming and going on convoy duties, Hudsons flying around, and Wellingtons – Wimpys – fitted with huge rings which seemed to embrace the whole of the aircraft. Being thoroughly bored with sitting around all day sun-bathing, we five all volunteered to fly in these shaky, not to say dicey, aircraft in whatever capacity required. I flew four such trips, on 27 April, 7, 8 and 10 May 1940, in Wimpys R2700 and P9223 (two trips in each). These went off more or less without incident, except we thought the Wimpys would never get airborne at times and the wings used to flap up and down like a frustrated duck as the aircraft tore down the airfield trying to get aloft. We would then navigate to a DR position off the coast and go down to 50 feet and sweep a section of the sea.

By 16 June the 'Powers' apparently decided that we had had enough time swanning at Bircham Newton and suddenly posted us to 15 OTU, Harwell where we were properly converted to Wellingtons, and on 8 August I joined No 99 Squadron at the race course at Newmarket. From 8 August 1940 until the end of January 1941 I completed my first tour with my skipper being Sergeant Kitely and second pilot Sergeant Ferguson. During the tour we went to Berlin five times, Frankfurt twice, Wilhelmshaven twice, and Mannheim twice. On our very first trip, which was to Hamborn, it proved to be a little hair-raising because our skipper, an experienced operational pilot, took us all round the houses and made our Wimpy do all sorts of aerobatics. I saw tracers going past us at a parallel level and remember thinking, *so* naively, 'What beautiful patterns and lights they form'! In those days we were not allowed to drop our bombs any old where. If you failed to identify the briefed target you were permitted to bomb an SEMO (Self-Evident Military Objective) and/or MOPA (Military Objective Previously Attacked).

During September 1940 we carried out raids on the Channel ports, returning to the Ruhr in October and Berlin. None of these trips were particularly exciting and were, to us, of short duration. By November we were visiting Berlin, Hamburg, Kiel, while in December our targets were Bordeaux, Lorient, Mannheim, and Wilhelmshaven. Our most eventful trip came on 16 January 1941

(Right) The proposed unit badge for aircraft of No.301 (Polish) Squadron, based on the pre-1939 badge of the 41st Karas Squadron, PAF.

(Below) No.304 (Polish) Squadron at Lindholme. Nearest, NZ—Q, was DV441.

(Far right) HF598,BH-E (later, BH-M) of 300 (Polish) Squadron, about to receive some parachute-retarded mines.

(Bottom right) No.305 (Polish) Squadron on church parade at Lindholme. Nearest Wellington is W5590, 'A', which crashed into the sea on night 3/4 May 1942.

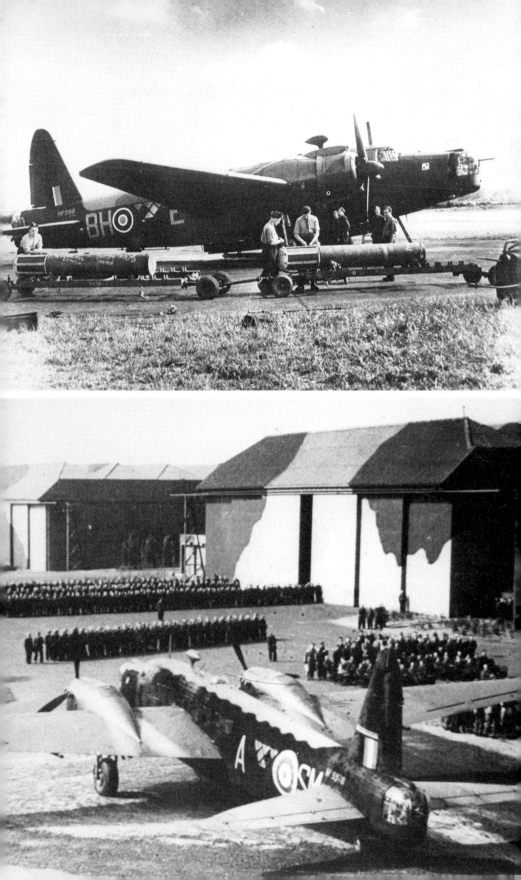

when, with Sergeant Ferguson as skipper and Sergeant Humphries as second dicky, we got hopelessly lost returning from an abortive trip to Wilhelmshaven, finally crashing our Wimpy, R3295,* at Kenley.

Although RAF aircraft had 'visited' the German capital, Berlin, for the very first time on 1/2 October 1939, when three Whitleys from No 10 Squadron dropped propaganda leaflets (but no bombs) on the 'Big City' (as Berlin was to become dubbed by Bomber Command crews in years to come) the first actual bombing attack was carried out on the night of 25/26 August 1940; a 'reprisal' raid for the Luftwaffe's attack on London the previous night. Nevertheless, from that date Berlin figured steadily more frequently among the bombers' targets, and one example of the skill and courage displayed by Wellington crews attacking the 'Big C' came on the night of 14/15 November 1940. Of some 82 Hampdens, Whitleys, and Wellingtons despatched to various objectives that night, 50 had Berlin as their briefed target.

Among the Wellingtons from Nos 9 and 115 Squadrons attacking the city was Wimpy W2509, 'W' of 115 Squadron, skippered by Sergeant H.J. Morson, with Sergeant E.A. Dean as his second pilot. Taking off at 1850 hrs, Morson reached Berlin, bombed a railway station there, then set off on his return trip. Passing over Hamburg his aircraft was hit heavily by flak and the starboard engine burst into flames. Maintaining control of the crippled bomber, Morson extinguished the fire and shut down the useless engine, then set a direct course for England, passing over the Heligoland Bight. Meantime his wireless operator, Sergeant D.H. Cleverley, kept up a constant series of messages back to base, keeping the base staff fully aware of the Wellington's position.

Inevitably, Morson had to ditch the stricken bomber in the North Sea, and in the crash his second pilot, Dean, was drowned, but the rest of the crew were rescued; their survival undoubtedly due to the efforts of Morson and Cleverley, both of whom were awarded immediate DFMs. One other Wimpy lost that night was L7852, 'P' of 9 Squadron, the aircraft's twelfth operational sortie since joining 9 Squadron on the day war was declared.

By the close of 1940 Bomber Command was only just beginning to

*Later 'P' of 101 Squadron, this Wellington ultimately ditched off the Dutch coast on 30 November 1941.

recover from its disastrous losses in mid-year, and was slowly building strength for what would now be, quite patently, a 'long war'. Actual bombing tactics were still somewhat haphazard, even leisurely if compared (with hindsight) with methods employed in 1942–45. Aircraft were still basically despatched as individual crews, rather than any attempted main stream formation concentrated on a single target. Briefings were still fairly basic, leaving the crews to work out their own means and methods of achieving the purpose of any sortie. Over enemy-occupied lands, particularly Germany itself, the greatest foes were German flak and, as ever throughout the war, the vagaries of weather. As yet the Luftwaffe night fighters were rarely encountered, although the overall night defences for the Reich were already extending their 'nets' of early ground radar installations, and were experimenting with radar-control and direction of airborne night fighters.

The first German claim for such a 'controlled' (from the ground) night victory came on the night of 1/2 October 1940 by a Leutnant Becker in a Dornier Do17Z–10; a Wellington, T2549, 'K', of No 115 Squadron, whose captain, Sergeant L.G. Goldie, and three of his crew were killed, with two other crew members surviving as prisoners of war. A second Wellington that night was fortunate not to have shared Goldie's fate, being attacked some two hours later by Unteroffizier Fick who opened fire too soon, allowing the Wimpy to evade further onslaught.

One raid, against Mannheim on the night of 16/17 December 1940, was significant for several reasons, not least for its *actual* results which exemplified the state of Bomber Command's accuracy in night bombing at that early stage of its offensive against the German homeland. A total force of 134 bombers – the largest such force despatched by the Command to date – comprised 61 Wellingtons plus 73 Hampdens, Whitleys, and Blenheims, and their briefing was to attack 'centre of the town'; a precedent for what would later be termed 'area bombing'. Leading the force were eight Wellingtons, each carrying a full incendiary load, to act as markers, while the remaining crews were briefed to bomb the fires started by those 'pathfinders'. Post-raid reports generally gave the impression that a majority of bombs had indeed created large fires in the centre of Mannheim. However, photo-reconnaissance photos taken five days later clearly revealed that the marker Wellingtons' fire-bombs had been placed inaccurately, causing widely scattered bombing by the following force; some bombs even hitting Ludwigshaven on the other side of the Rhine.

The poor results of this attack on Mannheim, added to similar PRU evidence of other targets, confirmed the vital needs for *effective* navigation aids and the use of night cameras. While production and issue of such cameras was given high priority, new aids to navigation, such as *Gee*, would not become available for operations until early 1942. Equally needed were better pyrotechnics, such as parachute flares, for illuminating targets prior to actual bombing, and more destructive high explosive bombs than the out-dated General Purpose (GP) bombs of ancient vintage still being dropped. Such improvements could hardly be produced overnight – thus the bomber crews had a long, hard struggle ahead of them.

CHAPTER SIX

Target Germany: 1941-42

By the start of 1941 Bomber Command's efforts were to a large extent dependent on the immediate weather conditions, particularly over Britain where fog became perhaps the greatest hazard for weary crews attempting to regain their base airfields after exhausting operational sorties to Germany. Indeed, for the first few months of the year casualties among returning bombers showed that almost three out of every four bombers 'lost' were due to crashes in the U.K.

A stark example of such conditions was the night of 11/12 February 1941 when, of a total force of 79 bombers despatched to bomb Bremen, 22 – including 11 Wellingtons – crashed in England due to fogged-in airfields; all but five of their crew members fortunately surviving by baling out. Bomber Command continued to send its aircraft out in relatively small 'packets' to a variety of targets rather than attempt total concentration upon one objective on any single operation; a form of tactics which produced negligible results in the context of significant destructions, and certainly gave no 'compensation' for the losses of many valuable, experienced air crews.

Although the 'new generation' of bombers – Manchesters, Stirlings, and Halifaxes – were slowly introduced to the sharp end, these were in very small numbers as yet, and in all cases beset by a crop of technical headaches and operating difficulties. Inevitably, the Wellington continued to shoulder the prime responsibility for taking the war to Germany, often comprising anything from 50 to 100 per cent of forces despatched on any night.

Added responsibilities for Bomber Command came with an Air Ministry directive dated 9 March 1941, which instructed the Command's AOC-in-C, Peirse to divert his prime efforts towards operations against German U-boat pens, docks, shipyards, and operational bases, and associated factory areas; the depredations of the German U-boats on Britain's vital merchant shipping supply convoys across the Atlantic had now reached a crisis peak.

This diversion for Bomber Command was not exclusive to maritime objectives, however, and included clear indication that the

HM King George VI (centre) with AM Sir Richard Peirse (1) and AVM J. Baldwin, AOC 3 Group, 1941.

'J-for-Jane' of 99 Squadron, Newmarket, Jan 1941; named after the very popular strip-cartoon heroine, Jane, in the contemporary *Daily Mirror* newspaper.

Air Staff wished for targets to be selected which would have the 'greatest moral (*sic*) effect' on the German civil populations resident in such target areas; a patent admission that 'area bombing' was now to be the Command's main tactic in view of the disappointing results of its overall bombing to date. Although such a heavy additional commitment was accepted by Bomber Command – it was to continue mounting small raids on Germany as before, intermingled with the fresh 'maritime' objectives – virtually no extra aircraft or squadrons were available to carry out any such expansion of effort. Dire situations in the Middle East had begun to necessitate the despatch of some aircraft and units to North Africa, thereby diluting the UK-based bomber forces, and in the context of Wellington strength, throughout 1941 only four new squadrons were to be formed, although existing units began exchanging their former Blenheims etc. for Wimpys and continued operations in these.

In small 'balance', a number of Merlin-engined, modified Mk II Wellingtons began reaching some squadrons, capable of lifting the latest weapon, the 4,000 lb High Capacity (HC) blast bomb, colloquially termed 'Cookie'. The very first 'Cookie' was dropped on Emden on the night of 31 March 1941 by Wellington W5439, 'X' of 149 Squadron *(Pilot Officer Franks) who had his target 'marked' by Wellington R1513 of 9 Squadron† (Squadron Leader K.M.M. Wasse) with a load of incendiaries. No 9 Squadron also began receiving Mk IIs in March 1941 and dropped its first 'Cookie' on Cologne on the night of 3 May (pilot, Sergeant Fairfax).

Of the new Wellington units for 1941, the first was No 104 Squadron. For the first 19 months of the war 104 had been a training unit, being absorbed by No 13 OTU in April 1940, but on 1 April 1941 it was officially reformed at Driffield as an operational bomber squadron again, having received its initial two Wellingtons, W5416 and W5417, on 20 March, then adding 14 more Wimpys to its strength by 27 April.

In the latter month a No 2 Group Blenheim unit based at West Raynham, No 101 Squadron, commenced conversion to Wellingtons, receiving its first two examples, R1700 and R1701, on 20 April and a further 16 by 22 May. Flying its ultimate Blenheim operation on 9 May 1941, the squadron quickly worked up on the new aircraft and mounted its initial Wimpy sorties on the night of 11 June when two

---

*Missing in action over Düsseldorf, 11/12 June 1941.
†Failed to return from Kiel, 12/8/41 after completing 36 sorties.

aircraft (Squadron Leader Jones and Sergeant Caunt) unloaded a total of 6,000 lb of HE bombs on Rotterdam. Ten nights later it made its first Wellington sorties to a German target, Cologne, then on 6 July moved base to Oakington where it now came under the aegis of No 3 Group, Bomber Command.

Even as 101 Squadron prepared to go to war in Wimpys, another unit came into being. On 23 April 1941, at Driffield, No 405 ('Vancouver') Squadron RCAF was formed – the first Canadian bomber squadron to be formed overseas – commanded temporarily by Squadron Leader D.G. Tomlinson, DFC, but from 20 May by Wing Commander P.A. Gilchrist, DFC. Its equipment was to be Wellington IIs, the first four examples, W5487, W5489, W5490, and W5491, being officially allocated on 6 May. By 5 June a further ten Wellingtons had been taken on charge, but on the previous day it suffered its first casualties due to enemy action when a German intruder attack damaged W5491 and completely burnt out W5487.

By 12 June eight Wellingtons and five crews were considered fit for operations, and on that night four set out to bomb marshalling yards at Schwerte, although one (W5484, 'G') had to abort early with mechanical failure. Four nights later the target was Cologne, but enemy fighters claimed one victim, W5522, 'Q', and damaged a second, (W5537, 'O'), which eventually force-landed at West Raynham with both engines damaged and numerous scars of cannon shell and bullet.

In pursuance of the 'anti-shipping' directive, a total of 18 bombers was sent out in daylight on 9 June 1941 to seek out enemy ships in coastal areas. Of these four were Wellingtons from No 9 Squadron, led by the unit commander, Wing Commander R.G.C. Arnold, with Squadron Leader P.C. Pickard, Flying Officer D.F. Lamb, and Pilot Officer K.E. Robinson as his other skippers. Off the French coast the Wellingtons were attacked by a gaggle of Messerschmitt Bf109s – with perhaps inevitable results. In the running fight which ensued, Pickard and Robinson managed to ward off the fighters while they gained the protection of cloud cover, but the remaining pair of aircraft, R1758 and T2620, 'G', were both shot down. Arnold managed to keep his crippled Wellington level enough to enable his crew – which included the squadron's navigation, bombing, and gunnery leaders – to bale out to safety, but left it too late to save his own life and perished in the subsequent crash.

Even with the golden advantage of hindsight, it is difficult to understand why, in view of the disastrous losses suffered on daylight

W5461 of 104 Squadron, which failed to return from Berlin on 12/13 August 1941.

Flt Lt Cowan, 9 Squadron, with his Wellington, X3794, 'Barbara & Mary', at Waddington, ca. Dec 1942.

(Above) R3295, SR-P, of 10
Squadron which was shot
down at Schienmonnihoog
30 Nov 1941. It had previou[s]
served as both 'J' and 'P' w[ith]
99 Squadron.

(Left) Canadian crew board[ing]
a 405 Squadron RCAF Welli[ng]
ton, Driffield, 12 June 1941

bombing sorties by the RAF during 1940-42, operations continued to be despatched – *without* fighter escorts in too many cases – in mid-1941 and later. Nevertheless, the campaign against German ships was to produce further daylight attacks – with concomitant casualties. One particularly outstanding example at that period took place on 24 July, aimed primarily at bombing Brest harbour with its resident battleships *Gneisenau* and *Prinz Eugen*, La Pallice with the incumbent *Scharnhorst*, with a so-termed 'diversionary' attack by escorted Blenheims against Cherbourg.

A force of 100 bombers – three B-17 Fortresses, 18 Hampdens, and 79 Wellingtons – was detailed to attack Brest, the Fortresses and Hampdens, accompanied by three squadrons of Spitfires, being intended to 'draw off' any Luftwaffe fighters and thereby leave the Wellingtons free to bomb – at least, that was the theory. In practice, however, the raid proved costly to the bombers. German fighter opposition was waiting for the bombers as these, in neat peace-time Vics of three, threaded their way out of a storm of flak over the harbour, and within minutes the sky over Brest became a sprawling battleground of fighters-versus-bombers.

Of the various Wellington units participating, No 405 Squadron RCAF had a particularly harrowing time. Sergeant Ken Craig, piloting W5581, 'V', was subjected to at least four separate Bf109 attacks, two of which were in turn shot down by Craig's nose and tail gunners, Sergeants Hughes and G.K. Higgins respectively, but suffered extensive damage, including a fuselage fire, and the rear turret being put out of action with its occupant, Higgins, wounded. Craig extricated himself from the battle and set course for home, ordering his crew back into the rear fuselage in order to help keep the damaged Wellington flying level. Craig eventually crashed into the sea some 300 yards short of the English coast but all the crew survived.

Another 405 Squadron Wellington, W5530, 'L', captained by Sergeant Scott, survived two fighter onslaughts, albeit having his rear gunner, Sergeant Dearnley, seriously wounded and his aircraft badly damaged. Scott managed to reach England where he crash-landed at Roborough, but Dearnley later died in hospital. Two of 405 Squadron's Wellingtons failed to return from Brest, these being W5537, 'O' (Pilot Officer Trueman) and W5551, 'U', piloted by the unit CO, Wing Commander Gilchrist. It was later learned that Gilchrist had become a prisoner of war, but had soon escaped captivity and reached Switzerland. In all, ten Wellingtons and two

Hampdens were shot down over Brest that day, either by fighters or flak.

The irony of the Brest raid was that weeks before, on 9 July, Bomber Command was officially relieved of its maritime commitment, and redirected to concentrate thereafter on 'dislocating the German transportation system, and to destroying the morale of the civil population as a whole and of industrial workers in particular'.* This meant a general return to night operations over Germany and, on occasion, Italy for the Wellington crews of Bomber Command, although the shorter summer nights tended to restrict target selections to comparatively short-range objectives. Another pragmatic reason for keeping the Wellingtons ostensibly protected by a cloak of darkness was the rapidly escalating opposition being met from Luftwaffe nightfighters during the latter months of 1941. Throughout 1940 German nightfighter pilots had claimed a total of just 42 aerial victories while defending the Reich. By the close of 1941 that annual gross claim was 421 such victories; a ten-fold increase which would grow even more dramatically over the following three years in the night skies over Germany. A favoured method of attack by German fighters by then was from the stern of a bomber, ideally from slightly below the rear fuselage. Such an approach meant that RAF bomber rear gunners – 'Arse-End Charlies' – were automatically the principal targets. Without a tail defender any Wellington was 'easy meat' for any determined fighter attack; thus the rear gunners held the lives of their fellow crew members squarely in their own hands on every sortie.

In August 1941 the first Australian Wellington unit joined the ranks of Bomber Command when No 458 Squadron RAAF was officially formed on 25 August at Holme-on-Spalding Moor under the command of Wing Commander N.G. Mulholland, DFC, an Australian-born RAF veteran.† The unit's first two Wellingtons, R1490 and R1695, both arrived on 30 August, followed by Z1272 and Z1273 the next day. Fifteen more Wellingtons arrived throughout September to bring the unit up to full strength, and the first operations were flown on the night of 20 October when ten Wellingtons, led by their CO, Mulholland, bombed Emden and docks at Antwerp and Rotterdam, and lost one aircraft, skippered by Sergeant P. Hamilton. The unit's second operation on 22 October –

*Directive dated 9/7/41 from DCAS to AM Sir Richard Peirse.
†See chapter *'Desert Queens'*

(Left) T2739, 99 Squadron, at Waterbeach on morning of 10 April 1941 after a clash with a nightfighter over Berlin the previous night. The officer examining the damage was Flt Lt K.T.A. Harvey, DFC. (Right) Plt Off Oliver Matheson of 75(NZ) Squadron surveys his aircraft's tasteful artwork, early 1941. Matheson (later, Flt Lt, DFC) was London-born.

115 Squadron crew, all Sergeants, and their Wimpy, R1501, 'X', at Marham, March 1941.

eight crews raiding Le Havre – cost another casualty when Flight
Lieutenant J. Sargeaunt's Wellington was hit by flak over the target
and managed to get back to Farnborough before having to order his
crew to bale out. Two men sustained leg injuries but the rear gunner,
Sergeant R.J. Hobbs, was still in his turret when the aircraft crashed
and was killed.

For the remainder of the year No 458 Squadron continued
operations against German objectives, rounding out the year with ten
aircraft being despatched on 27/28 December to attack both
Boulogne and some marshalling yards at Düsseldorf. Of the seven
Wimpys attacking the latter one, captained by Flight Lieutenant
D.T. Saville, after dropping its bombs, happened to pass over a
German airfield with its runway lighting switched on and a Heinkel
He111 in the process of landing. Saville immediately dived to come in
astern of the Heinkel, giving his nose gunner, Sergeant Howlett, the
chance to open fire. The Heinkel was obviously hit and plunged off
the runway. Saville and his crew then completed their 'night's
entertainment' (*sic*) by machine-gunning a train from caboose to
engine, and dropped their last bomb on a gasometer.

January 1942 proved to be a bitterly icy month but the squadron
managed to mount several operations, attacking targets at Brest,
Cherbourg, and other enemy ports. On 9 January the target was
Cherbourg, but of the three Wellingtons sent out only one returned;
one being hit by flak but returning over Dorset, only to hit a high
tension cable and crash in flames, while the second casualty was
never heard from again. The unit's ultimate operation from the UK
came on 28 January – two crews bombing Boulogne – after which it
was stood down in order to prepare for a move to the Middle East.

The initial formation process of 458 Squadron had taken place so
smoothly that on 24 November 1941 it was able to transfer four
officers and 117 non-commissioned airmen to a second newly-
forming Australian unit, No 460 Squadron RAAF, which was
officially formed on 15 November under the command of Wing
Commander A.L.G. Hubbard, DSO, DFC at Molesworth. Its first
Wellingtons, Z1284 and Z1334, were delivered on 30 November and
1 December respectively, followed by 17 more aircraft by 27
December. On 4 January 1942 the squadron moved base to Breighton
to join No 1 Group, from where it flew its first operations on 12/13
March 1942, an attack on Emden.

Though new to bombing operations, the quality of the unit's young
air crews was epitomised at an early stage by the actions of one

skipper, Sergeant (later, Warrant Officer) D.G. Kitchen, on the night of 26/27 April 1942. Detailed to bomb Rostock, he completed his attack and turned for home, passing north of Sylt at some 7,500 feet, when a Bf110 closed in from astern and seriously wounded the Wellington's rear gunner, Sergeant D.A. Black, a Canadian, apart from smashing the gunner's intercom. Kitchen's second pilot, who at that moment was standing in the astro-dome, was also wounded in the head and thigh. The Messerschmitt carried out three more determined attacks, smashing Kitchen's ASI, shooting away the elevator trimming gear, holing the port fuel tank, and slashing chunks of fabric off the upper port wing and port tail plane, apart from damaging the hydraulics which caused the bomb bay doors to flop open. Kitchen dived fast to sea level, shook off the persistent German fighter, then settled down for the 400 miles' sea crossing back to base.

Finally, after being at his controls for seven and a half exhausting hours, Kitchen achieved a safe landing, despite the lack of flaps and having both main wheels and the tail wheel flat from bullet damage. Although Kitchen received a Commendation from the AOC-in-C, he received no medal, and was destined to be killed in action on 20 June 1942 – just one of many thousands of young men to die unhonoured and unpublicised except among his peers.

Although any account of bombing operations necessarily highlights casualties among aircraft and air crews actually undertaking sorties over enemy territories, it should be remembered that many thousands of crew members were destined to die before ever commencing operations, or in flying accidents at their base airfields; such casualties being listed in official communiques as 'Died while on active service', the 'legal' euphemism to denote deaths unconnected with direct enemy action on actual operations. On 405 Squadron, RCAF, for two examples only, Sergeant Chandos survived an air collision while flying Wellington W5492, 'K' on 20 August 1941 during landing, but on 18 September, skippering the same (repaired) Wimpy on a local wireless test at 8,000 feet, was seen to go into a sudden, rapid dive which tore off the tail unit, followed by the port wing, then exploded into the ground in Northfield Farm, Pocklington, killing eight men aboard.

On 5 January 1942 Wellington W5589, 'F' took off for a mid-morning air test despite snow and sleet conditions, then developed engine trouble, and crashed near Strenshall village killing all its crew. Its normal wireless operator, Sergeant M.P.F. Robson, had been too late arriving at dispersal for this test – and owed his life to that lapse in normal punctuality.....

On the night of 17 January 1942 No 405 Squadron flew its 55th operation and thereby became the first RCAF squadron to drop a 4,000 lb 'Cookie'; this huge blast bomb being carried by Wellington Z8431, 'J' captained by Squadron Leader J.E. Fauquier.* The target was Emden but over that town Fauquier's electrical bomb release mechanism failed and the 'Cookie' had to be released manually. The same raid, however, cost the squadron a veteran pilot, Squadron Leader W.B. Keddy, DFC, flying Z8329, 'L'. Its starboard engine gave trouble over the target, oil pressure dropped, then the motor erupted in flames, and 'L-for-Leather' crashed into the sea, killing Keddy and three of this crew, the only two survivors being rescued by a British destroyer 14 hours later, both suffering from exposure, frostbite and minor crash injuries.

On 16 April 1942 seven of 405 Squadron's Wellingtons – four carrying 4,000 lb 'Cookies' – were detailed to bomb Hamburg. In the event two aircraft were cancelled for technical reasons, two more returned early with defective engines, two bombed alternative targets, and only one bombed the primary target. It was a somewhat 'damp squib' for what was the squadron's last Wellington operation, because on 18 April the unit began re-equipping with Halifax II heavy bombers and its faithful Merlin-Wimpys were transferred to other units.

Two other Wellington squadrons came into existence before the close of 1941. No 215 Squadron RAF, after various roles in training duties, was reformed at Newmarket on 9 December but was already ear-marked to be sent to India, commencing in January 1942. The other was No 419 RCAF which was born at Mildenhall on 15 December, 1941, with Wing Commander John 'Moose' Fulton, DFC, AFC as its first CO, and Squadron Leaders F.W.S. 'Roscoe' Turner and E.G.B. Reid as his A and B flight commanders respectively. It was the third RCAF heavy bomber unit to be formed overseas, and the first in No 3 Group, while its commander's orders were to have the squadron ready for operations within three weeks of initial formation.

Fulton's orders were hardly helped by the sluggish delivery of Wellingtons to the squadron. The first, X9748, arrived on 2 January 1942; followed by Z1145 next day; X9757, Z1077, and Z1083 on 8 January; X3201, Z1053, and X9874 on 9 January. However, on 11

*Later, Air Commodore, DSO, DFC.

(_ht_) Wing Commander John
ose' Fulton, DSO,
_,_ AFC, first commander of
419 'Moose' Squadron,
F, who was killed on
_ ations on 28/29 July 1942
bombing Hamburg.

_ ow_) T2961, LS–S, of 15
adron at Wyton, 1941.
r served with 57 Squadron
18 OTU.

January Fulton, at the controls of X9748, 'B', and Pilot Officer T.G. Cottier piloting Z1145, 'A', set off on the squadron's first operations, to each drop six 500 lb bombs on Brest. By the end of January 1942 the squadron was up to full strength in aircraft, but in late February began exchanging its Mk Is for Mk IIIs with a consequent all-round improvement in technical performance.

The contention, expressed several times in preceding text, that Bomber Command's backbone during the early years of the war was the doughty Wellington is borne out by a glance at the Command's firstline operations *available* strength in November 1941. Of a total of bombers available with crews, 250 were Wimpys. The remainder, for comparison, were:*

Hampdens.. 150
Blenheims 79
Whitleys.. 62
Manchesters.. 31
Stirlings 18
Halifaxes 17
B-17 Fortresses.. 3

If further confirmation of the Wellington's importance was needed, the opinion of the late Air Marhsal Sir John E.A. Baldwin, KBE, CB, DSI, will probably best reflect its status.† 'Jack' Baldwin was Air Officer Commanding (ACC) No 3 Group, Bomber Command from 29 August 1939 until 13 September 1942 – the prime Wellington Group with which Baldwin occasionally flew on operations to 'see for myself' – and was thus in virtually the best position to evaluate the contributions of the Wimpy in the context of Bomber Command's offensive during those critical years. In his view:

Without the Wellington during the first three years Bomber Command would have been totally ineffective, and could never have maintained its constant assault on Germany and occupied France. I would go so far as to say that had the Wellington not existed then, it is quite possible that the Command might well have been dismembered and split into mere elements of other

*Figures quoted in Appendix 39, Vol IV, *The Strategic Air Offensive against Germany. 1939–1945*; Webster/Frankland, HMSO, 1961.
†Correspondence with author, 1961-62.

Commands and even Services. Had that happened – and there were many politicians, including Winston Churchill, and high Army and Royal Navy officers who wished to do this at some stages – the eventual massive aerial attacks of 1943–45 would never have been possible and the outcome of the war in Europe could have been quite different.

The year 1942 saw Bomber Command, albeit still very much a sleeping giant, slowly but inexorably accumulate muscle with the new wave of four-engined heavy bombers gradually replacing the tired, obsolete Whitleys, Hampdens, and Blenheims. Only the Wellingtons of the 'old brigade' remained in quantity in firstline units and were supplemented by a further 14 squadrons of Wimpys before the end of the year. In addition to the new aircraft types, long-awaited accurate aids to navigation, target-marking, actual bombs and bomb-aiming began to appear, promising a far more effective destructive potential in the near future.

Two of the 'new' Wellington units joined the fighting ranks of the Command early in the year. On 14 February 1942 both Nos 156 and 158 Squadrons were officially reformed, at Alconbury and Driffield respectively. Although reformed on that date on paper, No 156 Squadron was 'built' from a nucleus transferred from No 40 Squadron and had already been allocated a total of ten Wellingtons, commencing on 18 January with R1168, Z1068 and Z1108, followed by receipt of Z1052, Z1114, X9975, Z1080, Z8969, and Z8973 by 10 February.

Once in 'legal' existence, the crews of 156 Squadron lost no time in becoming operational and their first sorties – three Wellingtons bombing Essen – were flown on the night of 16/17 February. No 158 Squadron's 'reformation' was in effect a straightforward retitling of the existing Home Echelon of No 104 Squadron on 14 February, on which date the 'new' unit took on charge a total of 21* of the Echelon's Wellington Mk IIs; and that same night seven Wellingtons set out to bomb Mannheim. This first operation by 158 Squadron was flown from Pocklington, due to the bad state of Driffield's runways at that time. All crews returned safely.

No 158 Squadron was to continue operating its Wellington IIs, commanded by Wing Commander P. Stevens, DFC, until 1 June, on

*See *In Brave Company (History of 158 Sqn)* by W. Chorley/R. Benwell; Private, 1977, for full list of aircraft serials etc.

which night the unit contributed six crews to 'Butch' Harris's second '1000-bomber' raid, on Essen. The unit's brief spell of operations on Wellingtons had lasted 108 days/nights, during which period it had participated in 32 raids (207 individual sorties) and lost 14 Wellingtons and crews on operations, apart from two crashes which killed 11 aircrew members, and other men injured and/or wounded to some degree; a fairly representative set of statistics for most operational bomber units during that period.

On 6 May 1942 a 158 Squadron Conversion Flight had been established to train the unit's air and ground crews in the use of Halifax IIs, the first example of which arrived on the Flight on 7 June, by which time the squadron had moved base from Driffield to East Moor from where it mounted its initial Halifax operations by despatching 11 aircraft to Bremen for the third of Harris's '1000-bomber' city assaults, on the night of 25-26 June 1942.

Undoubtedly, the major highlight operations in early 1942 were the three so-termed '1000-bomber' raids instigated by the AOC-in-C, Bomber Command, Arthur Harris; these taking place on the nights of 30/31 May (Cologne), 1/2 June (Essen), and 25/26 June (Bremen). In deference to the many published accounts of these particular operations (see '*Associated Literature*' at rear of this volume), only the relevant data for the Wellington units' participations need be presented here:-

Date	Target	Total a/c sent	Wellingtons
30-31 May	Cologne	1047	602
1/2 June	Essen	956	545
25/26 June	Bremen	1067	472*

The proportion of Wellingtons provided for the Cologne raid reflected the necessary scraping the barrel to achieve the magic '1000' figure; the firstline squadrons of Bomber Command put up 364 Wellingtons, while the OTUs and other non-operational units provided the balance of 238 Wimpys.

These highly concentrated attacks proved to be a turning point in many ways for Bomber Command. Apart from achieving Arthur Harris's intention of proving the need to retain his Command as a single entity, the tactics involved led to changes in future deployment

---

*Coastal Command also provided 7–10 Wellingtons, but these were recorded as a separate operation for statistical purposes.

bove) R1459, PM–X, of 103
uadron, 1941 which had
viously served with 301
uadron.

ght) Air Gunners of 149
uadron dressing in
ctrically heated flying
thing – which often proved
mperamental . . .

of bombing formations. The Cologne raid,* in particular, had used an advance force of 'illuminator' aircraft to mark the aiming points with incendiaries; a ploy which was to become the main *raison d'être* for the Path Finder Force (PFF) which came into being three months later. The sheer density of aircraft, flying along a relatively narrow breadth frontage meant that the bombers only traversed a few German flak and nightfighter defence zones, thereby reducing possible opposition, and by pure numbers tended to swamp those defence organisations.

Also significant was the grim fact that although RAF losses for all three attacks were classified as 'acceptable', the bulk of those losses had been directly attributable to the German nightfighters – a harbinger of the future for the RAF bomber crews who survived. And it is probably indicative of the Grim Reaper's catholicity in selecting his victims that Wellington (and other) losses were virtually composed equally of experienced and tyro crews. Moreover, despite the seemingly high odds of aircraft colliding in such a relatively close-packed bomber stream as that which flew to Cologne, only one such incident actually occurred, when Wellington X3670, 'F' of 101 Squadron collided with Stirling W7534 of 214 Squadron, and the Wimpy, captained by Pilot Officer A.D.F. Gardner, fell away and then exploded in mid-air.

Throughout June and July 1942 Bomber Command reverted to more 'normal' strengths in night raids, due partly to the shorter summer nights, and Wellingtons continued to make up anything from 40 to 65 per cent of the 'heavy' raids despatched. Then, on 11 August, Harris received a direct order to found a new 'Target Finding Force', which he personally retitled Path Finder Force (PFF) and established its headquarters at RAF Wyton under the command of Group Captain D.C.T. Bennett, DSO (later, Air Vice-Marshal, CB, CBE, DSO). The original PFF was to comprise one firstline squadron from each of Nos 1, 3, 4, and 5 Groups, these being respectively Nos 156, 7, 35, and 83 Squadrons, with No 109 Squadron on a 'detached' status for furtherance of *Oboe* experiments.

Of those 'founder-member' units, 156 Squadron, commanded by Wing Commander R.N. Cook, was equipped with Wellington IIIs and moved its base from Alconbury to Warboys in August. The squadron was destined to remain with the PFF until the end of the

---

*In fact, Harris's *first* choice of target for this first 1,000 bomber attack had been Hamburg, but weather conditions changed his choice to Cologne on the day.

war, exchanging its Wellingtons for Lancasters in January 1943. Those same summer months saw two further Wellington units within Bomber Command, when No 425 ('*Alouette*') Squadron RCAF was initially formed with Wellington IIIs at Dishforth on 25 June 1942, with Wing Commander J.M.W. St Pierre as its first Commanding Officer.*

Then, in August No 420 ('*Snowy Owl*') Squadron RCAF, already operating on Hampdens from Waddington under the command of Wing Commander D.A.R. Bradshaw, moved base to Skipton-on-Swale on 6 August to continue operations on Wellington IIIs. The changeover from their elderly Hampdens to Wimpys was slightly prolonged. 420 Squadron received its first Wellington, BJ644, on 4 August, followed by X3808 and X3809 on 11 August; X3814, Z1724, BJ717 on the 19th; X3963 on the 27th, and BJ966 next day. In September a further eight were received, X3800, BK235, BJ915, BK295, BK296, BK297, BJ917, and BK331 in that sequence.

By now the war had reached its halfway stage, and in the context of Bomber Command most aspects of the bombing offensive had changed quite radically from the near-pioneering operations of late September 1939–early 1940. The days (or nights) of sketchy briefings, despatch of aircraft in small formations and/or even singly were, by and large, over. Emphasis now was on fairly regular heavy, concentrated attacks on specific cities or industrial centres, led by specialist target-marking units, employing the latest radar aids to location and navigation. Crew briefings were far more detailed, giving specific altitudes, times, weather conditions, location of flak and nightfighter zones, and other vital facets to be taken into consideration.

For crew men, particularly pilots, fresh to the sharp end, the previous luxury of several second dicky 'fresher' or 'makee-learn' sorties to 'soft' targets before being entrusted to captaining their own crews was becoming reduced to one or at best two such trips before being thrown in at the deep end. Reg Williams, a navigator who had completed an operational tour in Hampdens in mid-1941 and volunteered for a second tour in the Spring 1942, recalls:†

The contrast in the preparations for an op in 1942-43, when compared to those of my first spell, was quite marked for me. In the

---

*See chapter '*Desert Queens*' for this unit's service in Middle East later.
†Interview by author, 1982

(Above) W5381, 'W' of 12 Squadron which carried a cartoon insigne of its namesake, J. Wellington Wimpy of *Daily Mirror* cartoon strip fame.

(Left) Erks and a pair of 25 GP bombs about to be loa into a 75(NZ) Squadron Wellington, which carried devil insigne.

old days everything was very leisurely, almost 'gentlemanly' in a sense. Once airborne *then* we were on our own with no real idea what was happening to the rest of our chaps, and were able to take our own decisions on how, where, and when to actually bomb any target specified. My first briefing of my second tour quickly dispelled all such notions. Now I became very conscious that I was merely a cog in a bloody great machine, slotted in precisely to a 'master plan' for each raid. In a curious way this comforted me because I felt not merely one of a single crew, but one of a much greater 'gang'. Naturally, my foremost loyalties were still to my own crew – in that respect nothing had really changed – but now I felt part of a great.... venture, if that's the right word.

The hazards now awaiting bomber crews over any important German objective during the closing months of 1942 may well be epitomised by the experiences of one Wellington crew on the night of 16/17 September 1942. The prime target was Essen and a force of 369 aircraft (including some from training Groups) was sent off initially, and 39 of these, including 21 Wellingtons, failed to return – virtually one in every ten despatched. One Wellington of 156 Squadron, 'F', skippered by Sergeant G.A. Proudfoot, did return – but only just. Proudfoot's aircraft had been detailed as one of the PFF element's illuminator force and was therefore carrying a load of 18 × 3-inch flares. Take-off went smoothly at 2002 hrs and he reached the target without incident at 2155 hrs, flying at 18,000 feet. In his own words:

> We 'stooged' around for about five minutes, saw two cones of searchlights and plenty of flak coming up on the starboard quarter. We decided we'd found the target; weather was 8/10ths cloud at 10-12,000 ft, moon up on the starboard quarter, and some ground haze. Ground detail was not visible and it was decided not to drop the marker flares as the aiming point could not be definitely identified. At approximately 2200 hrs at 18,000 ft, on a course of 160 degrees, with IAS (*Indicated Air Speed*) 160, the bomb doors were opened preparatory to releasing the flares.

At that moment Proudfoot was at his controls, the navigator, Sergeant B. Couchman, on the bomb panel, with the front and rear gunners – Sergeants Duke and Belton – at their respective turrets, and the wireless operator, Pilot Officer R.F. Tinkler, at the flare chute.

Seconds later the rear gunner reported an enemy aircraft – a Focke

Wulf Fw190 – dead astern and slightly above, which approached to within 150 yards and opened fire, to which the rear gunner replied. Cannon shells ripped into the Wellington, then the fighter broke away to port, turned, and bore in again from the port quarter, only to run head-on into the rear-gunner's fire. The 190 burst into flames and fell into a dive with flames coming from both wings and its fuselage, then disappeared into clouds at 8,000 feet. The German pilot's fire had been accurate. Tinkler, the wireless operator, had been hit in both feet by shell splinters but managed to push the photo-flare down the chute before staggering back to the astro-dome until the aircraft was well clear of the target area. From there he reported that fuselage fabric from the dome back to the tailplane had been sliced off by the cannon shells.

Meanwhile, Proudfoot, having seen the fighter go down, checked around for damage and found the starboard aileron unserviceable and had to use elevator and rudder to get the Wellington out of its diving evasion turn down to 14,500 ft. He then ordered his navigator to jettison the flare load and pulled his jettison toggles. Only as he left the target did the captain learn that his navigator was wounded and was 'flopped out on the bed' (*sic*) but decided to leave his injuries until the aircraft reached base. The rear gunner then reported his gun turret was out of action. Setting a course of 296 degrees for Kampen, Proudfoot found control difficult due to the missing fuselage fabric, and part of the starboard wing's trailing edge and aileron shot away.

At 2245 hrs the crippled Wellington was over Emmerich at 6,000 feet when the rear gunner reported a single-engined enemy aircraft approaching from dead astern, which soon gave the bomber one short burst but caused no apparent damage. Proudfoot side-slipped the Wellington down into clouds at 5,000 feet, despite the difficulty in control, and minutes later saw the oil pressure of his port engine rising sharply, then the engine cut out altogether. The bomber continued losing height until it was down to about 7,000 feet above the Zuider Zee. Proudfoot opened up the starboard engine and managed to gain a little height to 1200 feet as he crossed the Dutch coast, only to become coned by searchlights and flak. Again, no apparent damage was caused.

Plodding on across the North Sea, the Wellington reached about 20-30 miles from the English coast when the partially revived port engine cut out again. Proudfoot did a complete check of all systems and discovered that the undercarriage hydraulics were shot through, as well as its emergency system and hand-pump. He continued the

300 (Polish) Squadron Wellington, carrying a bomb log of 41 sorties, and the 'Great Bear' star constellation markings of the pre-war No. 212 Squadron, Polish Air Force, to which its air crew previously belonged.

WIMPYS WERE TOUGH. Wellington IV, Z1407, BH–Z of 300 (Polish) Squadron – named *Zoska* – after its return from Bremen on 4/5 Sept 1942 (Capt, Flt Lt Marian Wlodarczyk). It saw further service with 104 OTU.

flight on one engine, using rich mixture (as he had done since leaving the target) which necessitated him 'pulling' the nacelle tanks now. Arriving over base he next discovered that the TR9 set was useless and therefore fired a red Very cartridge to indicate his situation. Deciding to crashland rather than bale out – the wounded wireless operator might have suffered further injuries if he was parachuted out – Proudfoot ordered the crew to crash stations, then bellied in for a landing. On impact the flares, still in the bomb bay unbeknown to the skipper, were smashed up into the fuselage and immediately erupted in intense flames.

Proudfoot exited through his escape hatch and ran to the edge of the runway. Reaching there he realised that only two other crew men were with him and looking back into the blazing Wimpy saw someone crawling and being half-dragged along. He ran back to the inferno to find the nose gunner, Duke, helping the wounded Tinkler away from the fire and its exploding ammunition and other flares, assisted now by the navigator, Couchman, despite receiving burns. Eventually all were clear of the burning wreck, and Tinkler and Couchman were both taken to Ely hospital suffering from burns and other injuries. Proudfoot and the remaining two men were given treatment for shock but soon recovered – it had been an eventful night... but Proudfoot had the supreme consolation that he had brought his crew home – alive.

Wellington reinforcements for Bomber Command continued in late 1942. On 15 October, No 466 Squadron RAAF was formed at Driffield under the command of Squadron Leader R.E. Bailey (later Wing Commander DSO, DFC), and began receiving Wellingtons from 29 October (X3790 and Z1692), with a full complement of a further 24 Wimpys by the end of November. The unit then moved base to Leconfield on 27 December to commence operations on 13 January 1943 with five Wellingtons laying mines off the Frisians. On the same day as 466 Squadron's birth, two Canadian Wellington units also formed, these being Nos 424 ('*Tiger*') and 426 ('*Thunderbird*') Squadrons RCAF.

The '*Tiger*' squadron was formed at Topcliffe under the command of Wing Commander H.M. Carscallen and received its first Wellington III, BJ658, on 21 October, followed by a further dozen by 8 November. Its first operations were then mounted on the night of 15/16 January 1943 when five Wellingtons bombed Lorient. No 424 Squadron, commanded by Wing Commander S.S. Blanchard, came into being at Dishforth on 15 October and eight days later took receipt of its first four aircraft, BJ888, DF617, DF619, and DF620, then joined the 'Tiger' squadron on operations by bombing Lorient with seven aircraft on the night of 14/15 January 1943. By that date both Canadian units had transferred from the control of No 4 Group to the all-Canadian administered and controlled No 6 (RCAF) Group with effect from 1 January 1943.

On 7 November 1942 a further five Wellington squadrons were either formed or reformed within Bomber Command. No 199 Squadron was reformed at Blyton, equipped with Wellington Xs from 10 November, on which day it took delivery of BJ819, BJ960, BK366, and BK367, with eleven more being received by 22 November. Its first operations took place on 6/7 December when five Wellingtons bombed Mannheim. A second RAF Wimpy unit formed on 7 November was 196 Squadron, at Driffield, which began receiving its aircraft from 1 December (X3357) and had a total of 15 on strength by 7 December. The squadron first operated on 4/5 February 1943 when eight Wellingtons bombed Lorient. The other three Wellington units simultaneously formed on 7 November were Nos 427 ('Lion'), 428 ('Ghost') and 429 ('Bison') Squadrons RCAF. The 'Lion' squadron formed at Croft with Wing Commander D.H. Burnside, DFC as its first CO, and received a total of 16 Wellingtons on 9 November; commencing operations by despatching three aircraft to 'sow' mines off the Frisians on 14 December. Its 'Lion' motif was ratified in May 1943 when the squadron was adopted by the Metro-Goldwyn-Mayer film studios in Hollywood, and the unit owned a lion cub mascot.

The 'Ghosts' came into existence at Dalton on 7 November, commanded by Wing Commander A. Earle, RAF, and received its first pair of Wellingtons, X3545 and X3546, on 26 November (both aircraft being ex-466 Squadron Wimpys) followed by eleven more by 8 December. Operations began on 26/27 January 1943 when six aircraft set out to bomb Lorient (though one aborted with technical problems).

The third RCAF unit formed on the same date, the 'Bisons', was formed at East Moor with Wing Commander J.A.P. Owen RAF as its first CO, and took delivery of its first four Wellingtons, BJ798, BJ799, BJ908, and DF625, on 24 November, and by 10 December could boast a total of 26 Wimpys on strength officially. The unit's first sorties came on 21 January 1943 when three aircraft set out to lay mines at Terschelling. Of these, one aborted the operation and a second failed to return.

By the close of 1942 the veteran Wellingtons had been joined on
Bomber Command's firstline strength by Lancasters, Halifaxes, and
Stirlings in quantity, and were now officially classified as 'medium
bombers' (as opposed to 'light bombers' such as Mosquitos and
Bostons, and 'heavies' i.e. Lancasters etc). Even so, the Command's
official order of battle for 4 February 1943 still showed 15 Squadrons
of Wellingtons in frontline operations – a total of 258 aircraft on
actual unit strengths – of an overall Command strength of 62 bomber
squadrons (1091 aircraft of *all* bomber types). In addition, the
Command's ever-expanding training units – OTUs, Conversion and
other units – showed an aircraft strength (*all* types of trainers) of
1956, of which gross figure 841 were Wellingtons.* In down-to-earth
pragmatic terms, the average daily *availability* of bomber aircraft at
that time showed the following comparative figures.*

Lancasters	Wellingtons	Halifaxes	Mosquitos	Stirlings	Others
178	128	104	17	56	99

*All figures quoted from *The Strategic Air Offensive Against Germany* by Webster/
Frankland; HMSO, 1961.

CHAPTER SEVEN

Bomber Swan Song

The year 1943 was to see just three more Wellington units brought on the strength of the UK-based Bomber Command. The first of these was No 192 Squadron which was reformed at Gransden Lodge on 4 January under the command of Wing Commander C.D.V. Willis, DFC, with a mixture of Wellingtons and Mosquitos plus a Halifax, all inherited from its parent unit, No 1474 (SD) Flight. The initial squadron Wellingtons included Z1047, AD590, X3566, HE227, HE228, HE229, HE226,HE230, HE231, HE232, and HE233. The squadron's prime role for the remainder of the war was electronic intelligence (*Elint*), roaming over a wide variety of enemy-occupied territories to gain knowledge of enemy radar and radio wavelengths.

By November 1943 operational control of the squadron was transferred from No 3 Group to No 100 (Special Duties) Group, and involved a move of base to Foulsham. The ultimate Wellington sortie was flown on 7 January 1945, though the squadron continued its vital duties until final disbandment on 22 August 1945. The second unit came back to the operational scene on 27 January 1943, when the UK-based echelons on Nos 142 and 150 Squadrons were merged to reform No 166 Squadron at Kirmington. The 'new' squadron automatically took over the former units' total of 22 Wellingtons, and commenced operations on 27/28 January by sending out seven Wellingtons 'sowing' mines, followed by its first bombing sorties two nights later when 12 Wimpys set out to bomb Lorient. Of these, five aborted the raid, and a sixth (BK515) failed to return. By September 1943 the squadron began exchanging its Wellingtons for Lancasters.

The third new Wellington unit was No 432 ('Leaside') Squadron RCAF which was formed under the aegis of No 6 (RCAF) Group at Skipton-on-Swale on 1 May 1943 with Wing Commander H.W. Kerby as its first commander. Its initial complement of 18 Wellingtons were transferred from No 427 Squadron RCAF; this latter unit being in the process of converting to Halifax Vs. 432 Squadron commenced operations on 23/24 May when 15 Wellingtons were despatched to bomb Dortmund, although four of these aborted.

Wing Commander Kerby was destined to be killed in action on 29 July 1943, and was succeeded by Wing Commander W.A. McKay next day.

In October 1943 the 'Leaside' squadron relinquished its veteran Wimpys and converted to Lancaster BIIs, by which time the unit had become based at East Moor. 432 Squadron's ultimate Wellington operations were flown on the night of 8/9 October, bombing Hannover, and shared with No 300 (Polish) Squadron in putting up a total of 26 Wellingtons for what turned out to be the last time a Bomber Command raid was to include normal bombing efforts by a Wellington element. It was, however, by no means the last *operation* by Wellingtons over Europe under the aegis of Bomber Command, as will be seen.

By the spring of 1943 Arthur Harris was satisfied that his Command was finally in a position to commence a true strategic offensive against Germany. In his words:

> At long last we were ready and equipped. Bomber Command's main offensive began at a precise moment, the moment of the first major attack on an objective in Germany by means of *Oboe*. This was on the night of 5/6 March 1943, when I was at last able to undertake with real hope of success the task which had been given to me when I first took over the Command a little more than a year before, the task of destroying the main cities of the Ruhr . . . Essen had been named as the first town for destruction a year before, as it was the largest and most important manufacturing centre in the Ruhr, and Essen was the target on the night of 5/6 March.*

Harris was referring to the initiation of what has come to be titled the Battle of the Ruhr; a four months' bombing campaign deliberately aimed at a sustained, concentrated destruction of Germany's prime industrial area. It would mean challenging the most heavily defended targets within that vital area, and the Command's air crew casualty rates were to rise dramatically in consequence, but with the increasing influx of four-engined heavy bombers such as the Lancaster and Halifax the Command was now able to deliver far greater tonnages of bombs per raid, and with greater accuracy.

Despite the ever-increasing odds against survival in the night skies of Germany now, the bomber crews' resolution remained undiminished.

Bomber Offensive by Sir A. Harris; Collins, 1947

'G-George' of 432 Squadron RCAF, a Mk X, sets out.

420 Squadron RCAF crew. L–R: Sgts A.J. Soders & W.R. King; Fg Off G. Hubbell; Flt Sgt H.L. Davis; Sgt R.S. Hollowell – all Canadians. The whole crew were 'Missing in action' on 1 June 1943.

X3763 of 425 Squadron RCAF which failed to return from Stuttgart on night of 14/15 April 1943.

R1090, ED–K, of 21 OTU, Moreton-in-Marsh lands 'too low' . . . .

Just one outstanding, though not untypical, example of that prime quality occurred on the night of 23 May 1943 when the biggest raid of the Battle of the Ruhr – 826 aircraft despatched to attack Dortmund – took place. Seven minutes after bombing the target a Wellington of 431 Squadron RCAF was coned by searchlights and then thoroughly riddled by flak. Its pilot twice attempted to dive away from the cone, only to be further pinpointed by the flak gunners. An order to bale out was apparently given and the pilot duly abandoned the aircraft, but the English bomb aimer, Sergeant S.N. Sloan, slid into the vacant pilot seat, regained control, and with great difficulty finally flew clear of the target area. The escape hatch and rear turret door were open, creating a fierce slipstream wind through the fuselage during the return flight, while the navigator, Sergeant G.C. Parslow, despite having no electric lighting at his station, managed to plot a course to England. Helped by Parslow and the wireless operator, Flying Officer J.B. Bailey, Sloan eventually reached Cranwell where he accomplished a good landing without further incident.

Sloan was awarded an immediate CGM, while Bailey and Parslow received a DFC and DFM respectively. Sloan was also commissioned, given a pilot's course, and later flew operations with No 158 Squadron; but Parslow and Bailey were lost on operations on the night of 21/22 June 1943 over Krefeld.

The steady replacement of the Wellington in Bomber Command's firstline squadrons throughout 1943* did not mean the end of actual Wimpy sorties within the Command. By November that year only Nos 192 and 300 (Polish) Squadrons were still operating Wellingtons on frontline operations, and even these were either carrying out *Elint* duties (192) or mainly mining sorties in the case of 300 Squadron. Nevertheless, Wimpy crews were still being despatched over Europe by the various Command OTUs, primarily (but not exclusively) engaged in dropping propaganda leaflets on civilian centres.

Such 'bumf-bombing' trips were to continue spasmodically well into 1944, intermingled with very occasional 'special' operations; an example of the latter being the night of 17/18 August 1944 when 55 OTU Wellingtons, accompanied by 14 RCM-equipped aircraft flew a 'decoy' series of sorties over the North Sea with the hope of baiting German nightfighters into the air, and generally to confuse and alarm the German night defence systems. The actual final Bomber

*See Appendix 4 for dates of unit relinquishment of Wellingtons.

Command *squadron* sorties flown by Wellingtons were those by three aircraft from Ingham-based 300 (Polish) Squadron on the night of 3/ 4 March 1944 – a mining operation off French ports. Thereafter only the 100 (SD) Group's few remaining Wellingtons and Command OTU aircraft were to be sent into enemy skies in anger.

In May 1944 a Wellington unit, No 69 Squadron, commanded by Wing Commander T.M. Channon, DSO, which had given invaluable service in the Mediterranean theatre since January 1941, had become UK-based at Northolt where it was to operate Wellington XIIIs on specialist night duties over the Continent. Its prime role was reconnaissance, but included flare-marking and illumination of targets for other bombers, and particularly night photography. Operational control of 69 Squadron came from the 2nd Tactical Air Force (TAF) and from D-Day, 6 June 1944, the squadron 'partnered' Nos 16 and 140 Squadrons, flying Spitfire XIs and Mosquito XVIs respectively, to form No 34 (PR) Wing, 2nd TAF, still based at Northolt. On 4 September 69 Squadron moved base to an American landing ground, A.12, at Balleroy in Normandy; then on 25 September moved again to Melsbroek where it was to remain based until the end of hostilities in Europe. By then the unit commander was Wing Commander M.J.A. – 'Mike' – Shaw, DSO (later Group Captain), a veteran Wellington skipper who had served with No 221 Squadron on Malta previously. His memories of the Wimpy were affectionate and he recalled his service with 69 Squadron:*

Specially modified Mk XIIIs were used and these had clear perspex noses fitted to facilitate visual observation together with a moving film camera and a pistol discharger for letting off photo-flashes, so that photographic confirmation of visual sightings could be provided, and finally a flare chute for launching the load of 54 flares. One of the bonuses stemming from the selection of the Mk XIII Wimpy was the relative quietness of the aircraft from the ground observer's point of view. We were operating at pretty low level – below 3000 feet – and often ran into heavy ground fire from the German flak gunners. We dropped flares at about 3000 feet and then circled down below these to see what was revealed. If anything interesting was seen we were supposed to take photos with the special camera; an open shutter type with a moving film linked to a pistol discharger which was a sort of 'Mickey Mouse'

*Correspondence with author.

(*left*) Group Captain M.J.A.
, DSO, OC 221 and 69
drons.

(*below*) Aftermath of the
raffe's *Operation*
platte, 1 January 1945.
ins of 69 Squadron's
gtons at Melsbroek on
ay.

box with 12 photo-flash cartridges. These latter were small and did not give great illumination, but enable photos to be taken providing this was at low level – you couldn't take them above 1000 feet with any certainty of success.

No 69 Squadron's crews, eager for offensive action, later carried a load of 250lb HE bombs on moonlight nights, when visibility was good enough to dispense with flares; while early in 1945 some were modified to carry depth charges for use on patrols off the Belgian coast seeking German midget submarines. On 1 January 1945 the squadron's base at Melsbroek was one of several Allied airfields to be subjected to a mass Luftwaffe strafing – *Operation Bodenplatte* – and had 11 Wellingtons completely destroyed – HZ885, HZ769, ME950, MF128, HZ794, NC540, HZ862, JA629, HZ723, NC534, and one other – plus two more, MF129 & NC608, badly damaged. Five airmen of the unit's servicing echelon were killed and 25 other airmen wounded in some degree. Such was the RAF's supply organisation then that within 48 hours the squadron was up to full aircraft strength again. The squadron finally ceased operations on 7 May 1945, and was eventually disbanded at Eindhoven on 7 August that same year. Thus Wellingtons had given firstline service in the European theatre from the first to the very last days of that war.

The efforts – and especially, the sacrifices – of Bomber Command Wellington crews may well be illustrated by the records of just one veteran unit, No 115 Squadron, which between October 1939 and March 1943 flew the most raids, most sorties, and suffered the highest losses of any Wellington squadron under the aegis of Bomber Command. Its records show that its crews participated in 390 Command raids, involving a total of 3075 individual aircraft sorties, but lost 109 Wellingtons directly or indirectly due to enemy action. Of its air crew members, 421 men were listed as killed in action or just 'Missing, believed killed', apart from many others who received wounds and/or injuries in some degree. Such a human casualty rate was, statistically speaking, the rough equivalent of four times the normal squadron air crew establishment during those years. As one ex-member has stated to this author; 'That crew casualty figure might well have been much higher had it not been for the dependability and strength of the Wellington, which brought many crews home to roost safely in damaged conditions which would have meant certain crashes in most other types of bomber.'

CHAPTER EIGHT

For Valour

Of all the many possible honours, awards, and decorations able to be granted to members of the British and Commonwealth armed services over the years, one award has always stood apart, supreme, in a class of its own – the Victoria Cross. Since its inception by Queen Victoria in 1856, that tiny scrap of gun-metal in bronze has always been acknowledged as representing the epitome of human courage and, too often, selfless sacrifice. Indeed, among all ranks of the fighting Services, it was commonly held that for any man to 'earn' a VC, he must be 'either mad – or dead'. Throughout the 1939-45 global conflict a total of just 32 airmen, from all air services, were awarded a Victoria Cross, of which total 23 VCs went to members of bomber air crews. One of those bomber VCs was a Wellington pilot – Sergeant James Allen Ward, RNZAF.

'Jimmy' Ward was a New Zealander by birth, though his parents were English who had emigrated from Coventry. Born on 14 June 1919 in Wanganui, Ward grew up against a semi-idyllic backdrop of lush green pastures and majestic hill and mountain scenery, and quickly developed a love for his homeland with its ancient history and legends. He soon became fascinated with the Maori traditions, even learning something of Maori language, tribal chants and customs; while excelling in most forms of outdoor physical activities, including Rugby, tennis and swimming. His adolescent years were un-doubtedly strongly influenced by the staunch Baptist faith of his parents, giving him a strong sense of personal responsibility and duty to his fellow men which remained with him throughout his tragically brief life.

Educated initially at Wanganui Technical College, young Ward soon decided on a future academic career, and accordingly entered a teachers' training college at Wellington, where a fellow student was Edgar Kain, later to achieve fame as 'Cobber' Kain, DFC, the RAFs first fighter 'ace' of World War Two. On completion of his education at Victoria University College, Ward commenced his career as a teacher at the Castle Cliff School, Wanganui in 1939, but the outbreak of war in Europe later that year was destined to change not only Ward's but many thousands of his fellow countrymen's lives. In Ward's case he immediately volunteered to join the Royal New Zealand Air Force, and on 1 July 1940 was finally enlisted in the RNZAF for pilot training.

Ward commenced his air crew training at Levin Initial Training Wing, where one of his fellow trainees was another young Kiwi from Dunedin, James Fraser Barron, some two years younger than Ward, who was to continue training with Ward for the next year both in New Zealand and in Britain, before being posted to a different operational squadron. Barron was destined to rise to Wing Commander, DSO, DFC, DFM before his death in action on 19/20 May 1944 over France.

On 29 July 1940 Ward reported to No 1 EFTS at Taieri, completed advanced instruction at No 1 SFTS, Wigram, and on 18 January 1941 was awarded his coveted pilot's wings along with promotion to sergeant. Then, after a brief spell of embarkation leave, he boarded the *Aorangi* on 30 January to sail to England, via Canada. Reaching England eventually on 6 March, Ward and his fellow Kiwis were posted to No 20 OTU at Lossiemouth, Scotland for final crewing and training in Wellington aircraft, and on 13 June 1941 Jimmy Ward and his crew arrived at Feltwell, Norfolk to join their first operational unit, No 75 (NZ) Squadron. Next day – Ward's 22nd birthday – saw Ward detailed as second pilot in a Wellington for a bombing sortie against Düsseldorf – his operational blooding.

In the following few weeks Ward continued operating as a second pilot, accumulating experience, usually with a Canadian-born veteran skipper, Squadron Leader R.P. Widdowson, at the helm, and was detailed as second 'dickey' to Widdowson for an operation on the night of 7 July 1941. His Wellington for this sortie was L7818, coded AA-R, and the designated target was Münster, one of four targets due to be raided by Bomber Command that same night; the others being Cologne, Osnabrück, and Münchengladbach. L7818 was but one of ten Wellingtons put up by 75(NZ) Squadron as part of the overall force of 49 Wellingtons detailed to attack Münster, and with Widdowson and Ward in their Wimpy were two other New Zealanders, Sergeants L.A. Lawton (navigator)* and A.J.R. Box (rear gunner), with Sergeant W. Mason from Lincolnshire as wireless operator, and Sergeant T. Evans, a Welshman, tucked tightly in the nose turret. Ward took L7818 up for a 15-minutes night-flying test in

*Later, on 14 October 1941, commissioned and posted to 115 Squadron.

(*Right*) Sgt James Allen Ward,
VC, RNZAF.

(*Below*) 75(NZ) Squadron
Wellington AA–N being
prepared at Feltwell early 1941.

the afternoon, then at 2310 hours that evening Widdowson lifted the heavily-laden Wellington off Feltwell's runway and steadily climbed for height, heading for Münster.

The outward trip proved uneventful with no interference from nightfighters or other defences, and on reaching Münster Widdowson and his crew completed their bombing run successfully, then pulled away and headed back to base. The night was moon-lit, and as the Wellington droned across Holland at some 13,000 feet, Ward was standing with his head in the small astro-dome, looking at the Zuider Zee over two miles below shimmering silver in the light. Ahead he could see the Dutch coast getting nearer – not long now before they would be back in friendly sky.

Then it happened. From somewhere below the bomber came a hail of cannon shells, bullets, and tracers which riddled the Wellington from nose to tail – a roving Messerschmitt Bf110 *Nachtjäger* had evidently been stalking the lone bomber and now made its initial onslaught, catching the bomber's crew unawares. The German pilot's aim was deadly accurate. Shells rattled into the Wellington's starboard engine, shattered its hydraulic system causing the bomb doors to flop open, slashed through Mason's wireless equipment and cut off the crew intercommunication lines, filled the cockpit area with smoke and fumes, and liberally perforated the fuselage fabric.

In the rear turret Box, the nineteen-year-old gunner, was startled by the necklaces of tracers flashing by around his turret, then even more shocked when directly in front of his sights the belly of the German nightfighter suddenly appeared as it banked away. Instinctively Box fired all four of his Brownings and saw his bullets plunge into the Messerschmitt at near pointblank range. The fighter staggered, fell over on its back, and headed down pluming black smoke before disappearing from view as it merged with the earth below.

Though badly hit, the Wellington flew on, but now a five-feet long tongue of yellow-red flame was issuing from the split fuel lines of the stricken starboard engine, licking across the fabric-covered wing root and gaining in intensity. Widdowson took a good look at the fire and, knowing only too well how quickly that flame could soon spread to the rest of the canvas skin, pulled the Wellington round onto a course roughly parallel with the Dutch coast. With one engine out, and that one on fire, the pilot figured that any Wellington was hardly likely to remain airborne too long, so when Ward tapped him on the shoulder, Widdowson told him to order the rest of the crew to don their parachutes and be prepared to abandon their aircraft. As a final thought, the pilot added, 'and see if you can put out that bloody fire'.

Ward climbed back and passed on the order to put on parachutes, then with the help of Lawton and Mason, began ripping off the fabric of the fuselage nearest the upper starboard wing root in order to have a clear view of the engine fire. Trying first a hand extinguisher, then a thermos of coffee, they tried to dampen the flames, but the howling slipstream simply sploshed both containers' liquid contents back along the fuselage side.

Ward then heard his skipper's voice yelling and clambered forward again. Asked how the fire was going, Ward replied that it was still going, but had not worsened as yet. Widdowson thought for a moment. The idea of spending the rest of his war as a prisoner of the Nazis had no appeal to him. He made his decision and edged the nose of the Wellington round until he was heading out to sea again, heading home to England. Then, speaking to Ward again, he told him to cut a hole in the side of the fuselage and, if possible, lean out and smother the fire with something. Once more Ward returned to the mid-section and studied the engine fire. The flames had shortened but were still threatening to engulf the wing fabric surrounds.

Picking up a stowed canvas cockpit cover, Ward turned to Lawton and shouted that he was going to 'hop out with this' (*sic*). Lawton, horrified at such a prospect, argued fiercely with him not to try such a move, but Ward was adamant. Reluctantly acquiescing to the determined young Kiwi, Lawton at least persuaded Ward to attach his chest parachute pack to his harness, then insisted on tying a rope from the aircraft's dinghy around Ward's waist and wrapped the rest of the rope line around his (Lawton's) own chest as a form of anchor. The next step was to remove the 30-inch diameter perspex astro-dome bubble as Ward's intended exit.

Once this was done Ward, swaddled in full flying suit, parachute, and the bulky canvas cover, squeezed himself through the tiny hole head-first. As his head emerged Ward was blasted by the slipstream, almost robbing him of breath. Widdowson, unaware of Ward's intention, had realistically reduced speed as far as he dare for the journey back, but was still flying at near-100 mph; virtually gale-force as far as Ward was concerned as he inched his way outside onto the fuselage roof. With the top half of his body now outside the astro-dome aperture, Ward calculated his method of approach to that burning engine. It would mean letting himself down onto the wing root, then reaching across some three-four feet of the wing to get at the motor. With Lawton inside the fuselage clinging tightly to the rope tied around Ward's waist as his only life-line, Ward began his attempt to reach the stricken engine.

Lifting one booted foot over the side, Ward kicked a toe-hold through the fabric of the fuselage, then repeated this process with his other foot. He was now wholly outside, on the wing root, with the slipstream trying to pluck him away. Steadying himself, Ward slowly lowered himself to lie flat on the wing root, head forward into the teeth of the raging wind, still clutching the canvas cover. His chest parachute pack baulked his efforts to flatten himself properly on the wing, but Ward punched finger holds through the wing fabric for extra security.

Then slowly, literally inch by inch, he began pulling himself towards the burning engine. With only his left hand and both toe-holds to take the strain of the slipstream, Ward gripped the canvas cover in his free right hand and stuffed it into the flaming hole of the motor, holding it there until agonising pain forced him to release his grip. The hungry wind immediately began tearing the canvas cover free of the hole, but again Ward reached over and jammed it back in. Seconds later the slipstream finally triumphed, whisking the cover out of Ward's hand and away into the night sky. Ward looked helplessly at the fire, realised it had at least lessened in intensity, then knowing he could do no more, prepared for the hazardous move back to safety.

By now Jimmy Ward was on the point of total exhaustion. The combination of the howling, buffeting wind and booming engine roar had reduced him to a daze, but summoning strength from some unplumbed depth, he began his tortured, painfully slow return journey. Toe-hold by toe-hold, finger-hold by finger-hold, he retraced his short path to the fuselage. In the vacant astro-dome hole, Lawton kept the dinghy rope lifeline taut, braced for any sudden failure on Ward's part to retain his hold. Reaching the fuselage after what seemed an eternity, Ward gradually eased himself upwards, then managed to get his left leg into the astro-dome hole – then stuck there, too weary to continue. Inside, Lawton heaved and levered Ward's leg until he was able to pull the right leg in as well, then pulled Ward down into the fuselage.

Ward squatted on the fuselage floor, unable to speak or even move for the moment, wondering at the abrupt change from the roaring storm outside to the blissful peace and (relative) quiet of the

Sgt J.A. Ward, VC (centre) and his crew.

Damage to L7818, AA–R, 75(NZ) Squadron caused by Sgt Ward's attempts to douse the starboard engine fire.

Wellington's interior. Slowly he could feel the strength in his arms and legs returning, his breathing easing, his head clearing. Once Lawton was certain Ward would be all right, he went forward and reported to Widdowson, whose expression clearly showed the pilot's astonishment on hearing of Ward's efforts. Glancing out of the cockpit window, he could see the fire still burning, but with no real danger now of it spreading due to the adjacent fabric having been stripped away. He continued his course towards England.

When some ten miles from the English coast the engine fire suddenly erupted brightly again, then just as suddenly went out. The prime danger was over. Even so, other hazards remained. With its ruptured hydraulics, the Wellington's brakes and flaps were in effect useless, and shortly after 0430 hrs on 8 July Widdowson set the crippled bomber down on Newmarket's airfield, running the full length of the field before being halted ultimately by a wire-reinforced boundary hedge. Such was the aircraft's damage that it was returned to a maintenance unit for major overhaul and never used by the squadron again.*

Widdowson and his weary crew were given road transport back to their Feltwell base, arriving there shortly after 9 am, where they were greeted by their squadron commander, Wing Commander C.E. Kay, DFC who had remained awake all night anxiously awaiting their return. Once de-briefed the crew thankfully sought their beds – it had been a 'dicey trip', to put it mildly!

At that de-briefing Jimmy Ward had said very little, sitting quietly at one side, his reddened eyes and harrowed facial creasing the only clues to his recent ordeal. While the crew went back to their respective billets, Kay returned to his hangar office and immediately made out his personal recommendations to the Station Commander that Widdowson be awarded a DFC, Sergeant Box a DFM, and in the 'Award Recommended' column for Jimmy Ward Kay wrote without hesitation 'Victoria Cross'.

Kay's recommendations were swiftly approved at every stage as they wound through Service 'channels', and on 5 August 1941 the *London Gazette* announced the award of a VC to the shy young New Zealander. Two days later all station personnel at Feltwell gathered at a celebration dinner in honour of Jimmy Ward, yet when he was eventually persuaded to make a speech he confined his words to

*L7818 ultimately served again, with No 15 OTU, Harwell where, on 8 April 1942, it collided in the air with Spitfire R6686 and crashed at Cold Ashton, Glos.

'Jimmy' Ward, VC shaking hands with Group Captain Maurice Buckley, RNZAF at Feltwell, with Wing Commander C.E. Kay, OC 75(NZ) Squadron behind Ward with other squadron crew members.

praising the ground crews and their vital labours. Shortly after, however, a small incident betrayed the lasting effect on Ward of his ordeal. While lighting a cigarette from a petrol lighter a drop of the burning fluid fell on one of Ward's fingers – and he fainted . . .

Back with his squadron, Ward was now given his own crew and aircraft, as a captain in his own right, and on 13 September raided Brest in Wimpy X9757 with a load of six 500lb and one 250lb HE bombs. Hit by flak, Ward returned to make a safe emergency landing at Honington, then flew back to Feltwell next day where his aircraft was put into a hangar for repairs. On 15 September he was allotted Wellington X3205 for a sortie that same evening against Hamburg. Ward's crew consisted of Sergeants H.G. Sloman (second pilot), L.E. Peterson (observer), a Canadian, and H. Watson, R.W. Toller, and K.H. Toothill, and at 1945 hrs Ward left Feltwell. Over the target area Ward's aircraft was seen to be coned by searchlights with flak bursting around it, then fell to earth burning furiously.* Of its crew only two men managed to escape by parachute, Peterson and Watson – the rest perished in their burning aircraft.

Weeks later news filtered back to 75 Squadron via the International Red Cross organisation that Jimmy Ward, vc, and three of his faithful crew had been buried in the Ohlsdorf Cemetery at Hamburg.

*After the war, one of the surviving pair on return to England gave as his opinion that the Wellington had been the victim of a German nightfighter; though no positive confirmation of this has been unearthed to date (1986) by this author.

CHAPTER NINE

Desert Queens

At the outbreak of war in Europe in September 1939, the RAF
Middle East Command, commanded by Air Marshal Sir William
G.S. Mitchell, comprised a total of just 20 squadrons dispersed
among such areas as Aden, Sudan, Iraq, Transjordan, Palestine, and
Egypt. Actual equipment of those squadrons varied from the
antiquated Vickers Valentia 'bomber-transport' biplanes of No 79
Squadron to Gladiator fighters, Bombay transports, Wellesley and
Blenheim bombers; a 'firstline' total of (at most) some 200 machines
which might reasonably be called 'operationally fit' albeit obsolete
aircraft in many cases. The most 'modern' bomber immediately
available was the Blenheim with a relatively modest bomb load
capacity and limited operational range.

Reinforcement of the Command with more, preferably updated,
aircraft received low priority during the first nine months of the war
due, necessarily, to the immediate needs of the UK and French-based
RAF units. Fortunately, during that same period the Italian dictator,
Mussolini, preferred to bide his time in deciding which way the wind
was blowing before committing Italy to actual war, and a trickle of
aircraft despatched from Britain slowly built up the Middle East
RAF Command to a strength of 29 squadrons by the end of May
1940.

On 13 May, Air Marshal Mitchell was succeeded as AOC-in-C by
Air Chief Marshal Sir Arthur Longmore, who wrote to the Air Staff
for confirmation of the actual limits of his new command. The reply
said that he was in command of *all* RAF units stationed or operating
in Egypt, Sudan, Palestine, Trans-Jordan, East Africa, Aden, British
Somaliland, Iraq and 'adjacent' territories bounding the Mediterranean, Red Sea, and Persian Gulf – a geographical gross area of
almost five million square miles, greater indeed than the land area of
the United States of America. All with about 300 'firstline' and a
further 300 'reserve' aircraft of varying vintages!

At midnight on 10 June 1940, Benito Mussolini finally dragged
Italy into the hostilities with a formal declaration of war against the

Allies. Within hours a series of Blenheim formations drawn from Nos 211, 45, 55, and 113 Squadrons, had reconnoitred, then bombed the main Italian airfield at El Adem, destroying or damaging 18 aircraft on the ground, though at a cost of two Blenheims shot down by groundfire, a third crashing on return, and others damaged and scarred. This 'instant reaction' epitomised the RAF's policy of offence is the best defence, but the Middle East Command still lacked a truly long-range bomber to pursue any form of strategic offensive against Italian targets beyond the Blenheims' limited ranges. The most likely candidate for such a long-arm offensive was the Wellington at that date, and indeed four Wellingtons – L4227, L4235, L4374, and L7771 – were despatched from the UK on 20 June 1940 to Egypt, but these were destined to be converted to the DWI anti-magnetic mine configuration almost immediately for duties protecting the Suez Canal and its approaches, and the RN base port of Alexandria.

By September 1940, however, Wellington bombers had begun re-equipping No 70 Squadron, among the first arrivals being T2730, T2731, T2732, T2733, T2734, T2735, T2813, T2814, T2816, T2828, and T2832. No 70 Squadron promptly put their new aircraft to use, carrying out the unit's first Wimpy operations on the night of 18/19 September 1940 with an attack on Benghazi port – the beginning of a four years' association with the Wimpy by 70 Squadron.

Further reinforcements arrived within weeks. In the first week of November 1940, the Wellingtons of No 37 Squadron flew to Malta from where they carried out several operations against Italian targets such as Valona and Brindisi before moving to Shallufa, Egypt in December. A second Wellington unit, No 38 Squadron, was also despatched from the UK, with the advance ground crews' personnel leaving Glasgow on 13 November aboard a trooper, and transferring to HMS *Southampton* at Gibraltar for the final 'leg' to Alexandria. HMS *Southampton* set sail from Gibraltar, in convoy with HMS *Ark Royal, Renown, Sheffield, Ramilles, Berwick, Manchester, Coventry,* and *Newcastle,* on 25 November, and two days later, off Sardinia, the 700 airmen aboard HMS *Southampton* found themselves uninvited spectators to a naval and aerial clash with the Italian navy and airforce during the so-termed Battle of Spartivento.

On reaching Egypt the ground crews of 38 Squadron were taken to Fayid where they were reunited with the unit's Wellingtons and air crews; the latter having left Marham on 25 November and arrived intact except for one Wimpy destroyed by an enemy air raid on Malta en route. By 7 December No 38 Squadron was ready for operations

DWI Wellingtons on patrol over Suez, including L4374.

HF887, 'W' on arrival at 105 MU, April 1942. Later 'O', 70 Squadron, it crashed in the Qattara Depression on 8/9 Sept 1942 after raiding Tobruk, but its crew (skipper, Fg Off Elliott) walked back to safety.

(Above) Tight Trio. Wellingtons of 37 Squadron, May 1941, nearest T2875, 'B' which later served on 148 Squadron and ditched on 24 May 1941.

(Left) 37 Squadron Wimpy's insigne at Kabrit – *Der Oberhund II* ('Top Dog 2').

and next day ten of its Wellingtons joined ten more from 37 Squadron and other aircraft in raiding Benina airfield. For this they had first flown to LG 60 to 'top up' fuel, then attacked the target at heights between 5,000 and 9,000 feet, followed by a low-level 'strafe' of the ground defences.

Commanded by Wing Commander W.P.J. Thomson, DFC, No 38 Squadron spent the following weeks operating four or five nights per week, despatching up to seven Wellingtons on each sortie, despite 'a chronic shortage of spares and facilities – only one tractor and two bomb trolleys available to rearm, and no instrument or electrical ground equipment at all'.* On 17 December 1940, however, the squadron 'packed its bags' (*sic*) and next day travelled 20 miles further south to its new base, Shallufa, some eight miles from Port Suez. The move was completed by 1900 hrs on 18 December – and exactly one hour later the first Wimpy left for LG 60 en route to bomb Berka airfield, near Benghazi . . .

At Shallufa – where initially conditions were even more chaotic than at Fayid – No 38 Squadron joined No 37 Squadron which, after a few sorties from Malta had also settled at this airfield. By the close of 1940 the three Wellington units had already made an impact on the Italians, particularly in attacks on vital resupply ports such as Benghazi, and a deliberate campaign to destroy the Italian air force *in situ*; one attack by 11 Wellingtons from Malta on Castel Benito airfield on the night of 7 December destroyed or damaged 29 enemy aircraft, while ten more were destroyed at Benina the following night.

This form of semi-strategic air offensive was a preliminary to an Allied armies' offensive, *Operation Compass*, which was launched on 9 December, and the ensuing rapid westward advance along the North African coastal strip saw the army capture towns like Bardia (4 January 1941), Tobruk (22 January), and finally Benghazi (6 February). By the latter date, incidentally, the Italian air force in North Africa alone had lost more than 1,200 aircraft, either abandoned/captured, shot down, or wrecked by aerial assaults on landing grounds – a crippling loss from which the *Regia Aeronautica* in North Africa never really recovered fully.

On 14 December 1940 a 'new' Wellington unit was added to the Middle East RAF's strength when No 148 Squadron was reformed at Luqa, Malta for bombing duties, and which commenced operations that same night. However, even before *Operation Compass* was under

*No 38 Squadron, 1916-1963; 38 Squadron, 1964.

Breakfast à la carte – 38 Squadron crew in the Libyan desert, 1941

Wellington IIs of 148 Squadron flying above the Nile Delta.

way the RAF's relatively weak numerical strength in the Middle East had been further stretched by fresh commitments, when on 28 October 1940 Italian forces abruptly invaded Greek territory. Bound, at least in honour, by a guarantee of help to Greece dating back to 13 April 1939, the British government immediately promised 'all the help in our power' (*sic*), while Sir Arthur Longmore decided (with the approval of Winston Churchill) to detach some of his sorely-needed squadrons and other aircraft to Greece in support of the small Greek air services.

These detachments included an initial batch of six Wellingtons from 70 Squadron to Eleusis on 6 November, and next day these Wimpys carried out bombing sorties in the Valona area, losing two aircraft to Italian opposition apart from damage to others. Thereafter, the Wellingtons flew only by night. The arrival of Nos 37 and 38 Squadrons permitted further small detachments of Wellingtons to the ill-fated Greek campaign.

Even as *Operation Compass* was approaching its successful conclusion yet another element was introduced to the North African campaign – in the first week of January 1941 German forces began arriving in Tripoli along with the first units of the Luftwaffe to operate over the desert; these aircraft having already carried out raids on Malta and Allied shipping in the Mediterranean from bases in Sicily in preceding days. The German presence had no effect on *Operation Compass*, but was soon to prove its worth in North Africa when, commanded by General Erwin Rommel, who arrived in Tripoli on 12 February 1941, the Afrika Korps commenced a 'reconnaissance in strength' against Allied forces on 31 March which soon forced the Allied armies to retreat back beyond Tobruk.

Further German opposition followed when, in Greece, on 6 April, German forces came to the aid of the Italian forces there, heavily supported by the Luftwaffe. Only weeks later, yet another problem erupted for the Middle East RAF when, in early May, an anti-Allies' revolt, headed by the pro-Axis Raschid Ali, in Iraq included revolutionary troops investing the RAF training base at Habbaniya. This German-supported revolt, though soon defeated by the ragbag collection of aircraft at Habbaniya reinforced by other aircraft, including a few Wellingtons, from 37 and 70 Squadrons, flown in, was followed by a decision to occupy a hostile Vichy-French dominated Syria – yet another side-show campaign which drained the RAF's resources. Above all these one-off operations was the vital need for preserving Malta as a bastion of Allied defiance and springboard for aerial offensive operations against Axis shipping in the Mediterranean supplying Rommel's forces in North Africa.

The 'campaign' in Greece was brief once the German forces made their appearance, leaving the remnants of the RAF units involved to evacuate Crete, or in the case of the handful of Wellingtons to fly back to Egyptian bases from where they could continue operations over Greece and Crete during the final fateful weeks. One man involved in nearly all these side-shows was N.E. McIntyre, a sergeant observer who served with No 37 Squadron from August 1939 to September 1940. His first 12 operational sorties were from Feltwell, Norfolk against German targets, and he remained with the squadron when it was despatched to the Middle East:

In November 1940 I joined another crew – my first skipper, Sergeant D. Beddow, having completed his first tour – with Sergeant R.T. Spiller as my new captain, and the squadron was posted to the Middle East Command, with some aircraft stopping over at Malta, to boost the efforts against the Italians. The squadron flew individually at intervals to Malta, via Worthing, Marseilles, Bizerta, to Luqa. We made landfall at Bizerta at about 9000 feet to be greeted by a fair amount of 'friendly' French flak thrown at us, and as we scuttled away an Italian Macchi 200 jumped us. We dived to sea level and eventually shook him off, with the assistance of our phlegmatic New Zealander rear gunner and his Brownings, but not before collecting a few hits, one of these peppering the backside of an unfortunate armourer travelling with us. We made Luqa some two hours later and the armourer survived, despite his initial bleeding.

Whilst at Malta we flew sorties against Brindisi and Valona. This latter I particularly remember because of the severe thunderstorms we met over the Balkan coast, preventing location of both primary and secondary targets, and with the DR plot ending up like a spider's web due to the numerous changes of course we had to make. We left Malta on 20 December and flew to Shallufa in the Suez Canal area, which became our main base for the remainder of our Middle East tour. Targets from there included Benghazi, Derna, Tobruk along the coast, and Rhodes and Karpathos in the Dodecanese. From Shallufa we 'enjoyed' two detachments to Greece and a third to Iraq. Operating from Menidi, near Athens, and Paramythia, a landing ground in from the west coast towards Corfu. I particularly recall two sorties from

The Office. 148 Squadron Wellington's 'driver's' seat panorama, Kabrit.

POST 1941 (March).
LG09, LG167, OR LG237. !!)

Paramythia – the 'Valley of the Fairies', as its name translated. The first on 20 February 1941, in company with another Wimpy (Flight Lieutenant M. Baird-Smith), saw us drop bales of bread and bully-beef to the Greek Army at Kelcyre inside the Albanian border. We made it as low-level as possible and could almost see the joy on the faces of the men below us as they scampered through the snow to the drops.

The other was on 16 March when Intelligence learned that Mussolini was due in Tirana, the Albanian capital – we hoped that our bombs more than shook him at the royal palace! By then the Boche was coming down through the Balkans and we finished our stay in Greece with a raid on the Sofia railway yards, Calatos aerodrome on Rhodes, and German transport concentrations coming south through Ptolemais, Kozene, and Florina.

I well remember that last op. The CO, Wing Commander R.M. Collard, decided to skipper the aircraft and, after bombing and strafing the German transports on the road through the three locations, the weather closed in on us and, with Mount Olympus at 9,500 ft quite handy, we climbed in as tight a spiral as we dared, eventually breaking cloud, heading east, and (with a sigh of relief) pin-pointed the three-fingered peninsula south-east from Salonika. That was on 16 April and three days later we packed our bags and bade farewell to Greece, now being invaded by the Germans.

Just after leaving Athens, Ken Bevan, our Kiwi rear gunner, reported a fighter chasing us. We dropped to sea level and, with his customary cool commentary and marksmanship, he 'persuaded' the Messerschmitt to break off. A detachment to Iraq from 1 to 12 May gave us our first opportunity to be 'angry' during daylight. Based at Shaibah, we flew 'security patrols' over Habbaniya and bombed 'Raschid aerodrome' and the military installations and aerodrome at Mosul. In addition to bombs we dropped 'meaningful' messages addressed to one Raschid Ali . . .*

The Wellington crews of 38 Squadron were also involved in the Greek campaign, though not before being forced to join the general Allied retreat in North Africa before Rommel's forces; moving back to Shallufa eventually after three changes of airfield in just two days in early April 1941. On 10 April the unit received orders for yet another move, this time to an airfield near Athens. Arriving there on 11 April,

Wellington at War by C. Bowyer; Ian Allan, 1982.

Wellington victim on Crete.

X9889, 40 Squadron in the shadow of Gibraltar's Rock, late 1941, en route to Malta where, on 29 December 1941, it was destroyed on Luqa during an air raid by the Luftwaffe.

the crews only paused to refuel, then took off again to bomb the Sofia railway centre in Bulgaria; a raid repeated on 14 April, followed next day by nine Wimpys attacking the bridge over the Vardar at Veles and nearby troop concentrations. On 17 April the squadron detachment returned to Shallufa to join the rest of the squadron in attacking such targets as Derna, El Adem, and Rhodes; while in May 1941 the unit flew a total of 1085 operational hours in bombing targets both in the Western Desert and in Greece and – by 22 May – German objectives on Crete.

The shortage of Wellingtons at this period meant that squadron ground crews on all units were called upon for extraordinary efforts in ensuring that damaged aircraft were refurbished to firstline operational status as quickly as humanly possible. Merely one of many examples of this 'devotion to duty' by the anonymous 'Erks' was Wellington W5628,'Y' of 38 Squadron. Piloted by Flight Lieutenant Duder, 'Y' carried out an attack on Derna on 13 April 1941 and was badly shot up by flak, having its port aileron severed, rear spar and aileron hinge damaged, a three-foot hole in the fuselage caused by an explosive shell which severed the supply lines to the rear turret, and numerous damage to the geodetic structure, leaving the Wimpy dangerously left wing low.

Duder managed to reach Fuka safely, but knowing the vital need for every aircraft flew it back to Shallufa next day, landing at 1300 hrs. Within 30 minutes the Erks had started work on the ravaged Wellington and continued their work without let-up until 1600 hrs on 15 April – at which hour W5628,'Y' took off for its next operational sortie . . .

This overall shortage of long-range (*sic*) bombers within the RAF Middle East Command was recognised – albeit most reluctantly by the British Prime Minister, Winston Churchill – and measures were taken to establish a relatively safe method of transferring all necessary aircraft from the UK to the North African zones; once Italy had entered the war, transportation via the Royal Navy etc through the Mediterranean was a fraught prospect, while previous air routes crossing over France were, after June 1940, hardly advisable.

Accordingly, in July 1940 an advance party of technical tradesmen arrived at Takoradi in the Gold Coast (now Ghana) to supplement and expand an existing passenger/mail terminal of the Takoradi-Khartoum 'airline' originally established in 1936. By late September 1940 the first delivery flights to Egypt (eventually) had begun leaving Takoradi – some 3700 miles' route via Lagos, Kano, Maiduguri,

Geneina, Khartoum, and Abu Sueir. In later years this routing changed once the North African campaigns had been won by the Allies.

The more urgent need for aircraft to be provided for (primarily) the defence of Malta was undertaken by the Royal Navy's available aircraft carriers, strongly escorted, through the Mediterranean – often at relatively high cost in ships sunk or crippled; but a third means of reinforcement was by despatching Wellingtons (in particular) individually by direct air delivery, via Gibraltar as the main staging stopover. It meant risking solitary Wimpys across the Bay of Biscay, with its ever-attendant horde of Luftwaffe fighters based along the nearby French coastline; while, opposition or none, the sheer reliability of the Wellington on such an extended flight would be severely tested.

The 'Biscay Route' – or 'Junkers Alley' as some crews dubbed it – proved hazardous for many Wellington crews. The first leg to Gibraltar, particularly, meant having bomb bays filled with extra fuel tanks which offered an additional fuel capacity of some 1000 (or more) gallons. Gibraltar, the first intended refuelling stop, possessed a short runway completed on the old racecourse site by March 1936 and in the shadow of the towering Rock until, with the arrival of a detachment of No 233 Squadron's Lockheed Hudsons in August 1941, it was decided to extend the runway by reclaiming land from the sea westward; a scheme which eventually produced a total runway length of 1800 yards by July 1943.* For pilots making their first acquaintance with Gibraltar, particularly in 1940-42, the menacing Rock, some 1358 feet high, standing less than 600 yards away from the sole runway, produced no few qualms, especially with the not uncommon turbulence, strong cross-winds, and often flooded landing area they needed to cope with on first arrival. Moreover, on the runway itself, even after its extension, a fresh pilot often found himself running out of runway with an inevitable prospect of getting his feet wet at the far end . . .

The first nine months of Wellington operations in the Middle East had been, to say the least, testing. Inevitably, the various diversions to Greece, Crete, Iraq, etc had diluted the potential impact of long-range strategic operations in support of the Allied armies in North Africa, and had caused hard-felt losses which were not readily

*In July 1954 this was further extended to 2000 yards. RAF Station, North Front, Gibraltar came into official existence in May 1942.

replaceable. Due to enemy occupation of the western areas of the North African coastline, reinforcements flying out from the UK necessarily had to be staged through the bomb-racked, besieged island of Malta where virtually unceasing aerial bombing attacks quickly took toll of any aircraft parked in the open, especially during 1941-42.

No 148 Squadron, which had been reformed at Luqa in December 1940, remained on the island until March 1941, then shifted its base to Kabrit, Egypt, but continued to maintain detachments on Luqa throughout 1941 and early 1942. As a result of enemy bombing attacks the squadron lost many Wellingtons on the ground at Malta, including six destroyed in a single raid on Luqa on 25 February 1941 (R1247, R1381, R1382, R1383, R1384, T2955,'W'), while next day T2816 was added to the list of bombing victims. These losses were not the only casualties to be suffered by 148 Squadron during its early weeks of Wimpy operations since reformation. Wellington T2874,'W' failed to return from a sortie on 12 January 1941, while T2891 was lost over Tripoli on 24 February, and T2890 was destroyed at Gambut on 30 March. On 9 April Wimpy T2952 ditched in the sea, as did T2875 on 24 May, and on the last day of May L7860 was recorded as 'Missing in action'.

The other three existing Wellington squadrons also had their 'share' of casualties during the period September 1940 to May 1941. No 70 Squadron, the first Wimpy unit in North Africa, suffered its initial two losses on 7 November 1940 when T2731 (Flight Lieutenant Brian) and T2734 (Sergeant Brooks) were both shot down by Italian fighters while bombing Valona during the unit's first detachment to the Greek campaign. On the same detachment, T2827 (Sergeant Palmer) set out to bomb Durazzo but crashed in Yugoslavia on 18 November 1940. Among 37 Squadron's crop of casualties were L7865 which crashed at Sidi Barrani on 21 December 1940, N2757,'S', which crashed at El Zouara with an engine on fire on 17 February 1941, T2575 which mysteriously exploded in mid-air over the Mediterranean on 21 February 1941, and L7866 which was coded 'R' and failed to return from Scarpanto on 24 May 1941. No 38 Squadron's toll of war at the same period included L4391 which crashed on take-off at Bizerte on 26 December 1940, P9293,'S' lost over Tobruk on 7 January 1941, N2759 which crashed at Fuka and burned out on 15 January 1941, P9265 which was damaged beyond repair at Luqa on 3 February, and R1033 'Missing in action' over Derna on 14 April.

Such casualty figures did not wholly represent the overall picture in the context of any Wellington squadron's full operational capabilities. Apart from the actual losses of aircraft – and thereby, too often, experienced crew members – either on sorties or in serious accidents resulting in write-off action, each squadron perforce had to cater for its 'normal' quote of inevitable minor, albeit repairable unserviceabilities which temporarily reduced the unit's operational strength for any given operation.

Above all was the constant battle by the maintenance ground crews – the 'Erks' – with unforgiving Nature. In North Africa's desert regions the 'enemies' met *every* day and night were sheer heat by day which cracked perspex cupolas and windscreens, and the ever-present, invasive sand and dust which, when borne on the frequent storm-winds, could render any machine useless within mere minutes. Even without the winds sand penetrated every nook and crevice, seemingly delighted in clogging up aero engines, instruments, and hydraulic systems. As ex-Corporal 'Ben' Todd recalled:

If I have one overall memory of my three years in Africa it is of sand. It got into *every*thing – aircraft, MT, food, drink, clothes – you name it! And after only weeks of flying some Wimpys had their engine cowlings and other metal parts exposed sand-blasted down to the bare metal; the sand acting like heavy grade emery paper. The combination of boiling dry heat and sand often split fabric skins apart, and replacement fabric was never all that plentiful for immediate repairs by the riggers. The same applied to engine parts – spares were like gold in the early days and occasionally we had up to a third of our kites u/s simply awaiting some spare item. Whether working or 'off-duty' you just couldn't escape from that damned sand – in your bedclothes, you hair, your tea, your ears; it was a permanent part of your daily life and all you could do was try to ignore it.

On 1 August 1941 yet another Wellington unit joined the ranks of Middle East Command when No 108 Squadron was reformed at Kabrit, and commenced operations on the night of 27/28 August by despatching a single Wellington to bomb Benghazi. Two months later, in October 1941, further Wellington reinforcements reached the Mediterranean theatre when two UK-based units 'detached' aircraft, air and ground crews to Luqa, Malta. Of these, No 104 Squadron based at Driffield sent a total of 15 Wellingtons and crews, while No

40 Squadron, based at Alconbury, contributed 16 aircraft with air and ground crews. From Malta both squadrons' 'detachments' mounted full-scale operations against targets in Sicily, Italy, and North Africa; while the so-termed 'home echelons' of both units also continued sorties over Germany and France.

This division of effort was finally rationalised on 14 February 1942 when the UK element of 104 Squadron was retitled as No 158 Squadron, and on the same date the 'home echelon' of 40 Squadron became No 156 Squadron. By then the Malta-based detachment of 104 Squadron had moved its base to Kabrit in January 1942; being followed to Egypt later by 40 Squadron when it left Malta for its next base at Shallufa by July 1942. As with all units joining the Middle East theatre of war, both squadrons were quickly to suffer casualties.

No 40 Squadron, flying Wellington Ics, lost X9912 almost immediately after arrival when it ditched in the Mediterranean on 24 October, then on 12 November recorded X9765,'A' as 'Failed to return' from a raid on Naples. On 24 November Wellington X9662 blew up on dispersal while being bombed up, and six nights later Z1046 failed to return from a sortie to Benghazi. Enemy air raids on Malta accounted for Z9029,'T' on 19 December, and ten days later three more bomb victims, X9889,'D', X9907, X9919. December also saw the loss of R1066,'C' over Naples on 5 December. Three more losses occurred in January 1942, with Z1079 bombed on its dispersal on the 3rd, Z9036 'missing' on the night of 4/5 January, and Z8959,'B' suffering destruction on the ground on the 24th. No 104 Squadron, flying Merlin-engined Wellington IIs, had its share of problems in the context of losses and casualties during its first months in the Middle East too. Apart from the concomitant losses of actual operations, the squadron's air crews quickly adapted normal take-off and (especially) landing techniques to allow for the near-primitive 'runway' at Luqa which tailed off into a notorious quarry; this latter becoming a virtual graveyard for 'bent' Wellingtons and other aircraft. One early victim of Luqa's runway was Wellington W5398 on 26 October 1941, followed by Z8404 on 29 November.

At Shallufa, fast becoming the prime Wellington base airfield in Egypt, a detached Flight of the UK-based No 109 Squadron was formed with six Wellingtons by the end of October 1941. These Wimpys were specially modified for the tasks of radio counter-measures (RCM) i.e. discovering and the jamming enemy radio traffic. Flying its first sortie on 20 November, the unit suffered its first casualties the next day, when two Wellingtons flying in the Fort

Nose art of a 108 Squadron, B Flt Wimpy at Fayid, 1942.

108 Squadron Wellingtons at 'dispersal'. Nearest has an American Indian Chief's head, with full plumage, as its insigne.

Capuzzo area were jumped by three Messerchmitt Bf100s from JG27. One Wellington was shot down and a second damaged beyond repair when it crashlanded; both being claimed as victories by Leutnant Hans Remmer and Oberfeldwebel Otto Schulz. That same night two more of the unit's Wellingtons were badly damaged at a forward landing ground during an air raid. Within 24 hours, on 22 November, the Flight had further casualties, with one Wellington being shot down by Hauptmann Lippert of JG27 over the El Adem area, while a second received serious damage.

By 25 November this Flight was down to merely one serviceable and two repairable Wellingtons, and operations ceased temporarily. On 4 January 1942, however, the 109 Squadron Flight, commanded by Flight Lieutenant Willis, became the nucleus of a 'new' unit, No 162 Squadron, still based at Shallufa, and formally commanded by Wing Commander D.H.S. Rusher, DSO. Its role was a combination of radar calibration and *Elint* (Electronic Intelligence), and was initially equipped with Blenheim IVs for the former duties and Wellingtons for the *Elint* operations. At first *Elint* sorties were devoted to enemy installations in Greece and Crete, and on 6 March the squadron had its first loss when Z8905,'O'* (Sergeant Knowles) failed to return from a sortie over the Dodecanese.

The Wellingtons employed by 162 Squadron – successively Mk Is, IIIs, and Xs – differed little externally from standard marks, but usually carried an extra crew member, a set operator, stationed amidships. In contrast to its 'founding father', 109 Squadron's detached Flight, the squadron's 'cloak and dagger' operational duties meant that casualties were few relative to other Wellington units, though individual aircraft customarily penetrated hostile skies virtually unprotected. One example of the squadron's direct support of the land war in North Africa came prior to and following the battle of Alamein in late 1942, when 162's crews carried out sorties jamming the radio signal traffic of Rommel's *Panzer* forces. By early 1943 the squadron's aircraft were ranging as far afield as Italy, Sicily, Greece, Crete, Sardinia, Tripoli, and Tunisia in their investigations of enemy radar and radio sources, but throughout 1943-44 the tempo of operations steadily decreased until by 1944 that pace was little better than one sortie per month. Finally, on 25 September 1944, No 162

*Formerly 'K', 37 Squadron. Other Wellingtons used by 162 Squadron included T2878; W5679,'R'; X9986,'X'; Z1165,'M'; Z8765; Z8948; Z9034; AD589,'A'; AD630,'T'; AD643,'Q'; BB463,'O'; BB516,'F'; DV489,'A'; DV647,'D'; DV931,'V'; HD972,'U?H'; HF733,'L'; HX633,'F'; HX673; HX682; HZ123; LP238,'X'.

Squadron was officially disbanded at Idku.

In the latter months of 1941 the Shallufa-based No 38 Squadron, apart from its continuing pure bombing duties, began adding semi-maritime operational roles to its tasks by undertaking mining sorties; the first such operation taking place on 16 July when mines were sown in Benghazi harbour. Such sorties entailed the Wellingtons descending from some 5000 feet or higher to a mere 500 feet for the actual drop, inevitably in the teeth of intense flak opposition. Then, on 9 August 1941, the squadron despatched four aircraft for a one-off attack requiring accurate – and difficult – bomb-aiming. The targets were the near-vertical hillsides rising on each bank of the Corinth Canal, which were to be bombed in the hope of creating landslides which would effectively block the vital waterway to enemy traffic. The raid was completely successful and put the canal out of commission for at least a month.

Seven days later 38 Squadron sent two Wellingtons to bomb Derna harbour wherein an enemy submarine had been reported as lying on the bottom. After the raid considerable amounts of oil and wreckage debris were seen in the harbour, seeming evidence that the submarine was at least heavily damaged. Meanwhile, on 5 August, four of the unit's Wellingtons had been detached to Malta for three months, from where they participated in a number of attacks on Rommel's supply sea-routes as well as bombing objectives in Tripoli, Sicily, and Italy. On 12 September, for example, these Wellingtons bombed an enemy convoy comprised of five merchantmen escorted by six destroyers, claiming hits on at least four ships. Four days later came the squadron's first bombing raid on the Italian mainland, when 36,000lb of bombs were dropped on Naples, hitting the Royal Arsenal, railway station, and Valiana torpedo factory.

On 21 October 1941 the commander of 38 Squadron, Wing Commander R.J. Goswell, DFC, was succeeded 'in charge' by Wing Commander John Chaplin, DSO (later Air Commodore, DSO,DFC,BA). Chaplin took over the reins at a particularly busy period for the unit, which was averaging 80-100 sorties per month from the Shallufa base, attacking ports, harbours, and airfields along the North African coast in the preliminary offensive for an imminent Allied Land offensive *Operation Crusader*, which finally got under way on 18 November. Then, in December 1941, John Chaplin initiated a series of trials for yet another maritime role with modified Wellingtons converted as torpedo-bombers. This fresh role had originated from a request by the AOC, No 205 Group to Chaplin for an 'effective way of

'Fishington' – torpedo-Wellington of 38 Squadron at Shallufa, Egypt, 1942.

38 Squadron Wellington's full load of two torpedoes, Malta.

attacking with torpedoes at sea' (*sic*), to which Chaplin had replied:*

> The present torpedo-carrying aircraft suffer from the double handicap of a short range and the capacity to carry only one torpedo. There is a pressing need for an aircraft which has a longer range and can carry at least two torpedoes. The only aircraft at present in this Command which can satisfy such demands is the Wellington.

Modification of the squadron's standard Wellingtons entailed removal of the nose gun turret – better pilot vision forward – and conversion of the overall bomb bay to accept two Mk XII naval torpedoes; these being suspended two inches apart as a *vertical* pair, because space was not available to mount them side by side. Chaplin made the first practice-drop of a torpedo pair on 20 December, and during January-February 1942 more of his crews carried out dummy torpedo 'attacks', using a small yacht, HMS *Sagetta*, as their target.

Recognising a Wellington's limited manoeuvrability, as compared with normal torpedo-bombers like the Fleet Air arm's Swordfish and Albacore, 38 Squadron's crews devised a general tactic of long, low attack runs, releasing their 'fish' at about 1,000 yards' range from a height of 80 feet, then remaining low as they turned away from the target as part-protection from ships' flak guns. Chaplin also recommended that the best – and safest – times for such attacks should be either at dusk or by moonlight, whenever possible; in broad daylight the 'Fishingtons' (as torpedo Wimpys came to be dubbed) were patently too vulnerable to flak or enemy fighter opposition.

Using forward landing grounds at El Adem, Gambut, and Bu Amed, the squadron made its initial attempts to intercept enemy convoys in early 1942 but quickly realised that such targets were usually beyond the aircraft's range. Accordingly, the Wellingtons were fitted with long-range fuel tanks, and on 27 March three 'Fishingtons' attacked shipping in Patras harbour, with Pilot Officer Swingler sinking a 15,000 tons vessel – the unit's first completed torpedo sorties. Prior to that attack, however, Wing Commander Chaplin, flying Z9099, had left Shallufa on 9 March to fly to Bu Amed, from where he intended to carry out a sortie against enemy shipping with the two torpedoes in his bomb bay. South-west of Sidi Barrani he had the misfortune to be jumped by two Messerschmitt

*Report dated 26 December 1941.

Seldom-seen sight of 38 Squadron Wellingtons in neat formation, based on Malta.

'X' of unidentified unit, crashed at LG 09.

Bf109s from JG27 out on a *Freijagd* (*Free Chase*) patrol, piloted by Leutnant Friedrich Körner and Gefreiter Romeikat.

The latter attacked Chaplin's Wellington setting it on fire and forcing it to crashland, then both Bf109s proceeded to strafe the aircraft on the ground. Two of Chaplin's crew were killed, but he and the remaining members escaped injury and eventually 'walked back' to Allied territory. Chaplin's aircraft was one of several unit losses in early 1942.

On 17 March, Wimpy W5646 was a bomb victim on Malta; five days later Z9110 was lost in the Mediterranean; on 24 March the crew of Z9108 abandoned their aircraft; and on 28 March AD596 failed to return from a raid on Patras. On the night of 7/8 April, AD604 also failed to return from a sortie bombing Tripoli. No 38 Squadron continued to increase its commitments to maritime operations, and by the summer of 1942 was transferred to the aegis of the naval co-operation No 201 Group, based at Alexandria, for administrative and operational control. On 8 June command of the squadron had passed into the hands of Wing Commander C.V.J. Pratt, who was destined to be killed in action during a mine-laying sortie in Tripoli harbour on 14 December 1942, being succeeded as CO next day by Wing Commander B.C. Merharg.

The crucial necessity of attempting to nullify re-supply of men and materials to Rommel's Afrika Korps from Italy etc led to much reinforcement of RAF and Fleet Air Arm units operating from Malta and Egypt during 1941-42; hence (among others) the ready conversion of No 38 Squadron's Wellingtons. Another unit to join the struggle at sea was No 221 Squadron. Reformed at Bircham Newton on 21 November 1940 under the command of Wing Commander T.R. Vickers (later, Group Captain, DSO), the squadron was initially equipped with Wellington Ics fitted with ASV and commenced a successful year of operations within Coastal Command on anti-shipping sorties. In March 1941 the unit began re-equipping with Wellington VIII 'Stickleback' aircraft – nicknamed 'Goofingtons' – and in September moved base from the UK to Reykjavik, Iceland in order to extend its search areas for U-boats.

In December the squadron returned to Bircham Newton with orders to prepare for a posting 'overseas', though three crews were volunteers to go to Malta immediately, where they formed a so-termed Special Duties Flight (SDF), whose specific role was to fly Wellington VIIIs by night only, seeking and locating enemy surface ships by use of their ASV sets – the first seen on Malta. Among those three crews was Pilot Officer Anthony Spooner (later, Squadron Leader, DSO,DFC), whose subsequent six months' service on Malta are so well described in his autobiography*.

Arriving in Egypt in January 1942, No 221 Squadron, by then having Wing Commander A.M. Murdoch as CO, became based initially at LG87, then LG89, Shandur, Shallufa, and Gambut throughout the rest of the year. Its prime role was to use ASV to locate enemy convoys for other Wimpy torpedo aircraft, such as 38 Squadron, to carry out actual attacks. In between such night sorties, the squadron flew normal reconnaissance and anti-submarine patrols, claiming one U-boat as sunk on 21 August 1942. The co-operation with 38 Squadron's 'Fishingtons' is recalled by E.A. Sanders:

> 221 Squadron located any convoy and dropped flares, and we homed in on them and attacked either into the flares or along the moonpath. We had a sort of Heath Robinson-ish bomb-sight (home-made, I believe) mounted just outside the pilot's wind-screen, but it was not often used. Our method was to fly as low on the water as we could, aiming the nose of the aircraft about half the ship-length ahead, and drop the torpedo as near as possible to the target. The best 'way-out' afterwards used to be over the ship, down on the water again, then a steep turn away. The torpedoes could be released singly or together by the pilot. 221 Squadron's Wimpys had a massive array of aerials along the top of their fuselages and were nicknamed 'Sticklebacks', and in addition to their ASV equipment they carried a considerable number of parachute flares which they dropped for our benefit. 221 was usually airborne about an hour before 38 Squadron to enable them to search out any target convoy. Although we in 38 were based at Shallufa, we usually operated from LG226, Gianaclis, just over an hour's flying from base to the west of Cairo, where torpedoes were stocked for operations.

On 29 August 1942, Flight Lieutenant M. Foulis, DFC, of 221 Squadron set out as one of several Wellington skippers to attack an enemy convoy bound for Tobruk, which had already been attacked once on the previous evening with some success; the object of this second 'wave' being to 'finish the job'. His official report stated:

In Full Flight by A. Spooner; Macdonald, 1965.

'R' of 108 Squadron flying back to base, over the Nile Delta, 1941.

221 Squadron Mk XIII, JA416, above Malta on 3 Jan 1944.

We sighted the ships at 0015 hrs in the moonpath. There was no cloud and a bright moon. We could see the ship clearly, a vessel of about 8000 tons or perhaps a little less. There was one destroyer about two miles ahead of her, another about a mile on her port bow, and a third close in to her starboard quarter. I spent about 20 minutes flying across the moonpath on the west side to work out my line of attack. Eventually I made up my mind on the best approach and we commenced a long run-up on the ship's starboard bow. She was not fully in the moonpath but clearly visible. I could see no white wake astern of her, but the track in the sea along which she travelled could be seen. I dropped my first torpedo at a range of 700 yards, and the second at 400 yards. We flew ahead of one destroyer but were not fired upon until after our torpedoes had been released. As soon as the second torpedo was gone I pulled the aircraft up and we passed over between the centre and the stern of the ship.

The torpedoes were on their way but had not yet reached her. The destroyer close in and the ship herself both opened fire, the latter at point-blank range. My rear gunner could not fire at the ship because he could not depress his guns sufficiently. I took violent evasive action and we escaped damage. The navigator, in the astro-dome, reported two bright orange flashes on the vessel, astern and amidships. I swung the aircraft round and we could see two great columns of water going up above her masts – it was clear that both torpedoes had hit. We ran up and down on the west side watching developments. Very quickly thick grey smoke began to come out of the ship. The destroyers closed in on her and within five minutes a heavy smoke pall lay over all the ships. We could plainly smell this smoke in the aircraft – it smelt oily and acrid. We sent our first target report: 'Two hits on tanker, stationary, smoking'. After about 10 minutes the smoke cleared and a large oil patch was all that remained of the merchant ship. The destroyers were there but nothing else. We sent another signal: 'Tanker believed sunk, Large oil patch seen'.*

There was to be a tragic footnote. On 18 April 1943, Acting Squadron Leader M. Foulis, DFC, failed to return from a torpedo sortie, flying Wellington HX487,'Y'.

*RAF Middle East; HMSO, 1945.

221 Squadron 'Fishington' making a 'runner' drop practice attack on a British destroyer off Malta, December 1943.

221 Squadron at Grottaglie, late 1944.

Further reinforcements for the Middle East maritime Wimpys began to trickle through in early 1942, when the first detachments of No 458 Squadron RAAF arrived in the theatre. Based as a bomber unit at Holme-on-Spalding, the Australian squadron had commenced life in the UK on 25 August 1941, and begun bombing operations from 20/21 October. In January 1942, however, the unit was warned to prepare for overseas service, and on 22 February 1942 the unit CO, Wing Commander Norman Mulholland, DFC, led two other crews from England en route to Malta via Le Havre and Galita – a trip of some 1,460 statute miles – and though the other pair arrived intact, Mulholland's Wellington was shot into the sea by Ju88s, with only one survivor, Flying Officer Willis-Richards, the rear gunner, who was retrieved by an Italian destroyer and became a prisoner of war. Other 458 Squadron Wellington crews followed in batches later, followed by the ground crews, and eventually ferried a total of 36 aircraft safely. Unfortunately for the eager Aussies their aircraft on arrival were promptly 'borrowed' for other units, as indeed were many of the unit air and ground crews, and it was not until 1 September 1942 that the title 458 Squadron RAAF re-appeared justifiably when it was 'reconstituted' at Shallufa under the command of Wing Commander L.L. Johnston.

Here it was equipped with Wellington Ics and VIIIs for general maritime roles, and commenced such operations on 1 November 1942; a seven-hour strike against enemy shipping north-west of Tobruk. Though based at Shallufa, the squadron operated from forward airstrips at Gambut, Berka, and Malta during the winter of 1942-43; flying mining, torpedo, and general anti-shipping roles intermingled. Then on 17 January 1943 Wing Commander Johnston led a detachment of 12 of the squadron's aircraft from Gambut to Malta where they became based on Luqa as an addition to the island's offensive torpedo-strike forces savaging Rommel's sea supply convoys.

The closing months of 1942 brought sweeping changes in the tides of the war in North Africa. In the east the battle of Alamein initiated the Allied armies' eventual westward advance, while in the western territories of North Africa an Anglo-American invasion of Vichy-French occupied Casablanca, Oran, and Algiers – *Operation Torch* – aimed at providing a vast pincer movement to ultimately join hands with the advancing Eighth Army and crush Rommel's Afrika Korps between the two. *Operation Torch* commenced at 0100 hrs on 8 November 1942, as the initial troop landings went ashore at each of

HM King George VI shaking hands with Lt-Col B. McKenzie, DSO,DFC, third commander of 458 Squadron RAAF (though he was SAAF), when McKenzie boldly obtained royal permission to retain his unmilitary 'side-burn' whiskers . . . .

Fiume comes under attack by 104 Squadron on 15 Feb 1945 – view from 15,000 ft.

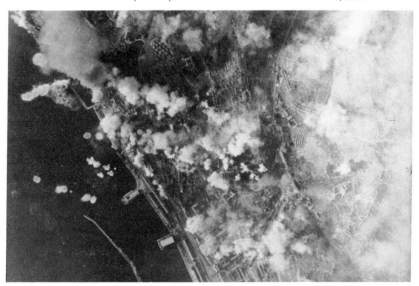

the three projected invasion areas. Within days several former French airfields were in Allied hands as operational bases, including Blida, 35 miles south-west of Algiers, and it was to this airfield that two more Wellington units were flown from England in December 1942. The two units involved were Nos 142 and 150 Squadrons based at Waltham and Kirmington respectively as part of No 1 Group, Bomber Command. The move started on 26 November when 12 crews and a ground crew echelon of about 100 men from each squadron were warned of an imminent posting abroad, followed by the arrival of brand-new Mk III Wellingtons bedecked in 'tropical markings' (*sic*).

Preparations were completed quickly and on 9 December the aircraft, each carrying a fitter and a rigger as passengers, flew to the intended 'jumping-off' airfield at Portreath. Here bad weather promptly delayed any attempts to leave for the next ten days, but on 9 December the first Wellingtons began landing on Blida, via Gibraltar with the remainder following suit within the next few days. Two Wellingtons crashed landing at Blida, leaving 22 aircraft immediately available for operations, and each squadron had brought a total of 24 'Erks' with them; the remaining ground crews arriving on Christmas Day. Sharing the muddy airfield with 142 and 150 Squadrons initially were three Coastal Command squadrons, two French units, and a flock of Douglas DC transport aircraft; the whole station being under the command of Group Captain W.V. Strugnell, MC.

Incessant rain precluded any operations until the night of 28/29 December 1942, when eight Wellingtons set out to bomb Bizerta docks, during which raid Flight Lieutenant Ronnie Brooks, DFC, dropped the first 4000lb 'Cookie' bomb on a Tunisian target – despite having his aircraft electric wiring freeze up so that his wireless operator had to be held upside down by his heels, hanging head-down into the bomb bay, to release the bomb manually!

At Blida the two squadrons formed No 330 Wing, and were nicknamed 'Cutie' and 'Janie' – a play on the official code letters used in the UK of QT (142 Squadron) and JN (150 Squadron), and both units soon made their presence felt. In January 1943, throughout that month a total of 231 sorties were flown (896,200lb of bombs dropped) on 22 nights attacking Bizerta, plus two other targets at Elmas and Medenine airfields. On 14 January, for example, 12 Wellingtons set out for Bizerta, duly bombed it, then ran into atrocious weather on the return leg. Flight Lieutenant Vincent, DFC, was forced to beach his Wimpy near Djidelli, without crew injuries, but Wing

Commander J.D. Kirwan, DFC, commander of 150 Squadron, was forced to bale out his crew over the Atlas mountains. Though all survived, some received injuries.

Four nights later Squadron Leader J.F.H. Booth attacked Bizerta, but was then attacked by a Ju88C of II/NJG2 piloted by Unteroffizier Tolksdorf. The German's fire set the Wimpy's starboard engine alight initially, then created further damage, including setting an oxygen bottle afire which the acting flight engineer, LAC J. Skingsley, coolly picked up and threw overboard. Tolksdorf, quite reasonably, claimed the aircraft as destroyed, whereas in fact, despite one crew man baling out,* the crew finally extinguished all flames and Booth, of 142 Squadron, accomplished a safe belly landing back at Blida. Booth was awarded a DFC, while Skingsley received a rare DFM for calm courage.

Booth's clash with a German nightfighter was not an isolated occurrence at this period. On the night of 17/18 December 1942, No 104 Squadron had two casualties from the guns of a Ju88C of 5/NJG2, piloted by Oberleutnant Schulz during a raid on Tunis docks and La Goullette; one Wellington being shot down, while the second, damaged badly, managed to return to base. Then on the night of 6/7 January 1943, the same squadron lost Wellington Z8496 to a Ju 88C of II/NJG2 piloted by Feldwebel Werner Heyne during a raid on Tunis. However, it seems probable that Heyne was a victim of the Wellington's air gunners, because his Ju88 crashed near Tunis, killing its crew. On the last night of January 1943 the 330 Wing Wellingtons extended their field of activity by bombing Trapani, Sicily – their first sorties to Italy since arriving in the Middle East. February proved to be a slightly less active month, although a total of 119 sorties 'delivered' a gross weight of 467,600lb of bombs on enemy objectives.

The month brought some further casualties to both units. On 22 February, Sergeant A.M. Jensen, RAAF, of 142 Squadron failed to return from a sortie against Bizerta, a victim of a Ju88C of II/NJG2 piloted by Hauptmann Dr Patuschka. Three nights later Pilot Officer J.G. Swain, DFC, of 150 Squadron, returning from a raid on Bizerta, flew into a mountainside some ten miles east of Blida, killing all aboard. A third, less tragic casualty was Wing Commander Kirwan, OC 150 Squadron, who injured himself baling out and had to be repatriated to the UK, his command passing to Wing Commander A.A. Malan.

*Having misheard Booth's order to *prepare* to bale out.

Continuing filthy weather conditions further depleted operations during March, with the two squadrons only able to operate on eight nights: a total of 155 sorties and 408,550lb of bombs dropped. During their first three months of operations, January-March 1943, no Wellington spares were received by the two units at Blida, and it speaks volumes for the labours and ingenuity of some 200 ground crew Erks that they still managed to produce an 85 per cent 'serviceable' state, averaging 20-25 Wellingtons fully operational, despite the extensive vagaries of tropical rains, winds, dust-storms etc.

April 1943 brought an escalating pace in sorties – totals of 247 sorties, dropping 935,230lb of bombs – but, perhaps inevitably, incurring more casualties. On 11 April, for instance, Sergeant J.C. Leckie, DFM, was in the process of bombing an enemy landing ground at St Marie du Zit when his Wellington was hit badly by flak. He ordered his crew to bale out, then successfuly crashlanded between the fighting 'lines' some six miles east of Medjez-el-Bab, without injuries to himself and three other crew members; these four being retrieved by a Guards' patrol that same morning. Leckie's rear Gunner, Sergeant T. E. Hewitt, RAAF, however, had broken an ankle on baling out, landing about a mile away from the Wimpy. It took him three days to reach the Wellington, then a further three days alone before being found by a patrol of the Grenadier Guards.*

Leckie and his crew were fated to survive for only another two weeks, being killed on return from a sortie to Bizerta on 29 April when their Wellington ploughed into a mountainside near Blida. On 17 April a force of 20 of 'Blida's bombers' were detailed to bomb Tunis docks and rail yards. Sergeant Chandler's aircraft was hit in the fuel tanks by particularly fierce flak and he ditched the Wimpy rapidly in Algiers Bay. The whole crew got out safely, then drifted in their dinghy for 36 hours before being picked up by a Polish destroyer, *Blyskowila*, and taken to Gibraltar, from where they eventually rejoined their squadron.

On 19 April a 'new era' (*sic*) commenced for the 'Cutie' and 'Janie' squadrons with the arrival of Group Captain J. A. Powell, DSO,OBE – known to all as 'Speedy'† – whose energetic, driving personality created an even greater intensity in operations, and he also

---

*Hewitt was later awarded a Military Medal (MM) for his feat of survival.
†Powell, then a Wing Commander, featured in the wartime film *Target For Tonight*, which starred another pilot destined for fame, Group Captain P. C. Pickard, DSO,DFC of the 1944 Amiens Gaol Mosquito raid epic.

immediately arranged for both squadrons to be moved nearer the battle zones – a move of base to Fontaine Chaude, some 15 miles from the French colonial town of Batna, being accomplished by May. The first operations mounted from the new base came on 6 May when 13 Wellingtons took off to bomb Trapani but ran into electrical storms and 10/10ths cloud conditions, and therefore aborted the raid. Nevertheless during that month 330 Wing flew 362 sorties overall, dropping 1½-million tons of bombs; operating on 73 of the succeeding 80 nights against such targets as Palermo, Naples, Alghero, Cagliari, Marsala and Trapani. In mid-May No 142's CO since arrival, Wing Commander T. W. 'Bas' Bamford, handed over his command to Wing Commander A. R. Gibbes, CF,RAAF.

On 16 May 'Speedy' Powell personally led an attack on Rome – the 'Eternal City' – to ensure that no bombs actually fell on the city but were dropped accurately on the briefed target, the Lido di Roma seaplane base at the mouth of the Tiber, 18 miles away. As the allied armies moved further eastwards, the Wimpy units were on the move again and moved base from Fontaine Chaude to Kairouan on 25-26 May.

With a further total of 373 sorties (1½-million lb of bombs) flown in June 1943, the two Wimpy squadrons brought their totals for the first six months of 1943 to totals of 1,447 sorties (7,005 flying hours) and over 5½-million pounds of bombs dropped. These included their part in the battering of Pantellaria in which, from 29 May until 11 June when its forces surrendered the island, they flew every night (225 sorties). As an indication of the personnel needed to sustain such operations, the two units in June 1943 could count totals of 297 air crew members supported indefatigably by 672 ground crew men. The combination of *Operation Torch* and Rommel's Afrika Korps' retreat back into Tunisia by early 1943 effectively set the seal on the Allies' triumph in North Africa, culminating in the surrender of all remaining Axis forces in Tunisia by General Messe on 13 May 1943.

That combination also brought a virtual cessation of Malta's prolonged agony as an unceasing target for Axis aerial assaults, leaving the RAF stationed on the island almost a free hand to complete destruction of Rommel's supply routes to Africa, and then become a foundation for the pre-planned invasion of Sicily and, eventually, Italy. The invasion of Sicily – *Operation Husky* – began on 10 July 1943, and by 14 August the island was to all intents and purposes in Allied hands; then on 3 September the Eighth Army gained its first toe-hold on the Italian mainland across the beaches at Salerno.

Further support for the Middle East RAF's bomber forces came in May 1943 in the shape of four more Wellington squadrons, three from the UK and a fourth from India. The three UK-based units were all Royal Canadian Air Force (RCAF), well-blooded in bomber operations over France and Germany, and were to form No 331 (RCAF) Wing in Tunisia as extra muscle for the Allied invasions of Sicily and Italy. Of these, No 420 ('Snowy Owl') Squadron was based at Middleton St George, commanded by Wing Commander D. McIntosh, DFC; No 424 ('Tiger') Squadron was based at Dalton (OC, Wing Commander G.S. Roy, DFC); while No 425 ('Alouette') Squadron was stationed at Dishforth (OC, Wing Commander J.M.W. St Pierre). As 331 Wing, the trio came under the overall command of Group Captain C.R. Dunlap.

All three units commenced their moves by despatching ground crews by sea on 16 May, and the air crews flew their Wimpys out to Tunisia starting on 5 June; both 'parties' had minor encounters with the Luftwaffe en route though without casualties. By 23 June all three squadrons, complete with ground crews, became based at Kairouan, and actual operations commenced on 26 June when both 420 and 425 Squadrons, led by their respective COs, attacked a landing ground at Sciacca, Sicily. One Wellington failed to return, but one rear gunner, Flight Sergeant J.P. Goyette, shot down a Ju88 which attempted to intercept.

Next night the target was San Giovanni on the Italian mainland, and again one Wimpy failed to return. Another Wellington, on take-off, unknowingly released its 4,000lb 'Cookie' bomb just as it became airborne! The 'Cookie' failed to explode and this crew flew on, unaware of their loss! The pace of operations for the three RCAF squadrons might be exemplified by the fact that from 26 June to 31 July they operated on every night except six, their main objectives during those weeks being enemy airfields and supply depots.

The Canadian squadrons were to remain based in Tunisia while carrying out their operations against Sicily and Italy, only moving base on 30 September to Hani East LG, but were all repatriated to the UK in October 1943. However, the fourth Wellington unit to reinforce the Middle East in May 1943 had been No 36 Squadron, which had been operating its Mk VIIIs on maritime duties from bases in India. On arrival in the Mediterranean zone of operations, No 36 Squadron was initially based on Blida, tasked primarily for anti-submarine patrols. The unit was to remain in support of the

(*right*) Wing Commander Dan
cIntosh, DFC, OC 420
quadron RCAF.

(*elow*) GRXIV of 36 Squadron
Reggizia, Italy on 2 August
44.

Sand-happy. 40 Squadron Wimpy HE108, 'L' and its crew at LG 104, Daba, Nov 1942. L–R: Sgts Cliff Mortimer (Capt); Reg Thackeray; Rowley Beatson (NZ); Wally Hammond; Bert Horton (NZ); F/Sgt Jeff Reddell (NZ).

HX392, 'K' of 40 Squadron with 'Saint' insigne and motto 'What the Hell' (pilot, Sqn Ldr J.E.S. Morton), ca, Oct 1942. Later served with 38 Squadron.

Allied advance up through Italy for a further year, still employed on maritime duties principally but mixing these on occasion with supply-dropping and other side-show sorties.

Yet another squadron in the Middle East to fly Wellingtons from 1943 was No 294, which formed at Berka on 24 September 1943, equipped partly with Wellington Ics and XIs and a number of Supermarine Walrus IIs for air-sea rescue duties. This unit was to continue operating its mixture of Wimpys and Walrus, later joined by Warwicks, with many detachments to such areas as Libya, Cyprus, Palestine, Greece, and Persia until its ultimate disbandment at Basra on 8 April 1946. Only one other unit was to be re-equipped with Wellingtons in the Middle East theatre*, this being No 244 Squadron; a veteran Middle East unit reformed at Shaibah on 1 November 1940 and eventually equipped with Blenheims from 1941 to early 1944, when in February it began receiving Wellington XIIIs for maritime roles, based at Masira, where it was eventually disbanded on 1 May 1945.

Once the Allies had invested Sicily and begun the invasion of Italy itself, the bombers intensified their pounding of vital and/or strategic targets in the Allied armies' paths as these slowly pressed northwards into the heart of Italy. The prime long-range bomber remained the doughty Wellington, although four-engined RAF bombers had been operating in the Middle East since July 1942 when detachments of No 10 and 76 Squadrons RAF, UK-based, began arriving in the Middle East theatre for operations†; while a handful of American Liberators had been flown by 108 Squadron from early 1942, and were later to equip No 159 Squadron fully. Other four-engined bombers to have flown a few sorties under the aegis of RAF Middle East were a few Boeing B-17 Fortresses in late 1941-early 1942, though these had by no means been an unqualified success. Thus the Wellington remained the RAF's chief strategic bomber in the Italian campaigns virtually until the close of the war.

Of the veteran Wellington pure bomber units, Nos 142 and 150 Squadrons were both disbanded at Regina on 5 October 1944, then reformed in the UK; No 37 Squadron replaced their Wimpys with Liberators from that same month as did 70 Squadron in January 1945; No 104 Squadron in February 1945; and 40 Squadron in the

---

*Two other Wimpy-equipped units, Nos 8 and 621 Squadrons, are dealt with in chapter *Above the Jungle*.
†These Halifax detachments were merged in September 1942 to form No 462 Squadron RAAF, based at Fayid, Egypt.

following month. In the cases of the maritime Wellington units, No 162 Squadron was disbanded on 25 September 1944; and No 36 Squadron was sent back to England, arriving at Chivenor on 26 September 1944 to join Coastal Command's unceasing offensive against enemy shipping and U-boats.

The extended battle for Italy proved bloody and glue-footed throughout 1943-45, particularly during the winter seasons, for the Anglo-American land forces; and no less intensive for the RAF, USAAF, and their allied air services. Luftwaffe opposition by early 1944 was outnumbered and outclassed, unable even to successfully defend its own airfields, and suffered lack of adequate reinforcement because of the German High Command's justifiable fears of an Allied invasion of southern France from the Mediterranean, coupled with the equal apprehension of an even greater invasion of northern France from England; apart from the ever-hovering threat of Russian advances on Germany's eastern fronts.

From March 1944 the Luftwaffe had no Fliegerkorps organisation remaining in the whole Mediterranean, and after the fall of Rome to the Allies on 4 June 1944 all single-engined German fighters were removed from the central Italian battle zones back to northern Italy for pure air defence duties – in effect, the Luftwaffe thereafter ceased to play any significant role in the Italian campaign. Nevertheless, German forces on the ground maintained a stubborn, occasionally near-frantic opposition, disputing the Anglo-American armies' advance, which meant no relaxation in the pace of air operations; particularly for the bombers which continue pounding away at enemy troop concentrations, communications, ports, harbours, and other vital targets. Among those bomber crews were the Wellington men.

Throughout the Wellington saga in the Middle East theatre of operations, 1940-45, the prime emphasis was patently upon the Wimpys' swathe of destruction among enemy objectives. Yet among the myriad tales that could readily be retold of bombing operations, death, dicey sorties, even near-miraculous escapes from the Grim Reaper, are a number of unpublicised mercy missions carried out by Wellington crews. If only to part-balance the record of Wellington achievements, one example of an operation designed solely to save, not destroy lives, may fittingly close this chapter on Middle East operational activities.

The area concerned was the southern Arabian district titled the Hadhramaut, a barren, sun-blistered desert region mainly occupied

NB895, 'G', and companion Wimpys of 38 Squadron.

by nomadic Bedouin. From 1941-44 this region had no rainfall which act of nature, combined with certain economic disasters, produced by 1944 famine conditions for the inhabitants which swiftly caused escalating deaths among the Bedouin. In early 1944 the British government responded by voting £300,000 for relief measures, and in April 1944 the Governor of Aden flew up to the Hadhramaut to gain on-the-spot understanding of the immediate needs. By then hundreds of sacks of millet and maize were reaching the port of Mukalla from Aden, and it only remained to set up some form of transportation quickly to get such supplies inland to the estimated 15,000 people on the verge of starvation and death. Accordingly, the RAF ME HQ formed a Famine Relief Flight on 22 April 1944, and three days later personnel of this Flight went to Aden, from where they were transported to Riyan airstrip on 27 April – the nearest landing ground to Mukalla.

Meanwhile six Wellington Xs, fresh from the UK, were rapidly modified at No 168 Maintenance Unit (MU) and flown to Riyan as soon as they were ready individually; the last Wimpy arriving on 7 May. At Riyan the Flight, commanded by a Flight Lieutenant, comprised both RAF and Army personnel; the latter mainly RASC men and parachute instructors from Ramat David, Palestine who had been trained in supply-dropping operations already.

In readiness for the air-relief operation a landing strip was prepared at Qatn in the Hadhramaut and on 28 April a successful test flight was made to this improvised 'landing ground'. Time being of the essence, the very next day three Wellingtons, each making two trips, delivered 216 sacks of grain. each sack weighing 168lb, and a Wimpy's normal load being 36 such sacks. These relief flights continued without pause until 18 May, after which date only one sortie per day was deemed necessary to Qatn, and the Wellingtons then proceeded to lift supplies to drop on other famine areas at Tarim, Ghuraf, Einat, and Seiyun; these last four venues receiving a total of 1936 sacks of life-saving grain, Overall, the relief flights were to continue until the last day of June 1944. Such flights usually commenced at 0430 hrs and the last aircraft landed at 1730 hrs each day, a punishing routine for both men and aircraft in the unrelenting, blistering heat.

By the end of May the Flight had flown 165 sorties, delivering totals of 5,505 sacks of grain and eight and a quarter tons of milk to the people of the Hadhramaut, but in June the strain on the aircraft began to tell. On 7 June one Wimpy force-landed at Qatn with a burnt-out cylinder and remained there unserviceable; on the 17th another Wellington's starboard engine failed in flight and it crashed at Riyan, a write-off; while a week later a third aircraft, on an evening sortie, crashed landing at Riyan thereby putting the sole 'runway' out of action for four days.

Other Wellingtons by then were displaying obvious signs of imminent problems – usually excessive oil pressures brought on by the fact that each aircraft was doing a heavily-laden climb to 6,000 feet, three times a day, in hazardous weather conditions. Thus, on 30 June orders came from Aden for the Flight to withdraw. The Political Officer in charge of the Famine Relief Commission had assured the men of the Relief Flight that due to their untiring efforts the people in the Hadhramaut now had sufficient grain to last for at least four months, apart from medical supplies, milk, etc. – the Flight had literally broken the back of the famine and saved untold hundreds, possibly even thousands of lives by their labours and skills. As ever, the Wellington had proved to be a great lady.

CHAPTER TEN

Webfoot Warriors

Although remembered primarily as a pure bomber or, perhaps, as a sturdy operational conversion trainer, the Wellington also earned proud battle honours in other equally important roles. Of these, probably the most surprising – in the context of the design's original conception – and certainly one of its least publicised operational roles was as an anti-submarine and/or anti-shipping hunter-killer; demonstrating yet again the Wellington's versatility in differing guises. The basic design's adaptability – and sheer rugged strength – was first manifested in a maritime-air configuration quite early in its wartime career. Within weeks of the start of hostilities between Germany and Britain, German U-boats and aircraft began sowing the south-eastern coastal approach waters to major ports and harbours of England with magnetic sea-mines; deadly effective weapons which could remain on the beds of shallow waters and lie in wait for Allied ships passing above them and then be detonated by the ships' magnetic fields.

The initial success of this type of offensive – by the end of November 1939 a total of 46 Allied ships (179,985 tons) had been sunk by this method – encouraged the German navy to extend these mining activities by sending out fast destroyers by night to concentrate in particular on mining the most vital sea areas, such as the Thames Estuary; this latter objective threatening to bring to a complete halt the use of London as the United Kingdom's premier reception centre for Allied merchant shipping. The potential scale of this form of blockade may be judged by the fact that by November 1939 German naval stores already held a stock of some 20,000 magnetic mines immediately available for 'distribution'.

On 23 November, however, the Allied authorities had a stroke of good fortune, when a German Kriegsmarine aircraft deposited two magnetic mines in very shallow water off Shoeburyness, with the result that once the tide had receded these mines were left high and dry on the mudflat. A Royal Navy mine disposal team from HMS Vernon courageously defused the mines – the first intact examples to come into their hands – and the mine's secrets were immediately passed to the Admiralty Research Department for examination and research into concocting an 'antidote' to this menace to shipping.

In close liaison with the Royal Aircraft Establishment (RAE), Farnborough, the Admiralty experts mooted several practical possibilities, including an idea for having an aircraft fitted with its own electro-magnetic field device which might detect suspected mined areas, then explode any mines *in situ* by flying over them at a calculated safe height.

This possible solution was given top priority by the Admiralty, under pressure from the (then) First Lord of the Admiralty, Winston Churchill, and the Vickers works at Weybridge was immediately instructed to prepare a Wellington ·to carry a huge electro-magnetic ring, measuring (initially) 51 ft in diameter,* affixed to the aircraft by attachments under each wing, nose, and rear fuselage. This 'ring' – dubbed 'Halo' or 'Electric doughnut' by anonymous wags – contained a paper-insulated aluminium strip coil, which was intended to be energised from an electric current produced by a 35kw Maudesley generator driven by a Ford V8 engine mounted inside the Wellington's rear fuselage.

Permission for Vickers to divert just one Wellington from their production line was given by the Air Member for Development and Production, Air Marshal Sir Wilfrid Freeman, KCB, DSO, MC originally because he did not want the flow of Wellingtons to Bomber Command to be interrupted. Indeed, Freeman would have preferred that either Handley Page Harrows, plentiful at that period, or the RAF's conscripted Armstrong Whitworth Ensign airliners be used rather than Wellingtons, but he was over-ruled. At Weybridge a team under the aegis of George Edwards took Wellington IA,P2516 off their production line and began modifying it to receive the new equipment, stripping out all armament, radio, and other surplus components in order to save weight and space for the bulky V8 engine and generator *et al* due to be installed, while Barnes Wallis tackled the various problems involved in the carriage of such a large electrical and magnetic device with its inevitable disorienting effect on the aircraft's compass etc.

As work proceeded at an intense pace at Weybridge, permission was given in mid-December for three more Wellingtons to be diverted and modified – these being P2518, P2521, & P9223 – with a provision

*Later modified to a 48ft diameter.

that any further requirements would be transferred to an outside firm, Rollasons of Croydon. At that same time, with effect from 15 December 1939, No 1 General Reconnaissance Unit (GRU) was formed at Manston, commanded by Squadron Leader John H. Chaplin*, as the first unit intended to be equipped with the modified Wellingtons.

The first four Wellingtons were allotted the Vickers Type 418 designation and code-named Directional Wireless Installation (DWI), Mk Is, and P2516 with its empty ring casing attached was first test-flown by Mutt Summers on 21 December 1939 at Boscombe Down. Actual testing of the complete installation, i.e. sweeps over minefields began in January 1940, with Squadron Leader H.A. – 'Bruin' – Purvis† as first pilot during the initial sorties. Experience gained during these first sorties led to replacement of the Maudesley generator by an English Electric type driven by a De Havilland Gipsy Six aero-engine in place of the V8 car motor; thereby increasing power output to 90kw and a 50 per cent increase in magnetic force – and, incidentally, offering a saving of roughly 1,000lb in overall installation weight. When fitted with these later components the modified Wellingtons became designated Type 419, DWI Mk IIs.

By mid-February 1940 No. 1 GRU had three DWI Wellingtons on strength and these were used singly or in toto to develop tactics for mine-sweeping thereafter. Throughout March and April 1940 the DWI Wellingtons carried out a number of successful sweeps around the south-east coast, though it should be noted that these were in the main unescorted by fighters, thus leaving the unarmed Wellingtons easy meat for any marauding German aircraft. Fortunately the Luftwaffe was not encountered, but on 10 May, when German forces invaded Holland, Squadron Leader Chaplin was detailed to lead three DWIs to Ijmuiden to sweep the approaches there prior to an RN evacuation of the Dutch royal family and a quantity of bullion. Despite being fired on initially by the Dutch harbour defences, all three Wellingtons completed their task and returned to base safely. Six days later No 1 GRU received orders to prepare for a move to Egypt, and on 20 May five DWI Wellingtons, led by John Chaplin, left Manston, eventually arriving at Ismailia alongside the Suez Canal on 23 May, minus one Wellington which had crashed on take-off from a staging stop-over at Bizerta, due to an engine failure.

*Later, Air Commodore DSO, DFC.
†Later, Group Captain, DFC, AFC.

Apart from the first four DWI Wellingtons produced by the Weybridge works, at least eleven more Wellingtons are known to have been converted to DWI Mk II standards in England, these being L4212, L4221, L4227, L4235, L4356, L4358, L4374, L7771, P2522, R2701, and later Z8772. Further examples were converted locally in Egypt from components sent from the UK, including HX682. The need for DWI aircraft around British coastal waters was relatively short-lived, due to the Admiralty Research Department's introduction of a de-gaussing system for ships which obviated the necessity of aircraft patrols. Nevertheless, the DWI crews had filled an important gap in UK defences during the winter of 1939-45, and for their parts in that pioneering venture John Chaplin and 'Bruin' Purvis were each awarded a DFC. Credit also went to the Vickers team at Weybridge who had worked unceasingly in November-December 1939 to produce the first DWI Wellington in complete form – virtually finishing the task in little more than a month from scratch.

In Egypt No 1 GRU*, based at Ismailia and Amriya, inaugurated airborne minesweeping on 11 June 1940, following Italy's declaration of war the previous day, by having a trio of DWIs search the approaches to Alexandria, followed in the next few days with thorough sweeps along the Suez Canal and its entrance and exit ports. It was a task that 1 GRU's handful of DWI Wellingtons were to continue into 1941 and 1942 until the final Allied victory in North Africa, 'cleaning' the harbour waters of each major port along the North African coastline as these came into Allied occupation. The last-known DWI Wellingtons in use in the Middle East theatre are thought to be single examples flown under the aegis of No 162 Squadron, a Wellington radio-countermeasures unit originally formed in Egypt in January 1942, which had at least one DWI Wimpy on strength in early 1944, still based in North Africa.

Actual handling of a DWI-festooned Wellington proved no great problem to pilots. John Chaplin, commander of the first DWI unit and later to command 38 (Wellington) Squadron in the desert campaign, had no previous experience of Wellingtons prior to joining No 1 GRU, but after a brief conversion course, quickly adapted to the 'Halo' DWI:

> Because of the angle of attack of the ring, take-off was an improvement on the bomber Wellington in spite of the weight

*When 1 GRU's five DWIs left for Egypt, all remaining DWIs in the UK went to equip newly-formed Nos 2 and 3 GRUs.

DWI Wellington, L4356 of No.1 GRU in Egypt.

DWI Wimpy with its 'Halo'.

which we never got rid of, as the bomber did of its bomb load. I understood that the ring plus the equipment inside the fuselage weighed just over two tons, which was quite an achievement for the early version of the 'Wimpy' with the early mark of Pegasus engine. In the air the aircraft was steadier. It was heavier on the turns, of course. I remember some of the pilots of the unit complaining about this, but personally, as I was a flying boat pilot accustomed to Sunderlands with overload tanks, this never worried me. Coming in to land was a different story. Now, the downward angle of the ring on the glide approach was pure drag. We had to be careful and watch our speed of approach. I remember being briefed by Coastal Command that we must not attempt to go round again. Once we had settled down to our approach speed and were less than 400-500 ft altitude, we were committed to making the best kind of landing we could in the circumstances, whatever might be the obstructions.

Presumably at that height, when there was little chance of increasing speed by diving, our engines were not powerful enough to overcome the very considerable drag which would have ensued from the abrupt change of angle from a fairly steep approach angle to the elevation necessary to level out and climb away. We would have lost speed and stalled. The actual touchdown was fairly normal, provided that one had sufficient speed in hand to overcome the drag caused by levelling out. The steadiness of the aircraft was a distinct advantage when it came to the actual minesweeping operations close to the water. There was little difficulty in maintaining a constant height of 30-40 ft above the sea. There was very little aerodynamic effect on the handling of the aircraft when we exploded a mine – except, of course, on the famous occasion* when 'Bruin' Purvis flew rather low near a wreck off the North Goodwins and we detonated a mine – which recorded over 10g on the accelerometer in the tail of the aircraft!†

By the autumn of 1940 RAF Coastal Command, in close liaison with the Admiralty, was urgently pre-occupied with the nullification of the greatest threat to Britain's vital merchant shipping supply life-lines – the U-boat. In August 1940 the Command had slightly improved its anti-submarine 'armoury' by stocking some 700 modified standard Mk VII naval depth charges to replace the virtually useless standard

*On 13 January 1940
†*Air Pictorial*, May 1979

RAF 500lb anti-submarine high explosive bombs used hitherto; but a satisfactory means of actually *locating* U-boats, particularly at night, was yet to be made available for Coastal Command aircraft. Developments in radar research had by then already produced working 'black boxes' of ASV (Air-to-Surface Vessel) and airborne AI (Airborne Interception), but the latter was firmly and wholly earmarked for equipping the RAF's somewhat makeshift nightfighter force then engaged in attempting to combat the Luftwaffe's night aerial *blitz* on Britain during the winter 1940-41.

Thus, while impatiently awaiting its turn to receive some form of maritime-air radar, Coastal Command's AOC-in-C, Air Chief Marshal Sir Frederick Bowhill, cast around his Command for any bright ideas for tackling U-boats, especially by night. Ironically, within his own headquarters staff was an administrative officer, Squadron Leader Humphrey de Vere Leigh who on first learning about the highly secret ASV research promptly, and purely privately initially, applied his fertile mind to the problem of anti-submarine warfare; in particular how to adapt ASV or some-such radar installation to actual location of a U-boat.

On 23 October 1940, Leigh wrote a paper outlining his suggestion for fitting a 90cm searchlight 'either in the nose or the underside of a Wellington bomber'; having in mind the now-unused DWI Mk I and Mk II Wellingtons readily available with their installed generators and motors. Leigh also specified:

The searchlight would not be fixed but would be mounted in a swivel ring to allow at least 20-degrees downwards or sideways movement. The 15 cwt, 90cm Army type searchlight as at present used for ground defence gives an effective beam of about 5000 yards with a two-degrees dispersion. It is suggested that a searchlight of not less than this power . . . would be most suitable for this purpose.*

In essence, Leigh's intention was to close the gap between an ASV set's ability to pinpoint a U-boat at night only to within one mile range of its location – at which point the U-boat just 'disappeared' off the radar screen – and the U-boat itself, by lighting up that one-mile stage of projected attack.

With Bowhill's firm support – and despite distinct reservations by

*Quoted in *Instruments of Darkness* by A.W. Price; Wm Kimber, 1973

certain scientific staff at the RAE, Farnborough – Leigh was detailed to work full-time on his project. Modifying his original proposal, Leigh now suggested the use of a smaller, 61 cm (24 inches) naval searchlight as fitted on RN destroyers, which would be fitted into an adapted Frazer Nash FN25A gun turret for lowering through the under-belly fuselage hole which had been designed for the Mk I Wellington's initial dustbin gun turret. On 22 November 1940 Leigh visited the Vickers works for a conference to iron out modification details, including an ingenious system of ducting air to the under-turret to ventilate heat fumes from the light when in operation.

Early in 1941 a Wellington, P9223, was set aside for installation of both the Leigh light and ASV search radar, and was initially code-titled as DWI Mk III to camouflage its true purpose. Operational trials soon proved that Leigh's idea was workable, but in June 1941, when ACM Bowhill was succeeded in his post as AOC-in-C, Coastal Command by ACM Sir Philip Joubert, Leigh was somewhat shocked to be ordered to return to duty in his former job as Assistant Personnel Officer! Joubert fresh from the Air Ministry had recently been involved with a similar proposal for an airborne searchlight put forward by a Wing Commander (later, Group Captain) W. Helmore, although in Helmore's idea the light was to be fixed in the nose of a nightfighter Douglas Havoc – being code-named Turbinlite – and had a far wider beam of greater illumination. It was to be a further two months before trials of the Turbinlite idea made Joubert realise his error in thinking Helmore's project could be more effective than Leigh's for Coastal Command's requirements, and in mid-August 1941 Leigh was permitted to resume work on his suggestions.

In the following months Leigh modified and refined his installation, in particular dispensing with the bulky motor/generator power source and substituting a battery of seven standard RAF 12-volt accumulators, charged from a small aircraft engine-driven generator – this new installation weighing only some 600lb. Once all these improvements were ready for production, the Wellington Mk IC conversion having the Leigh Light and search radar installations became titled Wellington Mk VIII; early versions of which could be readily identified by their 'stickleback' array of antennae along the fuselage top associated with their ASV Mk II radar sets.

To introduce the Leigh Light Wellington to firstline Coastal Command operations, No 1417 Flight was formed at Chivenor on 18 March 1942, but this embryo unit was quickly expanded to full squadron status and on 4 April 1942 the unit became retitled as

No 172 Squadron, commanded by Wing Commander J.B. Russell (later, Air Vice-Marshal AVM, CBE, DSO). The squadron mounted its first Leigh Light Wellington operation on the night of 2/3 June 1942 – and made an immediate claim. Squadron Leader Jeff Greswell* took off in Wellington ES986, 'F', as one of four aircraft despatched to recce near the Spanish coast, and at shortly before 0230 hrs detected an Italian submarine, the *Luigi Torelli*, commanded by Lt-Commander Augusto Migliorini, which was surprised on the surface by Greswell's Leigh Light as Greswell's wireless operator sent off a coded signal back to Chivenor – '472' – meaning 'Sighted sub. Am attacking'. The Wellington duly depth-charged and strafed the submarine, then left it to attack a second U-boat nearby. Although badly damaged, and forced to seek a nearby port for repairs, the *Luigi Torelli* survived this 'maiden' Leigh Light Wimpy attack and continued a chequered career until 1946.†

In the following four weeks two U-boats were actually discovered and attacked without visible results, but on 5 July the squadron claimed its first confirmed 'kill' when Pilot Officer W. Howell, an American serving in the RAF, flying Wellington 'H', trapped *U-502* (Kapitänleutnant Rosentiel) on the surface as it sped eastwards after a sortie in Caribbean waters. Howell's depth charges were dropped in a perfect straddle and *U-502* was sunk with all hands.

Only days later, on 12 July, Howell surprised *U-159* (Kapitänleutnant Witte) and depth-charged accurately in the face of defensive gunfire, fracturing the submarine's batteries and forcing it to crash-dive for safety. *U-159* finally made a safe harbour but was *hors de combat* for several months. In the same month Pilot Officer D.E. Dixon ran into fierce opposition from two Arado Ar 196 aircraft, having two of his crew members mortally wounded but seeing his gunners shoot one Arado down in flames.

Prior to those early successes the air crews of 172 Squadron had completed several months of intensive training for their future role, as one pilot, Warrant Officer Don Fraser, RCAF remembers:

The Helwick Light Vessel in the Bristol Channel served for practice detection at night. Practice bombing was done against a floating target off the steep cliffs of North Devon. The aircraft would approach from the land, dive towards the floating target to

*Later, Air Commodore CBE, DSO, DFC.
†For detailed account see *Wellington at War* by C. Bowyer; Ian Allan, 1982.

Wellington XII, MP512, which served as 'A', 172 Squadron, and with 432 Squadron RCAF. Note under-fuselage retracted Leigh Light.

Wellington XII, HF113, 'P' of 407 Squadron RCAF flying off the estuary of Taw/Torridge, west of its Chivenor base.

simulate an attack on a surfaced U-boat from 1000 ft altitude and one mile distance. This training was not without its casualties. One Wellington, with the squadron's gunnery and navigation officers, a Flight commander, and a full crew, homed in on a blip which they thought was the Helwick Light Vessel. Unfortunately, the blip was an American tanker steaming up the Bristol Channel. Its alert crew opened fire – the burning Wellington* fell into the sea with no survivors . . .

Training went on. Squadron Leader Leigh periodically showed up on the station to oversee developments. The three-tiered bomb bay held four Torpex-filled depth charges, the long case of batteries for the searchlight, and an overload fuel tank. The Wellington flew tail-down even with trim. Pilot Officer Blackmore, my skipper, and I worked on an obvious solution by moving the batteries into the nose of the machine. A wooden case for the batteries was built under the searchlight operator's seat in front of the pilot. The aeroplane now flew better. with an all-up weight of 33,000lb, the two 980hp Bristol Pegasus engines were severely tested. Even in Bomber Command the same aircraft had an all-up weight of only 29,500lb. The unfavourable power/weight ratio affected single-engine flying characteristics of the aircraft, but this was later rectified when 1425hp Hercules engines replaced the old Pegasus plants.

From 17 August a detachment from 172 Squadron was sent to Skitten, Caithness, some three miles north-west of Wick in Scotland, and on 1 September 1942 this detachment became the nucleus of the second Leigh Light Wellington unit, No 179 Squadron, commanded by Wing Commander A.N. Combe, AFC (later, Group Captain), and sharing the airfield with No 489 Squadron's torpedo-strike Hampdens of the Royal New Zealand Air Force. Little time was wasted in getting 179 Squadron onto a full operational basis. During a steady routine of extended patrols in October 1942, two attacks on U-boats were recorded; one of these by Flight Sergeant A.D. Martin piloting Wellington HX776, 'B', on 22 October when he sank *U-412*. Tragically, this same aircraft was fated to be shot down by a 'friendly' trawler's trigger-happy gunners off the Shetlands on 8 November, with all six crew members being lost with their aircraft. A week later 179 Squadron stood down temporarily from operations to prepare for

*Wellington HX482, on 19 August 1942.

a move of base to Gibraltar – a shift in scenery completed by the end of November.

In the meantime Flying Officer D.E. Dixon of 172 Squadron, in Wellington 'D', claimed a U-boat as 'damaged' on 10 November, his near-victim being later identified as *U-66*. By that date command of 172 Squadron had passed to Wing Commander J.B. Brolly, though this change in leadership did not affect the pace of squadron operations. By November 1942 the squadron was flying some 90 sorties per month, and its crews – possibly frustrated by the apparent 'lack' of U-boats to attack and therefore determined to 'hit something' (*sic*) – coolly used their depth charges to 'bomb' enemy surface vessels on occasion . . . !

Leigh Light Wellingtons were, patently, intended for night work in the Allied offensive against Germany's U-boat fleet, but further development of the Mk VIII Wimpy continued apace and produced a day strike variant, armed with two torpedoes in place of depth charges, and fitted with gun turrets in the nose and tail (FN7As each with a pair of Browning 0.303-inch), but still regarded as Mk VIII Wellingtons. Still striving for higher performance and load-carrying capacity, the Vickers design team next produced the Mk XI Wellington – a daylight torpedo-bomber which incorporated the basic strengthened fuselage of the Mk X bomber, and the more powerful Hercules VI or XVI engines of 1675 hp. The Mk XI was fitted with ASV Mk II or the improved Mk III centimetric radar, and it needed only (primarily) a change of power plants to Hercules XVIIs of 1735 hp to 'produce' the Wellington Mk XIII. Of the other two main Wellington variants employed by Coastal Command, the Mk XII was a Leigh Light-equipped Mk XI with a chin-mounted housing for its ASV Mk III radar; while the Mk XIV was in effect a Leigh Light-fitted night attack variant of the Mk XII day torpedo version. The combination of Leight Light, depth charges or torpedoes, and ASV search radar in any Coastal Command Wellington comprised, in essence, what in later years was to be dubbed a weapons system, i.e. both the means of locating a target *and* the means of destroying that target all in a single aircraft.

The use of Wellingtons by Coastal Command by no means commenced with the formation of the Leigh Light units. On 21 November 1940, No 221 Squadron was reformed at Bircham Newton under the command of Wing Commander T.R. Vickers (later, Group Captain, DSO), and received its first Wellingtons, N2910 and R2700 on 29 November, with a further eight aircraft being added to unit

Mk VIII 'Stickleback', W5674 which served with 221 Squadron and 7 OTU at various periods.

Mk XIII, MF639, NH–H of 415 Squadron RCAF at Bircham Newton, ca. May 1944.

strength by Christmas Day. These were Mk ICs, but in January 1941 the squadron began installing ASV in their aircraft – the first Wellington thus fitted being T2919 – and from 2 March the crews began operations, reconnoitring the length of the Dutch coast seeking out enemy shipping. Among the crews who made up the squadron's original complement were several men destined to gain high rank and honours later in the war, including a 'sprog' Pilot Officer, Anthony Spooner, later to finish his war as Squadron Leader, DSO, DFC.*

In the event 221 Squadron was destined to continue flying succeeding Marks of Wellington until its ultimate disbandment in North Africa on 25 August 1945; changing from its initial Mk ICs to Mk VIIs in March 1941 – these ASV-fitted aircraft being nicknamed 'Goofingtons' by the crews – then changing to Mk XI and XII in mid-1943 and slightly later Mk XIIIs; the torpedo-Wimpy being titled 'Fishingtons'. The squadron's operations from UK bases and Iceland ceased by the start of 1942 when 221 Squadron moved to the Middle East.

The crucial need for strengthening Coastal Command's UK-based frontline forces for the Battle of the Atlantic had become a priority by late 1941, resulting in several units being 'milked' from other Commands. Two such units were Nos 311 (Czech) and 304 (Polish) Squadrons, both Wellington units serving with Bomber Command at that period. No 311 Squadron was officially transferred to Coastal Command on 30 April 1942, on which date it became based at Aldergrove, near Belfast, from where it began operations in its new role on 22 May.

On 12 June, the squadron moved again, this time to Talbenny, Dyfed, from where on 27 July Squadron Leader J. Stransky piloting Wellington DV664, 'A', sighted and attacked *U-106*, but could only claim the submarine as 'damaged'. In the following month, however, came a confirmed 'kill' when on 10 August Flying Officer Nyvlt in HF922, 'H', sank *U-578*. By that month the squadron's Wellingtons had begun encountering stiff opposition not only from any U-boat attacked but also from roving packs of Luftwaffe aircraft, recording several clashes with small formations of Junkers Ju88s and Arado Ar 196s from French bases.

No 304 (Polish) Squadron was 'legally' transferred to Coastal Command with effect from 7 May 1942 and left its bomber base at

*See *In Full Flight*, by A. Spooner; Macdonalds, 1965

Lindholme on 13 May to fly to Tiree in the Inner Hebrides, from where it commenced operations on 18 May. Sharing the remote airfield at Tiree was No 224 Squadron (Lockheed Hudsons) and the two squadrons quickly formed a firm friendship and good-natured competitive rivalry. Tiree itself, an isolated, even desolate spot, offered little in the way of physical or 'spiritual' comforts for the squadrons' personnel – as one arrival quipped, pointing to a framed portrait of Queen Victoria in the Mess, 'The only woman on the island – and she's dead!' Indeed, the only locals were some obstreperous goats, under-sized cows, and thousands of squawking seagulls . . . Maritime operations came as a new way of life to 304's air crews – one crew on a training flight quite seriously reported a U-boat ahead and proceeded to carry out a full-scale attack – only to find they were attacking the rock peak of Rockall! On 31 May the squadron lost a Wellington at sea – due it was suspected to being shot up by 'friendly' ships – but Flight Lieutenant W. Waltera and his crew were soon retrieved thanks to an intense search set up by Hudsons and Wellingtons from their own airfield.

Two weeks later, on 13 June, the squadron left Tiree for rather more hospitable surroundings at Dale in South Wales, where it was henceforth to operate mainly over Biscay, under the control of No 19 Group, Coastal Command. The Poles arrived at Dale at a crucial stage of the Battle of the Atlantic – in the same month Dönitz's U-boats sank 144 ships in the Atlantic theatre, i.e. 700,235 tons – the greatest monthly figure attributed to U-boats in the war to date* – while U-boat losses had been few.

Luftwaffe opposition to Coastal Command's patrols, especially over Biscay Bay, steadily increased in the late summer and autumn of 1942, until reports of attacks by formations of four or more German fighters became almost a corollary to any sortie. No 304 Squadron's Diary records one particularly heavy encounter when Wellington 'E', skippered by Flying Officer S. Targowski, was engaged by six Ju88s. The navigator, Flight Lieutenant Minakowski made the following report:

As we approached position 'A' near Spanish waters on 16th September 1942 at 1612 hrs, six aircraft appeared; one starboard, three to port, and two far astern. The sky was cloudless and the

*Only in November 1942 was this figure bettered throughout the entire war, when U-boats sank 729,160 tons of Allied shipping.

'Stickleback' Wimpy with full ASV Mk II aerial display.

Wellington GRXIV with under-wing rocket projectile (RP) batteries.

'weather was very fine, with visibility between 25 and 30 miles from our altitude of 1500 feet. Flying Officer S. Targowski, our pilot, descended to 500 feet when the aircraft were sighted and, when we identified them as Ju88s, jettisoned our depth charges and went down to 50 feet. The enemy fighters closed in rapidly. Three of them attacked from port at 1615 hrs, one after another. Our pilot evaded them, keeping from 15 to 50 feet above the waves so as to rule out attacks from below. We often had the impression that our wings were skimming along the water. Whenever a Junkers attacked, Targowski turned the Wellington head-on to meet the enemy in order to present the smallest possible target and to decrease the duration of the attack.

The front gunner gave two short bursts at point-blank range and the rear gunner a long one during the first attack. Our wireless operator signalled to base about the attack and gave the dead reckoning of our position. He then manned the side machine guns. Five minutes later the front gunner hit the second attacker, who turned away steeply and fell into the sea. Two Junkers – those originally farthest away – now closed in from starboard, passed us and then attacked. They nearly succeeded. As one of the fighters attacked on the starboard beam and our Wellington turned head-on towards him, it was struck by cannon shells and a machine gun burst. One of the tanks was damaged and the cabin was filled with smoke from the explosions. All our machine guns were blazing away furiously. Another Hun was hit, and pieces fell off him as he turned for France with smoke streaming out of his starboard engine. Shortly after this a crash resounded in the Wellington and dense smoke filled the fuselage. There were no flames, however, and nobody was wounded. I ordered the co-pilot and the wireless operator to take the reserve ammunition to the front and rear gunners. Some clouds appeared on the horizon and we made for them.

Two fighters now attacked us time after time from astern. Our gunners greeted them with accurate fire at close range and both Junkers were hit. The enemy's attacks thereafter were half-hearted. The clouds were now much closer, about 1500 feet up, so Flying Officer Targowski made for them at full speed. He reached them safely and we broke away from the enemy. We fixed our position and informed base we would land at Portreath in Cornwall, owing to shortage of fuel. The petrol in the starboard tank had all leaked out and the auxiliary oil-tank delivery had been damaged. We landed at 1750 hrs after being airborne eight hours and 20 minutes. None of us was hurt but our Wellington had been hit as follows; Starboard propeller-boss, three hits; starboard engine nacelle, three hits; starboard engine collector, two hits; starboard wing and fuel tank holed by cannon fire (tank had a hole 6" x 6" and smaller ones), with fabric about three feet by six feet torn from the upper surface, with geodetic airframe damaged; fuselage, 18 hits; astro-dome, one hit.*

Just one month later, on 16 October 1942, came a tragic footnote to Targowski's superb skippering on that occasion. On that morning he had received a letter from his wife in Poland – his first news from her since he left his native country in 1939 – and thus set out on a sortie in high spirits. Some two hours later his squadron office received a signal announcing the award of a DFC to Targowski, and his fellow crews immediately prepared a celebration party to greet Targowski upon his return. The party never took place – Targowski, a veteran of air operations in Poland, France, Bomber and Coastal Command, failed to return from patrol, being shot down into the sea.

By the end of 1942 No 304 Squadron's crews had flown 549 sorties (some 4500 flying hours operationally) during its seven months in Coastal Command to date; dropping 78,100lb of explosive stores and actually attacking nine U-boats apart from others sighted and forced to submerge. Of its crew members, 24 were killed, drowned, or missing. Before the year was out Coastal Command acquired three more Wellington units for frontline operations. At Holmesley South No 547 Squadron came into existence officially on 21 October 1942 as a maritime recce unit, commanded by Squadron Leader H.N. Garbett, (later, Wing Commander, DFC, AFC). Its equipment, Wellington VIIIs, began arriving in November and, on moving to Chivenor in December, the squadron commenced operations on 17 December with some air-sea rescue (ASR) sorties which acted as familiarisation flights for its crews. A second unit, No 612 Squadron, Auxiliary Air Force (AAF), based at Wick in November 1942, and commanded by Wing Commander R.M. Longmore, CBE (son of ACM Sir Arthur Longmore), was already within the aegis of Coastal Command flying ageing Whitleys on coastal patrols *et al*.

On 5 December 1942 this squadron began receiving Wellingtons

*No 304 'Silesian' Squadron War Diary

GRXIV QD–V of 304 (Polish) Squadron, May 1944, receiving a load of depth charges.

GRXIV, HF330, '2N' (later, 'QD–N') of 304 (Polish) Squadron displays its flak damage on return from an attack on a U-boat, 5 May 1944, in Bay of Biscay.

Ready for the Off. 304 (Polish) Squadron Wellington raring to get away, May 1944.

GRXIV, HZ258, 'S' of 304 (Polish) Squadron. Note beam gun near roundel. This aircraft had served with 280 Squadron, Dec 1943 – March 1944.

to replace its Whitleys – the first nine aircraft, ES986*, HX379, HX436, HX504, HX512, HX575, X629, HX690, and HX771, all arriving on that date – with a tenth Wimpy, HX444, following on 11 December. These were Leigh Light Wellingtons and 612's crews, after a brief conversion course at nearby Skitten, began Wellington operations on 13 December, mainly in the form of recces along the Norwegian coastline zones of the North Sea.

In February 1943, however, 612's Wellingtons were transformed to Nos 172 and 179 Squadrons and the unit reverted to Whitleys until April 1943. Then, on 15 April, the squadron was moved south to Davidstow Moor for reconversion to Wellingtons – only to suffer the loss of its latest commander, Wing Commander J.S. Kendrick, in June when his aircraft, on a training flight, dived into the river at Barnstaple. Temporary command passed to the Leigh Light pioneer Wing Commander J.B. Russell, DSO, who remained in command after the next officially appointed commander, Wing Commander Palmer, was killed in an accident.

A third Wellington unit to join Coastal Command in late 1942 was No 544 Squadron. Officially formed at Benson on 19 October, this squadron comprised merely two Flights – A Flight operating a mixture of Avro Ansons and Wellingtons from Benson, while B Flight was based at Gibraltar, flying Spitfires in the photo-reconnaissance (PR) role. The Wellingtons of A Flight began operations in January 1943, flying experimental night photographic sorties over France, but by April 1943 these aircraft were withdrawn and replaced by D.H. Mosquitos. Thus, by January 1943 a total of six Webfoot Wimpy squadrons had joined Coastal Command's firstline offensive against the U-boats, and had well established their effectiveness by claiming three U-boats definitely sunk, at least five others severely damaged, apart from many others attacked with unseen or unconfirmed results.

Inevitably perhaps the Wellington crews had suffered losses – 172 Squadron alone had lost seven aircraft – but in the arithmetic of war they had already shown a good profit on the balance sheet. Moreover, and in common with other Coastal Command aircraft engaged in the battles of the Atlantic and Western Approaches, Wellingtons now added to the overall deterrent effect that any patrolling aircraft had on a surfaced U-boat, forcing the submarine to seek safety immediately in the ocean depths on sighting any aircraft. With the

*The Wellington which, with 172 Squadron on 3/4 June 1942, had made the first part-successful attack by a Leigh Light Wimpy on a U-boat, it will be recalled.

Leigh Light, Wellingtons now precluded the hitherto safety factor of a U-boat surfacing by night, thereby forcing a change in overall strategy and tactics upon Dönitz's plans for his force.

One pilot who had joined 172 squadron in its early days was Flying Officer Peter Stembridge (later, Group Captain, DFC, AFC), who recalls the initial problems and tactics involved in flying Leigh Light Wellingtons.*

> I was posted to 172 Squadron at Chivenor in July 1942 and, because I had been flying Lockheed Hudsons, proceeded immediately to the Wellington/Whitley OTU at Cranwell for Wellington conversion – the start of some 1100 hours on various Marks of Wellington. I soon developed a great affection for the Wimpy. It was an easy aircraft to fly and virtually 'vice-less' – I was *very* glad to be posted to Wellingtons and not Whitleys! On return to 172 Squadron in August 1942 I was appointed captain of aircraft, flying LL Wellington Mk VIIIs, with Pegasus XVIII engines, on anti-submarine operations in the Bay of Biscay. The aircraft were under-powered in that they could not maintain height on one engine – one could not feather the props, and the extra weight of the searchlight and batteries was virtually unjettisonable in any reasonable time; it was estimated that it would take two and a half hours, armed with a hand-axe, to jettison the searchlight/turret and numerous batteries in the nose. It meant that an engine failure at a patrol height of 800 – 1200 ft (and perhaps down to 50 ft in an attack), hundreds of miles from land, was unfortunate, necessitating a ditching, at night, probably into rough or very rough seas. We reckoned that our Pegasus engines were not designed for long flights – eight-and-a-half to ten-and-a-half hours – low over the sea; the fairly salt-laden air seemed conducive to 'sticky valves' problems. The Mk VIII Wimpy had, of course, besides the Leigh Light, the 1½ metre Mk II ASV with all its associated fishing rod aerials sticking out in virtually all directions – one heard that some local civilians in the Barnstaple area reckoned we were spraying poison gas over Germany from these prominent 'rods'!
>
> I had carried out, with my crew, many night anti-submarine sweeps/patrols over the Bay of Biscay before we sighted and attacked our first U-boat during the night of 22/23 December

*Correspondence with author

'1942. On many sorties we had investigated, with the Leigh Light, a considerable number of ASV contacts but virtually all proved to be French or Spanish fishing boats. Many of those boats carried lights but obviously we had to illuminate and investigate all ASV contacts; a U-boat with no lights might be hiding alongside a lighted fishing boat, or be in the midst of a group of such boats. Carrying out the homing and investigating procedures every time – sometimes 20, 30, or more during one sortie – was very frustrating, and one wondered at times if the searchlight and/or its batteries would pack up. Our luck changed on the night of 22/23 December 1942 – an early Christmas present! At this stage I had a very competent crew who flew some 500 operational hours with me and, in particular, Sergeant Eddie Goodman (later commissioned on our crew) was an 'ace' on both ASV Mk II and Mk III. Anyway, just after 0315 hrs we got an ASV Mk II contact at six miles. We switched on the Leigh Light at one mile and there was a fully surfaced U-boat heading west at good speed! It is, and was, difficult to describe one's feelings on seeing an enemy submarine for the first time, especially after many long hours on sorties without a sighting and particularly at night – a very sinister sight, I recall. In brief, I felt a combination of surprise, excitement, elation, intense satisfaction, etc, but all subordinated to carrying out *immediately* the correct attack procedure in the ensuing seconds – after all, we might never sight another U-boat!

The U-boat started to dive as soon as it was illuminated but its conning tower was still visible when I dropped a stick of four DCs at an angle of about 60-degrees (because of the 'stick' spacing and because the lethal range of our DCs was only six yards) just ahead of the U-boat. The rear gunner reported that the DCs had exploded across the centre of the conning tower swirl. Flame floats had been dropped with the DCs and we homed back over the position but saw nothing of the U-boat. We backed up the flame floats with a marine marker. Shortly after, when the marker was to port of us, we came under fire from the starboard side – it appeared to be cannon and/or machine gun fire from about two miles or less away. As we had already used our one and only stick of DCs, I made a diving turn to port from 500 to 100 ft, during which the firing followed us round, and then after a brief deliberation on tactics returned to the estimated position of the source of the firing. Though we searched the area for 50 minutes nothing further was seen, either visually or on ASV. It was assumed that two U-boats had been in company about two miles apart. Anyway, it proved to ous conclusively that there *were* really such things as U-boats in th Bay!

On 29 January 1943 yet another Leigh Light Wellington unit was added to Coastal Command's strength. No 407 ('*Demon*') Squadron, RCAF based at Docking, Norfolk, had been with the Command since its formation on 8 May 1941, flying Blenheim IVs and Lockheed Hudsons, but on 29 January its role was changed to General Reconnaissance and on the same day it received its first Leigh Light Wellington. Commanded by an RAF officer, Wing Commander J.C. Archer*, the squadron quickly converted and worked back up to operational fitness, then commenced Wellington sorties in anger on 7 March with a series of anti-submarine patrols.

On 1 April, 1943 the squadron moved to Chivenor in order to operate over the Bay of Biscay and Western Approaches, and three weeks later, on 22 April, made its first U-boat claim when Flight Lieutenant D. Pickard attacked and strafed a surfaced U-boat, though without tangible result. By then, 192 Squadron had added two U-boats confirmed as sunk and two others at least seriously damaged to its tally. The first of these claims happened on 19 February 1943 when Flying Officer G.D. Lundon,† flying Wellington MP505, 'B' attacked and sank *U-268*. On 3 March, the same aircraft, now skippered by Flight Sergeant J.L. Tweddle, attacked and at least damaged *U-525*; while on 21 March Flying Officer I.D. Prebble in Wellington 'T' damaged *U-332*.

The next kill for 172 Squadron came on the night of 22 March 1943, when Flying Officer Peter Stembridge, flying MP539, 'G', made a contact. In his own description:

> Soon after midnight on 22 March, height 1000 ft and visibility one mile, we had an ASV Mk III contact at seven miles. We homed and at one mile, height 350 ft, turned on the Leigh Light. At half a mile we sighted a U-boat in the act of crash-diving with its conning tower and stern still visible. I dropped six DCs from a height of 70 ft ahead of the conning tower swirl, the stern still visible. Due to the angle of attack the DCs had more of a 'cluster' effect than a spaced 'stick', and the rear gunner reported what appeared to be one large

*Killed in action 27 September 1943.
†Wellington MP505, 'B', (Flying Officer Lundon and crew) shot down by *U-333* on night 4/5 March 1943.

explosion, with the full length of the U-boat visible in the trough caused thereby. As he could not see the conning tower or the hydroplanes, he thought the U-boat was keel uppermost. He fired a burst of about 50 rounds from his guns for good measure! I made a wide circle and came back at 250 ft over the flame floats three minutes later with the Leigh Light on. We saw two separate patches of very large bubbles, but no sign of any part of the U-boat.

It was later confirmed that Stembridge and his crew had sunk *U-665*, commanded by Oberleutnant Haupt. It might be pertinent to point out that *U-665* was the only U-boat sunk between 20 and 28 March, during which period no less than 41 U-boats crossed Biscay in one direction or another, of which 26 were sighted by aircraft and 15 actually attacked – a slight indication of the enormous task undertaken by Coastal Command's air crews, and no less the extreme difficulty in merely finding let alone destroying a U-boat, by night or by day.

In April 1943 three more submarines were credited to 172 Squadron crews. On 10 April Pilot Officer G.H. Whitley, skippering Wellington 'C', sank *U-376* (Kapitänleutnant Marks), while on 26 April Sergeant A. Coumbis in aircraft 'R' succeeded in at least damaging *U-566**, and three nights later Peter Stembridge in Wellington 'H' attacked an ASV Mk III contact shortly after midnight, dropping his stick of six DCs in a 'cluster' proximity despite heavy defensive cannon and/or machine gun opposition from his target. The ASV contact then remained stationary for an hour while Stembridge continued circling the area, before suddenly 'disappearing' from the radar screen. *U-437* had escaped death for the moment, but was re-sighted in daylight later and promptly attacked by Liberator 'D' of 224 Squadron. By that time 172 Squadron had replaced its Mk VIIIs with Mk XII Wellingtons, the first examples of these arriving on the unit in late January 1943.

Four of the squadron's aircraft and crews were detached to Luqa, Malta in April too, but the bulk of the unit's aircraft continued their offensive over the Bay of Biscay, commanded from March 1943 by Wing Commander R.G. Musson. The latest commander took a full part in his unit's operations and was responsible for having a single

*__U-566__ was fated to be sunk on the night of 23/24 October 1943 in the Straits of Gibraltar by Wellington HF132, 'F', 179 Squadron (Sergeant D.M. Cornish)

0.303-inch machine gun being fitted in the nose 'turret' of 172's Wellingtons – a somewhat dubious form of offensive armament with which to respond to any U-boat's multi-cannon defences, but no doubt a morale-booster. With the increasing daylight hours of summer the squadron now flew both day and night sorties, and one such day operation on 24 July 1943 proved tragic for one crew.

Flying Officer W. Jennings, piloting Wellington MP514, 'H', discovered the U-boat tanker *U-459* and immediately pressed home his attack in the teeth of a fierce defensive cannon hail of fire which caused plentiful damage to the incoming aircraft. Sweeping in at zero height the Wellington hit the U-boat head-on, crashing into the boat's starboard side and smashing the cannons and their gunners into the sea, then disintegrating, leaving part of the fuselage embedded at the rear of the conning tower after impact, killing all the aircraft's crew except the rear gunner, Sergeant A. Turner. The U-boat crew immediately began to dump the tangled aircraft wreckage clinging to the U-boat superstructure over-board, including two unexploded depth charges from the Wellington's bomb load. The DCs promptly detonated at their depth-setting of a mere 25 feet, right under the submarine's hull! The explosion wrecked the U-boat's steering gear and created havoc inside the engine room, leaving the vessel to circle uncontrolled and helpless.

At that stage a second Wellington, 'Q' of 547 Squadron (Flying Officer J. Whyte) arrived on the scene. *U-459*'s commander, von Wilamowitz-Möllendorf, promptly realised the hopelessness of his situation and ordered his remaining crew to abandon ship. He then returned inside his vessel, set off the scuttling charges and went down with his ship. The sole Wellington survivor, Turner, and 44 German seamen were rescued some ten hours later by a Royal Navy warship.

Just five days later, on 29 July, 172 Squadron's commander, Wing Commander Musson, extracted revenge for the loss of Jennings and his crew by flying Wellington MP539, 'G' on a Biscay sortie and sinking *U-614*. Such were the vagaries of war, that on 24 August 1943, while piloting Wellington MP624, 'R', Wing Commander Musson failed to return from a sortie, and command of 172 Squadron duly passed into the capable hands of Wing Commander E.G. Palmer (later, Group Captain).

In April 1943, No 179 Squadron returned to Britain, being based at Predannack, Cornwall. One of its members, Flying Officer Donald McRae, a Canadian from Stavely, Alberta, attacked and sank the *U-134* on 24 August 1943, the first of several submarines to be sunk or damaged by McRae over the coming months. On 3 September he attacked a surfaced U-boat without visible result, then three days later surprised *U-760* and damaged it, sufficiently so that the U-boat was forced to seek shelter in Vega harbour, Spain, where it was interned for the rest of the war. As a result McRae and his set operator, Flying Officer Senior were each awarded a DFC in October 1943, but in the following month McRae scored again, sinking *U-211* on 18/19 November while acting as aerial escort to a merchant convoy. McRae's remarkable successes – two U-boats definitely sunk and several others damaged – were rarely matched by *any* pilot in Coastal Command, and even more rarely surpassed, no matter which types of aircraft or operational roles were flown. For the vast majority of air crews engaged in anti-submarine operations within Coastal Command's aegis, their war careers comprised hundreds of hours flying over featureless ocean without even a sight of a U-boat; yet their very presence above any U-boat action zone was a definite deterrent, as many surviving U-boat crewmen were to affirm after the war's end.

In August 1943 further improved-equipped Wellingtons began reaching the Coastal Command Wimpy units. No 172 Squadron began receiving Mk XIVs from that month, while No 407 Squadron RCAF also took delivery of some Mk XIVs from June and continued flying a mixture of these and Mk XIIs for the following six months. On the night of 6/7 September the Canadian squadron claimed its first confirmed U-boat sinking when Pilot Officer E.M. O'Donnell at the helm of Wellington HF115, 'C1-W', attacked and sank *U-669* in the Bay of Biscay. In the same month, September 1943, a second Canadian unit joined the ranks of the Command's Wellington anti-submarine force when No 415 'Swordfish' Squadron RCAF received its first Wellington, DV762 on 3 September, and added 15 more Wimpys by 25 October.

The 'Swordfish' squadron, based then at Thorney Island under the command of Wing Commander C.G. Ruttan, DSO, had been a torpedo-bomber unit with Coastal Command since its formation on 20 August 1941, and had flown Beauforts and Hampdens until the arrival of the Wellington VIII, Leigh Light aircraft. Moving base to Bircham Newton on 15 November 1943, the squadron then flew both Wellington VIIIs and biplane Fairey Albacores on anti-shipping sorties along the Channel and Dutch coastal areas – their prime targets being German E-boats roving in those areas – using the Leigh Lights to illuminate targets for the Albacores to actually attack – in some ways a parallel to Wing Commander Helmore's earlier project for his 'Turbinlite' nightfighters. No 415 Squadron was to continue in this one-off role until after D-Day (6 June 1944), after which, with effect from 12 July 1944, the unit was retitled as a pure bomber squadron and re-equipped with Handley Page Halifax B.IIIs and, later, B.VIIs on being transferred from Coastal Command to No 6 (RCAF) Group, Bomber Command.

From September to December 1943, in addition to McRae's and O'Donnell's claims Wellingtons accounted for six more U-boats – four of these sunk, a fifth scuttled by its crew, and the sixth, *U-667*, damaged in the course of separate attacks on both 24th and 26th of September. All six had been victims of No 179 Squadron crews, assisted in three cases by other Coastal Command aircraft and/or RN vessels. In that same period 179 Squadron had shifted base to Chivenor, then Benbecula, with a detachment on the Azores for greater range of action. By April 1944, however, the Azores detachment had returned to the UK to participate in Allied preparations for the Allied invasion of Normandy – D-Day. Its prime role in those preparative operations was maintaining Rover patrols over the Channel approaches and adjacent areas, attacking all and any types of enemy shipping, surfaced or otherwise; a role shared by 172 Squadron and others during the same period. The 'run-up' months to D-Day in early 1944 brought reasonably rich pickings for Coastal Command in the context of U-boats being sighted, attacked, damaged and/or sunk, with no less than 15 such victims being credited to Wimpy crews up to and including the night of the Allied invasion.

The first claim for 1944 was made by Wing Commander J.B. Russell, DSO, by now commander of No 612 Squadron AAF, who attacked *U-373* on 3 January but could only report it as 'damaged' – an action in which he was helped by Liberator 'H' of 224 Squadron. In fact, *U-373* had indeed escaped fatal damage on this occasion, but was fated to become one of two U-boats sunk within 22 minutes of swift action by the Canadian K.O. Moore of 224 Squadron in his Leigh Light Liberator in the early hours of 8 June 1944. On 4 January, Flying Officer H. Czyzun of 304 (Polish) Squadron, flying Wellington HF185, 'B', attacked and damaged *U-629* – one of several U-boats attacked without positive results during that month by the eager Polish crews. Four days later, on 8 January, Flying Officer W.F. Davidson of 179 Squadron in Wellington 'R' joined with Catalina 'J' of 202 Squadron in attacking *U-343*, but Davidson's aircraft was shot down by flak, with only himself surviving the crash.

Before January was out, however, two positive kills were registered by Wellington crews. On the 14th Pilot Officer W.N. Armstrong, flying HF168, 'L' of 172 Squadron trapped *U-231* and sank it; while on 30 January Flight Sergeant L.D. Richards, skippering MP813, 'K', sank *U-364* to add to 172 Squadron's tally – but Richards and his crew failed to return from this sortie. February 1944 saw two more confirmed sinkings – *U-545* on the 10th by Pilot Officer M.H. Paynter of 612 Squadron in Wellington 'C', and *U-283* on 11 February by Flying Officer P.W. Heron piloting MP578, 'CI-D' of 407 Squadron RCAF. Heron's success came as something of a morale-raiser for his squadron which had suffered several months of fruitless operations (in the context of U-boat claims) and had several crews lost over the oceans. Moving from its base at Chivenor, the Canadian unit settled into Limavady from 29 January 1944 and almost immediately began a series of U-boat sightings and actual attacks.

On the night of 11/12 March, Flight Sergeant D. Bretherton flying Wellington 'C' of 612 Squadron discovered *U-629* and damaged it with his attack. (In the event *U-629* became the second sunk victim of Flying Officer K.O. Moore of 224 Squadron on 8 June 1944, as previously mentioned.) On 13 March, however, *U-575* was not to escape from the combined attentions of Flying Officer F.P. Finnessey in Wellington HF183, 'B' of 172 Squadron, two Boeing B-17 Fortresses and some naval warships, being sunk. April 1944 brought just one confirmed U-boat kill, when Flying Officer C.C. Punter in Wellington 'W' of 612 Squadron sank *U-293*.

The following month added two more tangible results for the UK-based Wimpy units. The first of these came on 4 May when Flying Officer L.J. Bateman, piloting HF134, 'M' of 407 Squadron RCAF, took off from Chivenor – to where his unit had moved from Northern Ireland on 28 April – and eventually sighted a U-boat in his patrol area. His attack approach got within 500 yards of the submarine before the 'target' put up any opposition with a fierce flurry of flak. The Wellington's nose gunner started to reply, only to have his gun jam immediately, but Bateman attacked straight along the U-boat's track and dropped his depth charges accurately. Swinging away and circling, he returned to the target but could only see a 100-yards wide oil slick stretching for about half a mile. Later in the day a patrolling Sunderland flying boat reported three surviving and numerous dead German crew men in the same area as the oil slick. *U-846* had indeed been sunk, and Bateman was later awarded a DFC. The other May

1944 claim was for *U-736*, damaged in an attack by Flying Officer K.M. Davies from 612 Squadron, but Davies and his crew failed to return to base.

If much emphasis has been put upon the Wellingtons' unceasing offensive against U-boats as their prime objective, other equally hazardous and successful anti-shipping operations were also flown by Coastal Command's Wimpy warriors. A prime example was No 415 'Swordfish' Squadron RCAF's activities during the early months of 1944 during the pre-invasion operational effort by all units. Though nominally based at Bircham Newton at the start of 1944, the squadron's mixed bag of Wellingtons and Albacores were in fact spread around various locations during the period 8 May to 12 July. The torpedo-strike Albacores – nicknamed 'Applecores' by their crews – were divided between Manston, Thorney Island, and Winkleigh, Devon; while the Leigh Light Wellingtons were dispersed between Docking and North Coates. The Swordfish Wellingtons began a series of sweeps over the North Sea off the Dutch coast, interspersed with anti-E-boat patrols in liaison with RN warships from early November 1943, but for the first four months found few targets until on 1 March 1944, a Wellington skippered by Flying Officer K.T. Ashfield completed the destruction of an enemy merchant vessel off Den Helder – it had already been damaged by Beaufighters – by dropping bombs on the ship.

Over the following weeks the Wellingtons found a succession of likely targets – sometimes bombing these on their own, but more often acting as 'spotters' for Beaufighter strike units with whom they could join in the actual attacks. The results were usually successful, with one or more vessels left burning and/or sinking after being bombed by the Wellingtons, apart from any Beaufighter 'scores'. Among many successful Wellington skippers on these types of operation by the Swordfish crews, one of the most prominent was Winnipeg-born Squadron Leader Hubert G. Keillor who was to finish the war with a DSO and DFC for his courage and determination. Tragically, Keillor, who continued in RCAF service, was killed on 17 May 1949 in an accident while flying an Auster training aircraft from the RCAF base at Trenton.

In June 1944 Coastal Command's activities reached a peak, with particularly an intense concentration on operations to protect and isolate the English Channel from any form of German naval intrusion. By the evening of 5 June 1944 Coastal Command's Wellington units were disposed as follows:

Squadron	Base	CO
172	Chivenor	Wg Cdr K. Petrie
179	Predannack	Wg Cdr R.R. Russell
304	Chivenor	Wg Cdr J.M. Kranc
407 RCAF	Chivenor	Wg Cdr R.A. Ashman
415 RCAF	Bircham Newton	Wg Cdr C.G. Ruttan, DSO
524	Davidstow Moor	Sqn Ldr A.W.B. Naismith
612 AAF	Chivenor	Wg Cdr D.M. Brass, DSO

No 524 Squadron had only recently rejoined Coastal Command, having been reformed at Davidstow Moor on 7 April 1944 and equipped with Wellington XIIIs for anti-shipping operations along the French coast, beginning this role on 30 April. Of the former Wellington units in UK-based Coastal Command, Nos 311 (Czech) and 547 Squadrons had exchanged their Wellingtons for Liberators in June and November 1943 respectively.

On the night of 5/6 June 1944 the Allies launched their air and seaborne invasion of German-occupied Normandy – the greatest invasion force ever assembled in the history of human conflict – and to Coastal Command fell the crucial responsibility for ensuring that the highly vulnerable and massive fleet of vessels bearing the Allied forces across the Channel to Normandy was not subjected to interference from Germany's navy, especially its U-boat forces. To this end a system of so-termed 'Cork' patrols had already been instigated, whereby a continuous aerial patrol of designated areas of sea stretching from Eire's south coast to the shores of Biscay, covering the whole western approaches to the Channel, was flown by day and by night – the prime onus for this vital protection screen being on the 'shoulders' of No 19 Group, HQ of Coastal Command at Plymouth. It meant that Coastal crews were expected to cover some 20,000 square miles of sea with barely 400 aircraft in toto, and in practice required aircraft to be despatched singly or in pairs to patrol particular stretches of the 'Cork' pattern of mapped oblong areas, working in overlapping shifts.

With the eastern approaches to the Channel already well mined and guarded, the main threat would patently come from the bulk of Dönitz's U-boat forces based around the Brest and Biscay areas. Shortly after 5 am on the morning of 6 June, Dönitz's orders to his U-boat men were flashed to all boat-commanders to sail and to make every possible effort to intercept the Allied seaborne forces in the

Channel – 'regardless of danger from shallow water, possible minefields, or anything else' (*sic*).

In response to that 'do-or-die' order, a total of 15 U-boats set sail that evening as the vanguard of a mini-fleet of 49 submarines intended to be despatched to the Channel zone.* Seven of that initial 15-strong advance force were fitted with *Schnorchel* 'breathing tubes', meaning these could remain submerged on their journey, but the remaining eight had no such apparatus and perforce had to stay on the surface to preserve their batteries for an intended submerged daylight assault on the invasion force.

Shortly before 2 am the next morning these surfaced U-boats met their first opposition from Coastal Command aircraft, in the shape of several Liberators from 53 Squadron and 179 Squadron Wellington, 'G', piloted by Pilot Officer W.J. Hill. The Liberators immediately attacked two leading U-boats, *U-256* and *U-415*, losing one Liberator to *U-256*'s flak gunners. Pressing home their attacks, however, the aircraft quickly inflicted serious damage on *U-256*, forcing it to submerge and shakily make its way back to port, abandoning its sortie. *U-415* was attacked by a Liberator initially, then by Pilot Officer Hill's Wellington. Hill came in low over *U-415*'s starboard beam and dropped six depth charges across its midships section. The force of their explosion in unison lifted *U-415* bodily out of the sea, stopped its diesels, and jammed its rudder to starboard, leaving the submarine curving out of control and at the mercy of any further attack.

Fortunately for *U-415* the Wellington now had no more depth charges and could merely drop a marine marker on the spot, hoping other aircraft might 'finish the job'. Instead *U-415*, badly damaged, was forced to abort its mission and join *U-256* in a retreat to safe harbour back at Brest. One more U-boat of the pack was attacked by a Wellington when Squadron Leader D.W. Farrell, flying Wimpy HF149, 'C' of 407 Squadron RCAF, tackled *U-989* and damaged it. Farrell, who had made several attacks on U-boats in preceding months, though without positive results, failed to return from this sortie.

The pressure of the 'Cork' patrol system was maintained throughout the critical weeks of June and July 1944 and reaped a rich harvest of U-boats sunk, damaged and/or forced to abort their missions. Among those successes were two U-boats seriously

*For further details, see *Men of Coastal Command* by C. Bowyer; Kimber, 1985

damaged (*U-270* by Wellington MP789, 'Y', 172 Squadron Pilot Officer L. Harris; and *U-971* by Wellington HF286, 'L' of 407 Squadron RCAF, Flying Officer F.H. Foster), and one confirmed as sunk. The latter was the *U-441*, commanded by Kapitänleutnant Klaus Hartmann, which was merely 50 miles from its intended harbour at Brest after a two-weeks' patrol when it was spotted at 2254 hrs on 18 June by Flight Lieutenant J. Antoniewicz piloting Wellington HF331, 'A' of 304 (Polish) Squadron.

The Wellington quickly started an attack run, only to see a second U-boat nearby and surfaced. Ignoring this one for the moment, Antoniewicz continued his run-in to *U-441* and could see it slowly submerging. At 100 ft he dropped six depth charges spaced 60 ft apart and fuse-set to detonate at 14-18 feet depth. His aim was accurate and the resulting explosions combined to completely obscure the submarine for a moment, then as the sea spray died down no sign of the U-boat was visible, only the flickering flames of two flame floats dropped with the depth charges now marking the spot. Between these floats appeared a widening circle of oil, tinged with iridescence, with various pieces of wreckage swirling in the vortex. The oil patch continued spreading to well beyond 500 ft diameter, so the Polish pilot had marine markers dropped to mark the location, then left for base. The whole episode had lasted merely 18 minutes.

There was a certain irony in *U-441*'s demise – it had chosen to submerge on being sighted, instead of remaining surfaced and relying on its defence flak guns to ward off Antoniewicz's Wellington. Yet *U-441* had been the first U-boat deliberately given extra-deadly flak guns to act as a *surfaced* 'aircraft-trap'; coolly inviting any aircraft to a slugging match when such an occasion arose. A U-boat's ability to hit back was formidable in the latter war years, and many aircraft were lost to the deadly accuracy of the German gunners. Such situations often resulted in mini-epics of human courage, endurance, and self-sacrifice among aircraft crews brought down in the sea, and probably no finer example of those qualities could be found than the final hours in the young life of Roderick Borden Gray, a Canadian air observer from Sault Ste Marie, Ontario on the night of 26/27 August 1944.

In the evening of 26 August, Gray was among the crew of Wellington NB798, 'B' of 172 Squadron (skipper Flying Officer Whiteley) who left for an anti-submarine hunt over the Bay of Biscay. Within minutes of midnight a blip appeared on the aircraft's radar screen indicating a contact about 11 miles ahead. At one mile range the 20-million candle-power Leigh Light was switched on and almost immediately revealed a surfaced U-boat. It was *U-534*, captained by Kapitän Nollau, armed with four 20mm and two 37mm cannons for self-defence on its *Wintergarten* – the crew's nickname for the railed gun platform on which these cannons were mounted. Nollau's crew were well-drilled for such situations and alert, and as soon as the Leigh Light beam appeared the gunners were at their posts, sending up a steady hail of cannon shells at the incoming Wellington.

The first flurry of shells hit the aircraft's port engine which immediately erupted in flames, then seconds later the starboard engine was hit and spewed a roaring trail of smoke and flames. Undeviating, Whiteley continued his attack run-in, released his stick of depth charges in a straddle of *U-534*, then thundered low over the vessel and stayed airborne for another half-mile before diving head-on into the sea. The impact killed some crew men but four finally managed to extricate themselves from the wreckage, including the pilot and Roderick Gray. Despite a severely injured leg – survivors later recorded their conviction that Gray's leg had in fact been severed – Gray inflated a dinghy, then assisted his pilot and a second injured member into it, while he refused to overburden the dinghy and remained in the water, clinging to the side along with the fourth survivor of the crash, Warrant Officer G.H. Bulley, RCAF. As the hours slipped by Gray, in particular, remained in the water, refusing appeals from those aboard the dinghy to 'spell' him, and he eventually lost consciousness, being supported thereafter by the grip of the others' hands. When dawn came on 27 August the men aboard the dinghy realised that Gray was now dead, and with the greatest reluctance let his body slip into the depths.

The three survivors were to suffer for a total of 14 hours before hope was revived of being rescued. Shortly after 2pm a Sunderland from No 10 Squadron RAAF (EK573, 'P') hove into view over the dinghy, skippered by an Australian, Flight Lieutenant 'Bill' Tilley, DFC, who was shortly after joined in his circling above the dinghy by a second Sunderland of his unit, ML856, 'Y' (Flight Lieutenant M. Ryan) and Wellington 'A' from 172 Squadron. After circling for an hour to reduce fuel slightly, Tilley proceeded to land on the sea* and achieved this without damage to his Sunderland. Taking on board the three surviving Wimpy crew men, Tilley then got airborne again, despite a

---

In spite of a general order forbidding Coastal Command flying boat captains from attempting landings in open ocean seas.

(right) Flg Off Roderick Borden Gray,
RAF, awarded a posthumous
George Cross.

(below) Leigh Light GRXIV of
Squadron at Chivenor, 1944.

battering from the angry ocean swell, and flew directly to Mount Batten, Plymouth where the retrieved crewmen were immediately whisked away to hospital.

Once recovered, the survivors all spoke of Gray's deliberate self-sacrifice in attempting to succour his comrades, and later the *London Gazette* announced the posthumous award of a George Cross (GC) to Flying Officer R.B. Gray, RCAF, while Warrant Officer Bulley received a DFC.

By September 1944, with the Allied invasion armies well established on the European mainland, Coastal Command units were re-allocated operational patrol areas to continue their watch-and-ward roles, protecting merchant convoys and seeking out U-boats, *et al.* Accordingly, in September Nos 179 and 304 Squadrons moved to Benbecula, Nos 172 and 612 Squadrons to Limavady (though 612 Squadron moved on to Langham on 18 December); No 407 Squadron shifted base to St Eval on 3 November, then moved again, to Limavady on 2 December; while 524 Squadron went to Langham in November 1944. The previous main Wellington base at Chivenor was, however, a continuing host to Wimpy units, because in September 1944 No 36 Squadron, which had just returned from operations in Italy, moved to the Devon base, equipped with Wellington Mk XIVs; and on 24 October it was joined by No 14 Squadron, an ex-Martin Marauder unit in the Middle East theatre, but now re-equipped with Wellington XIVs for anti-shipping/submarine work over the Western Approaches and into Biscay.

By the close of 1944 the former U-boat havens along the west coast of France had long been evacuated in advance of imminent Allied armies' occupation, leaving mainly only the various ports and harbours around the Baltic and Norway as continuing operational bases for Dönitz's submariners. By then too Allied aerial supremacy over the Luftwaffe was reaching a peak of ascendancy, thereby permitting – in the maritime/air context – an even greater concentration of aircraft for hunting U-boats and other German shipping.

For the Wellington crews the closing months of the war were to bring only two more confirmed U-boat sinkings. On 30 December 1944 the *U-772* was destroyed by Wellington NB855, 'L' of 407 Squadron RCAF, piloted by Squadron Leader C.I.W. Taylor; while the ultimate Wimpy kill was *U-321* which became a victim of Wellington HF329, 'Y' from 304 (Polish) Squadron, skippered by Warrant Officer R. Marczak, flying from St Eval where his squadron had been based since 3 March 1945. On 2 April 1945 Marczak had found the *U-321* at a position of 50° 00' N/ 12° 57' W and laid his depth charges in a close straddle. This attack was in fact No 304 Squadron's final attack on any U-boat during the war. On 4 May 1945 Grossadmiral Karl Dönitz sent out an order for all U-boats still at sea to cease operations immediately and return to base, then followed with a second order for all U-boat captains to surrender their vessels *intact* to the nearest Allied 'authority'; this last order being in direct variance with an existing secret naval plan, code-named *Regenbogen* ('Rainbow') for scuttling in the event of Germany's defeat. Nevertheless, some 200 U-boat captains did scuttle their submarines before 5 May 1945.

For Coastal Command Wellington crews – in common with all others – May 1945 brought to a close over five years of unrelenting vigil and no small human sacrifice. Perhaps the operational statistics of just one Wellington unit in Coastal Command can be taken as representative of such effort and losses. From 7 May 1942, when it was transferred to the Command, until 30 May 1945, the date of the unit's ultimate operational sortie under the Command's aegis, No 304 (Polish) Squadron's crews had flown 2451 individual sorties (21,331 operational flying hours), attacked 34 U-boats (apart from others merely sighted), and had lost 106 air crew personnel killed or presumed dead.* The end of European hostilities brought a swift rundown of Coastal Command's Wellington units, as the following table indicates:

Squadron	C	Remarks
14	Wg Cdr G.I. Rawson	Disbanded Chivenor, 1/6/45
36	Wg Cdr G. Williams	Disbanded Benbecula, 1/6/45
172	Wg Cdr S.R. Ramsay Smith	Disbanded Limavady, 4/6/45
179	–	Converted to Warwick a/c, Nov '44
304	–	Transfer to Transport Command, 14/6/45
407	Wg Cdr K.C. Wilson	Disbanded Chivenor, 4/6/45
524	Sqn Ldr G.E. Willis, DFC	Disbanded Langham, 25/6/45
612	Wg Cdr G. Henderson	Disbanded Langham, 7/7/45

*As quoted in *Destiny Can Wait*, PAF Association/Heinemann, 1949

CHAPTER ELEVEN

Above the Jungle

In comparison with the Middle East Command, the introduction of the Wellington to the Far East theatre of operations came late and, in relative terms, only in small numbers; a circumstance dictated purely by questions of contemporary priorities and difficulties of supply. Thus, it was not until early 1942 that Wellingtons were considered plentiful enough to be spared for the 'Forgotten War' in India/Burma. Initially, two units became involved almost simultaneously i.e. Nos 99 and 215 Squadrons.

No 99 Squadron, based at Waterbeach at the beginning of 1942, still operating Wellington Ics and IIIs, was warned for an overseas posting, and began the projected move to India in late January 1942 when advance ground crew parties left England. The air crews commenced flying Wellingtons to India, via the Middle East, from the first week in February, although too often their aircraft were promptly annexed by authorities in the Middle East to boost strengths of local squadrons. This ferrying operation was to extend over most of February 1942 and in the following months No 99 Squadron tended to be split up into various parties and detachments in India, such as Ambala, Solan, and Pandaveswar, until the squadron was finally brought together as an entity again at Pandaveswar in mid-September, then moved base to Digri in October 1942 to commence full operations as a complete squadron.

The second unit involved in reinforcing India was No 215 Squadron which had reformed as a bomber squadron at Newmarket on 9 December 1941 after some 19 months of chequered existence as a training unit of various guises. In January 1942 the 'new' squadron despatched its initial ground crew parties by sea to (eventually) India, while its air crews spent some three months working up at Waterbeach and 15 OTU, Harwell, before beginning the ferrying of Wellingtons via the Middle East to India in late March 1942. Again, RAF commanders in the Middle East had few qualms about acquiring some aircraft for local use as these arrived, particularly on Malta, but by the close of April 1942 the unit was gathered together at Asansol, India and began operations on 24 April after moving base to Pandaveswar.

The two squadrons' arrival in India came at a period of Allied recuperation from a series of disastrous retreats and repletion of resources, as General Wavell patiently began to rebuild Allied strength with a view to going over to the offensive by the end of 1942. To the air and ground crews fresh from England their arrival in the sub-continent of India coincided with an ultra-sultry summer during which even the natives were dying from heat exhaustion, while a further hazard to health was a malaria epidemic – the worst known for many years – which laid low nearly 40,000 Allied troops by November 1942.

On arrival, the Wellingtons were earmarked as the nucleus of an eventual night bomber force, and indeed were the only long-range bombers available within the theatre until a few Liberators began trickling through to India before the end of the year. For the air crews, flying over Burma proved to be a continual struggle with raw nature primarily. Cumulo-nimbus clouds of towering heights above the hills and mountains contained inner currents of terrifying violence which had been known to tear the wings off large aircraft, while occasional cyclonic winds at ground level could lift a loaded bomber off the ground bodily. And to most crews' amazement, their aircraft often iced up at height even in monsoon conditions. They also flew with the certain knowledge that any descent into the jungle meant probable death either at the mercy of the impenetrable jungle itself, or at the hands of a Japanese foe whose ideas of 'chivalry' and 'Bushido' for a captured enemy included brutal torture and bestial treatment, if not immediate barbaric execution.

Nos 99 and 215 Squadrons remained the only Wellington units in India throughout 1943, and by May that year were both based at Jessore, forming No 175 Wing. Their prime targets on operations were the various Japanese communications routes, by river, rail, and road, but occasionally acted as freight supply-wagons for individual army formations. In the same year the overall Allied fighting organisation in the Far East was drastically restructured when, in August 1943, the Quebec Conference created a new South East Asia Command (SEAC) as a totally integrated Anglo-American organisation, with a single Supreme Commander, Admiral Louis Mountbatten – the youngest such appointment since Napoleon's heyday.

Within that command was born Air Command South East

(Top right) Squadron Leader Jones and Sgt Dichiel, 99 Squadron at Digri, 1942

(Bottom right) 99 Squadron crew, Rear: Sgts Dacey, Radmore, Chopping. Front: Fg Off David Allan; Laurie Butler.

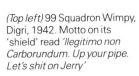

(Top left) 99 Squadron Wimpy, Digri, 1942. Motto on its 'shield' read *'Ilegitimo non Carborundum. Up your pipe. Let's shit on Jerry'*

(Bottom left) Wellington with appropriate Bengal tiger insigne, India, 1944.

Indian pastoral scene, 1943.

215 Squadron crew. L–R: Plt Off Ruwald; Fg Off Rogers; Sqn Ldr J.R. Sutton, DFC; Flt Sgts Leigh & Mather. Jessore, 1943.

Asia (ACSEA), commanded by ACM Sir Richard Peirse, which included the USAAF units of SEAC, and had Anglo-American integration at all levels of administration and operational control. This also now brought certain peripheral areas and units, formerly under the paper control of the former RAF India, under the aegis of ACSEA, including No 8 Squadron, based at Khormaksar, Aden since May 1942, and No 244 Squadron, based at Sharjah in 1943 with a detachment at Masira.

Both units were by 1943 engaged in maritime reconnaissance and anti-shipping roles covering areas of the Indian Ocean and the Gulf of Oman respectively, and both began receiving Wellingtons for such duties by February 1944; No 8 Squadron at that period was commanded by Wing Commander D.W. Reid, DFC, and No 244 squadron by Wing Commander R.C. Rotheram, DFC.* In the case of 8 Squadron, its first Wellington, a Mk XIII, JA209, arrived on 14 December 1943, and the unit mounted its first Wimpy operation (JA210) on 2 January 1944. By the end of that month the squadron was up to its full 16-aircraft strength.

Another maritime Wimpy unit, No 621 Squadron, commanded by Wing Commander P. Green, OBE, AFC, which had been formed originally at Port Reitz, Kenya on 12 September 1943, was also based at Khormaksar by December 1943, with detachments at various landing grounds along the southern Arabian coastline, wholly engaged in general maritime operations. Although enemy submarine activities in the area were not comparable in intensity to, for example, the Biscay Bay, they were by no means minimal – in January 1944 alone 16 U-boat sightings were recorded – and therefore every air crew kept fully alert throughout every patrol.

Patience was rewarded on 2 May 1944 when Flight Lieutenant R.H. Mitchell of 621 Squadron, flying Wellington JA107, 'E', was carrying out an anti-submarine search just south of the Gulf of Aden and suddenly came upon a U-boat, fully surfaced and making some 12 knots. Mitchell and his crew instantly swung into an attack; the nose gunner opening fire at 800 yards' range, and a stick of six depth charges straddling the U-boat as it attempted, too late, to crash-dive.

Mitchell's aim was deadly accurate, damaging the submarine's hull sufficiently to prevent it submerging and leaving it wallowing helplessly on the surface. Unable to inflict further damage, Mitchell

*Later, Wing Commander, OBE, DFC.

(Above) Setting out.

(Left) 99 Squadron Wim
prang, February 1944.

circled the 'sitting duck' and sent off urgent signals for other aircraft and/or RN vessels to come and complete the destruction.

Over the next 48 hours six further aircraft attacks were made on the U-boat, while HMS *Falmouth*, escorting a convoy from Mombasa to Aden, was ordered to the scene to administer the *coup de grâce*. The aerial attacks were made by 621 squadron crews, but included one by an 8 Squadron Wellington, HZ703, 'B', skippered by Flight Sergeant McGivney on 3 May. When HMS *Falmouth* finally reached the area, and before it could engage, the submarine's commander, Heinz Eck, ordered his vessel, *U-852*, to be scuttled and set afire. Subsequently, Flight Lieutenant Mitchell and one of his Wop/AGs, Flight Sergeant W.R. Stevenson, were awarded a DFC and DFM respectively, while the U-boat commander, Eck, along with two of his senior officers, were eventually sentenced to death by a military court in Hamburg after the war for the murder of British and Allied seamen from the steamer *Peleus* which *U-852* had encountered only weeks before its ultimate action.

A further addition to Wellington units in the Far East zones was No 203 Squadron, a former Martin Baltimore unit based in North Africa, which was moved to Santa Cruz in November 1943 and re-equipped with Mk XIII Wellingtons for maritime roles over the Indian Ocean, commanded by Wing Commander C.A. Masterman, OBE,DFC (later, Group Captain). Like its counterpart anti-shipping squadrons, Nos 8, 244, and 621, the squadron flew consistent operational sorties with little material success for the remaining months of the war, yet all performed a vital 'deterrent' to enemy shipping in the vast areas they patrolled. In the event Nos 8 and 244 Squadrons were disbanded, both on 1 May 1945; 203 Squadron exchanged its Wellingtons for Liberators in November 1944; while 621 Squadron ceased maritime operations by the end of May 1945 and took up more sedentary transport roles until November 1945, when it moved back to North Africa, based at Mersa Matruh, and then in the following month converted from Wellingtons to their stablemates, Vickers Warwicks.

In India the two Wellington bomber units, Nos 99 and 215 Squadrons, remained operational until the autumn of 1944 before re-equipping with Liberators. Prime targets, as with all strike aircraft serving in the Far East theatre of operations, tended to be all forms of enemy lines of communications – rivers, roads, railways, bridges, etc – but were by no means confined to them. On 10 February 1944, for example, a daylight raid was mounted against a

Japanese headquarters and troop concentration at Godusara near the Arakan front. Flight Lieutenant J.R. Sutton, skippering a 215 Squadron Wellington LN703, 'A', accompanied by two more 99 Squadron Wimpys and nine USAAF B-25s, set out at 1520 hrs. Sutton's Wimpy was a modified variant, carrying a 4000lb 'Cookie' bomb, and he scored a direct hit on the south-east village area, totally devastating the eastern half as well as obliterating the nearby road. Once the smoke and debris settled, the crews reported that the eastern half of the target was now just a 'large brown patch'. On that occasion the bombers had been shepherded by a fighter escort of 35 Spitfires, though no opposition was met.

Next day, Wimpy LN703 in company with three other Wellingtons and escorted by six Hurricanes and six Spitfires, attacked Hparabyin village with its adjacent enemy troop concentration and stores depot, north and south of the Nyaung Chaung. LN703's 'Cookie' landed just north of the Chaung, throwing up a huge mushroom of smoke and debris which lingered, preventing observation of results.

The legendary ability of a Wellington to absorb damage and/or technical problems and yet still fly was exemplified on many occasions in India and Burma. In the evening of 7/8 February 1944, for an instance Flight Sergeant J.W.C. Nixon took off in Wellington 'K' of 215 Squadron intending to attack Toungoo airfield, but some 40 minutes after leaving Jessore part of the fabric skin of the starboard wing calmly detached itself, leaving the geodetics exposed. Nixon decided it was unsafe to continue to the primary target – and coolly proceeded to attack Akyab instead, where his bombs started a series of fires visible 30 miles away! His eventual return to Jessore at 2034 hrs was 'uneventful' (*sic*) . . .

A previous raid against Akyab which set out from the same base, Jessore (roughly 80 miles north of Calcutta), had a rather different conclusion. On 7 September 1943 Flying Officer David M. Allan, DFC, of 99 Squadron left base in Wellington HE663, 'T' at dusk with Akyab as his primary objective. The subsequent events are described by Allan's Wop/AG, Laurie Butler:

We set off about 1800 hrs but had not reached the target when the port engine failed. David (Allan) decided to return to base, so we jettisoned the bombs in the bay and threw out anything we didn't need including the guns and ammunition etc. It was to no avail and we slowly lost height. Dave gave the 'Prepare for ditching'

NC828, 'H' of 621 Squadron at Khormaksar, Aden, May 1945.

Flt Lt R.H. Mitchell, DFC (R) and Flt Sgt W.R. Stevenson, DFM of 621 Squadron, Aden, 1944.

order, which I may add was a well rehearsed procedure by us, having practised it many times on the ground, so we all knew what to do. The navigator, Sergeant Chopping, gave me our position and I sent that with an SOS for as long as I was able – the message was in fact received at base and in other areas, as we were told later.

The pilot remained in his seat, naturally, while the navigator left his normal position and sat next to the skipper. I sat on the floor with my back to entrance to the cockpit, and the bomb aimer, Sergeant Dacey, and rear gunner, Sergeant Radmore, sat in the centre of the fuselage with their backs to the main beam, just below the astro-dome. Obviously, it was always difficult for a pilot to know how high he was above the sea, so we usually got the wireless operator to lower the training aerial, continuing to send the SOS, and when the aerial touched the sea we knew we'd be 80 feet above the water, or thereabouts. I can remember calling out to Dave that we were '80 feet' – the set went dead – when there was an almighty crash as we hit the sea in the dark. I also remember getting up and attempting to get out of the door when I realised I was going the wrong way – I should have been going towards the rear to follow the bomb aimer and rear gunner out of the astro-dome. Then a rush of water enveloped me and I was convinced I'd had it and was drowning.

The next thing I knew I was floating about on the surface, though how I got there I'll never know. I couldn't hear or see anyone, but after shouting for some time I heard an answer in the distance and swam towards that sound. When I reached it I found Dave and the navigator together, but not in the dinghy which was uninflated, just a mass of rubber floating onto which they were hanging. I joined them and we all three started shouting for the other two – but received no answer. Both had apparently gone down with the aircraft.

Butler and Allen spent the next few hours trying to inflate the dinghy by the hand bellows attached, and on initially achieving this, tried to get the navigator aboard – he had seemingly broken one or both legs – only to have the dinghy immediately deflate. An examination found an 18-inch rip in the dinghy side, but by experimenting they soon found that if they kept that side under water the dinghy would retain its air. Having reflated the dinghy, the injured navigator was shoved aboard, then Butler and Allan took turn and turn about to 'spell' each other either on board or clinging to the side ropes in the sea. With the dawn the sea was rough and it rained hard, but the survivors now sorted out the emergency kit aboard – Very pistol, cartridges, a mirror, tins of fresh water, some Horlicks tablets, and a small medical kit. Giving the injured man a morphia shot, Allan and Butler settled down to (hopefully) await rescue, scanning the skies.

In mid-morning, as the sea got rougher, they saw about a mile away a waterspout stretching up to some 2500 feet coming towards them. The whirling spout came close, then actually circled the dinghy, before finally collapsing about half an hour later, leaving the sea with mountainous waves in its wake. A little later an aircraft was spotted and several Very cartridges fired but they were not seen by the searching pilot. However, shortly after a second aircraft flew over the dinghy at very low altitude and Butler fired one of the last three Very cartridges, which described an arc right over the aircraft's rear gun turret! It was now about 1 pm and Butler signalled to the aircraft that the dinghy was leaking and there were no provisions aboard. Two hours later a DC3 arrived and dropped a number of packs including an inflated dinghy. Laurie Butler concludes his description:

We were unable to get that dinghy because the sea was too rough and it floated away; while of about seven packs dropped I only managed to retrieve one. To our disgust this only contained drinking water – we found later that the others contained hot soup, food, coffee, clothing, etc!

The aircraft continued to fly round us and when dusk came he started to drop flame floats around us. We thought we were in for another night in the dinghy and, to be quite honest, we doubted if we could make it. However, a little later – I was in the water at the time – I saw a light in the distance which eventually transpired to be an Air Sea Rescue Launch. This picked us up and took us to Chittagong, 163 miles away. Next day they flew the navigator to Dacca, and a 99 Squadron Wellington picked Dave and me up and returned us to the squadron, where we spent two weeks in hospital and then were sent on leave before resuming flying.

Laurie Butler, despite a later bout of illness, completed his first tour of operations with 99 Squadron, then eventually flew a second tour with No 117 Squadron's Dakotas, supply-dropping to the 14th Army. It should be added that he had the 'honour' of being among the crew which flew the ultimate Wellington bombing sortie over

JA259, 'N–Nan', 621 Squadron, en route Salalah-to-Khormaksar on 14 May 1945. This aircraft also served on 8 Squadron.

Burma, on 15 August 1944 attacking Pinlebu.

Laurie Butler was also one of many Wellington crews of 99 and 215 Squadrons who played a small but vital part in the crucial Battle of Imphal during March to July 1944. In the initial phases of that battle – which was coincidental with a siege of Allied troops at Kohima – supplies were air-dropped in primarily by Dakotas of the veteran Nos 31 and 194 Squadrons, but by mid-May the need for supplies of bombs for the Imphal Hurricane fighter-bombers brought the Wellingtons of 99 and 215 Squadrons into the fray directly; whereas until then they had been mainly engaged in normal long-range straight bombing support operations.

The first Wimpy bomb-delivered sorties commenced on 19 May when both units carried stocks of 250lb HE bombs from Jessore to Kumbhirgram where they (the bombs) were stock-piled ready for actual delivery. On 21 May the Wellingtons were 'detached' to No 177 Wing for immediate control, and next day began the delivery of the bombs into the valley. Over the following weeks such flights continued, despite the ever-looming possibility of aerial attack by Japanese fighters each day and a gradual deterioration in weather conditions, in addition to the 'normal' hazards of operating low over the Burma jungle.

Yet in spite of such daily dangers, only one Wellington was actually shot down by the Japanese during those re-supply sorties. On 17 June Squadron Leader Anthony S.R. Ennis, DSO, DFC of 99

Squadron set out in Wimpy MZ719 and made three delivery flights of bombs, then took off again to fly to Kumbhirgram. Shortly after mid-day his Wellington was seen to fall in flames into Japanese-held territory, a victim of roving enemy 'Oscar' fighters.

Apart from operating their own Wellingtons for these supply sorties, a number of Wimpy air crews were 'lent' to the Dakota squadrons temporarily to replace exhausted 'Dak' crews or at least supplement them while the Imphal battle was at its peak. Once the siege of Imphal had been 'lifted' and the Japanese besieging armies forced to retreat, the Wellingtons returned to their prime roles of attacking the enemy by long-range bombing in support of the Allied offensive during the height of the July-August 1944 monsoon.

These last operations proved to be the virtual swan-song for the Wellington as a pure bomber in the Burma campaigns. By November 1944 their task had been taken over by specially modified B-24 Liberators which could penetrate far deeper into the back areas and attack strategic objectives. Thus, on 1 December 1944, the ACSEA Order of Battle included just three Wellington units: Nos 8, 244, and 621 Squadrons, all under the aegis of No 222 Group HQ, Colombo. By 1 May 1945 only 621 Squadron with its establishment for 16 aircraft remained within the control of the Command; and by 1 August that year no Wellington units appeared on either ACSEA or RAF Burma strength.

CHAPTER TWELVE

From the Cockpits

What was the Wellington like to fly? Any individual answer to such a generic question will patently depend upon a combination of variables. Which Mark? Which operational role? Which war theatre? With or without a 'war load'? And for that matter, how experienced was the pilot before he first piloted any Wimpy? Perhaps the overall comment of one ferry pilot in the Air Transport Auxiliary (ATA), Hugh Bergel, may epitomise the views of the vast majority of Wellington pilots, when he recorded*:

> The Wellington was universally loved. It was the first big aeroplane flown by ATA pilots who had converted to Class IV on the Blenheim, but it was such a docile and friendly thing that this worried nobody. Because, I suppose, its unique geodetic construction was more flexible than the normal all-metal monocoque construction, it had the habit – not in the least disconcerting – of twitching slightly from time to time as it rattled along; it was almost as if it was wagging its tail at you. It was very easy to fly (though a bit marginal if one engine failed), and the view from the cockpit was good enough to make it one of the better aeroplanes for bad weather flying. And it was exceptionally easy to land.

Bergel's opinion was shared by a fellow ferry pilot, H.A. Taylor:

> Once a pilot had become accustomed to its minor quirks of behaviour and its oddly assorted controls, he found it to be a delightfully easy and forgiving affair. However much the structure quaked in rough air – with the control column wandering erratically backwards and forwards as the elevator cables moved to match the flexings of the fuselage – no one ever had any doubt about the strength of geodetic construction. We knew, too, that it

*Flying Wartime Aircraft by H. Bergel; David & Charles, 1972 was *meant* to flex.*

However, flying a Wellington, lightly loaded, across peaceful skies over Britain can hardly be compared with piloting a maximum-loaded Wimpy through flak and nightfighter air over Germany, or in any other operational theatre. Yet pilots' opinions remained remarkably consistent in praise and affection for the design, A.J. Payne – 'Tony' – first met Wellingtons in April 1942 when he joined No 26 Course at Edge Hill, satellite to 21 OTU, Moreton-in-Marsh:

Rumour had it that our course, No 26, was the first to pass out without a fatality; if this was so it soon became plain that luck played as big a part as judgment. The Wellington proved to be a good-natured beast, of aluminium extended basket-weave construction with a fabric skin which absorbed a great deal of abuse before complaining – from friend or foe! However, it drew the line at towing gliders; it was reliably reported that after the ignominy of having its tail jerked a few times by a Horsa glider on tow, the fuselage was found to have stretched by 18 inches! To a pilot new to twins it proved easy to fly and I surprised everyone – including myself – by going solo in less than three hours. Take-off and landing were leisurely, viceless affairs in contrast to, say, the Harvard.

With the tail up the view over the front turret was comprehensive, while satisfying three-pointers soon became second nature, though without flaps the landing attitude was struck as one crossed the boundary hedge at an indicated 100 mph. Clottishly, I failed to appreciate this at the first attempt, banging the tail-wheel down first and ruffling the rear gunner's feathers. Single-engine procedures were not mentioned; it was just accepted that with an engine out one was faced with a gradual loss of height†, but fortunately the Pegasus was very reliable, even the much-travelled ones put out to grass at OTUs.

The part played by luck showed up on our first night solo trip. The captain had first go and after a couple of circuits under the instructor's gaze we were on our own. VAs completed, we received our 'Green' from the caravan, swung onto the runway, lined up and applied the brakes. At this point the damage was done. Unhappily,

* *Test Pilot at War* by H.A. Taylor; Ian Allan, 1970
† Referring only to the Mk Ics flown at the OTU here.

the button on top of the control column was slipped across so that when – at zero boost and 2000 revs – the spectacle grips were released, we stayed put with the brakes locked on. Nothing daunted, more coal was poured on until we were at full power – 2600 revs and max boost. Still no joy.

At this point everything happened at once. Deciding, as the subsequent Court of Inquiry made clear, that full flap had been selected instead of five degrees, the hapless pilot went to take corrective action to reduce the impeding drag. In the gloom he chose the wrong lever and retracted the undercarriage. Came a crash which broke the aircraft's back. The props, spinning at peak revs, snapped off, thereby allowing the thus uninhibited engines to achieve unheard-of decibels. The propellers were found next morning a good 200 yards up the runway. The starboard one in its highly dynamic state took great bits out of the nose of the aircraft as it rocketed forward – the first bare inches in front of my right knee. The various crew members ejected rapidly through sundry orifices into a dust-laden environment none the worse – and two days later I found myself promoted to the left-hand seat.

Luck was around on another Edge Hill occasion. Back from a solo night cross-country, we were cleared to land but on the final approach descended into an inversion so that all the windows of our chilled Wimpy misted up completely in the warm air just as we were lining up with the runway. The goose-neck flares, usually sharply defined, were reduced to a cluster of smudgy blobs, so that a relative certainty was switched to a wild gamble. Obliged to go by the book, as the blobs gradually converged, a tentative round-out was begun and we waited somewhat breathlessly for the bump or bumps. None came, but suddenly we were straddling the line of flares as we veered onto the grass. In all honesty I can say that nobody on board detected the touch-down – my guardian angel was obviously working overtime that spring night! However, the expletives which accompanied our arrival went out over the air-waves – after requesting landing clearance I'd omitted to switch off my microphone, to the considerable embarrassment of the station WAAF R/T operators . . .

H.D. Rogers flew Wellingtons from an OTU in early 1940 to January 1941, and again in 1942-43, and after re-enlistment postwar, yet again on his refresher course in 1949. Just a few of his impressions of those early Mk I, IC, and Mk II Wimpys remain clear:

How heavier on the controls the Mk Ias and Ics were after the Mk I . . . how noisier, and with more vibration, were the Mk IIs . . . the mid-under 'dustbin' turret, when lowered, dropped the speed by some 20 mph, while visibility from this turret was poor, and if one includes its weight, it was a pretty useless appendage. It was impossible to land with the turret down, even with its footwell retracted, and at least one crew, having suffered hydraulic failure, cut the rear hand-rail ropes off and attached rope to the turret, then passed the rope over the overhead geodetics and hauled the turret up into a locked position in order to land . . . the earlier Marks of Wimpy had no cabin heating and were *very* cold and draughty, leading to some cases of frostbite, particularly among crew members taking part in the leaflet raids, with aircraft flying higher than when carrying a bomb load; 12,000 feet was the practical cruising height for a Mk Ic with a bomb load . . . the propeller de-icing fluid tanks carried only a limited supply of fluid, so one waited until ice formed, then turned the fluid slingers on . . . the ice flying off the props broke through the fuselage side fabric and put the wireless operator in some danger. Eventually, metal plates were fixed to the fuselage to prevent this . . .

We were issued with 'hot bags', which consisted of a double-lined rubber bag containing lime. Water was poured into the bags and, when placed in the Sidcot suit leg pockets, enabled one to warm one hand at a time. An occasional shake-up helped the reaction between lime and water and warmed the bag up. As their useful time was short, we used to take some with us dry and use a drop or two of coffee – or other fluids I'd better not mention – to warm up the bags . . .'

'Artie' Ashworth, later Wing Commander, DSO, DFC, AFC, was born in Gisborne, New Zealand, and joined the RNZAF in September 1939, then transferred to the RAF in June 1940, and as a sprog Pilot Officer, joined his first operational unit, No 75 (NZ) Squadron on 25 January 1941 to fly Wellingtons – until which date he had only *seen* inside a Wimpy once. By his 21st birthday, on 3 May 1941, Ashworth had flown a total of 12 operational sorties as second pilot to three different skippers, and accumulated 77 hrs 45 minutes flying time as 'second dicky', plus 10 hrs 55 mins as captain of a Wellington – yet had never landed a Wellington at night!

His first *operational* sortie as a Wimpy captain came on 8 May – to bomb submarine yards at Hamburg – which he completed, despite flak damage, safely. His 65th Wellington operational sortie – his last at the helm of a Wimpy – was flown some 16 months later, by which time 'Artie' was a Squadron Leader on the Air Staff of Don Bennett's PFF HQ at RAF Wyton. It very nearly proved to be his ultimate flight in *any* aircraft . . .

19 September 1942 began as a normal wartime day. The target for the night came through from Bomber Command to the Operations Room at PFF HQ, Wyton where I was one of Group Captain (later, AVM) Don Bennett's merry men. The target was Saarbrücken and I got permission from the Group Captain to fly that night. So I rang Wing Commander T.S. Rivett-Carnac (always known as 'Nuts & Bolts'), the CO of No 156 Squadron at Warboys, and asked for the loan of a Wellington and a crew. This was readily agreed. Unexpectedly, later that morning, my brother, a fighter pilot in the RNZAF, 'phoned from the railway station to say that he had arrived to see me.

We took off from Warboys with a load of 12 three-inch flares and six 250lb bombs. The flares were to be used to illuminate the target for the rest of the bombers. I'd never seen the crew before – and it was to be quite a long time before I wanted so to do . . . The first sign of trouble was a smell of burning – no smoke, or at least none where I was. We were somewhere near the target at the time and had been for quite a while, flying up and down and trying to get the reflection of the moon in the river. There was haze on the ground and we needed the river to pinpoint our objective. A few seconds after I'd noticed the smell of burning, the wireless operator came through the intercom with the information that sparks were coming through the floor. I wasn't all that worried – it might have been anything, say, an electrical fault; all sorts of odd things happened to one in the air over wartime Germany. So we went round again, still searching for the river, which took about five minutes, then the wireless operator came through again, saying that there were more sparks coming through the floor. He also said he was standing by with a fire extinguisher. I realised then that we must be on fire somewhere and guessed it was one of the flares – these being in the bomb bays and unreachable from inside the aircraft – so decided to jettison the flares. The bomb aimer let them go and suddenly there was a blinding light all round the aircraft and what appeared to be flames underneath us. Looking over my shoulder through the window it seemed to me that the whole of the

(Above) Crews of 75(NZ) Squadron, early 1941.

(Right) Wg Cdr A 'Artie' Ashworth, DSO,DFC,AFC.

rear of the aircraft was on fire. I had enough experience – this being my 65th op in a Wimpy – of watching Wellingtons destroyed by fire in the air – they seldom lasted long – so right away said, 'OK. Bale out!'

I felt the rear gunner go at once because his turret turned. The rest seemed to take a devil of a long time. I yelled and swore at them to get on with it but I doubt if they heard me. It was possibly here that the confusion over parachutes arose, and one of them may have got the impression that I was telling him to take mine. At last all the others were clear – I saw a couple of them sliding out in the light from underneath me, just for an instant, I could see their bodies falling. It was now my turn and I came dashing out of my seat to follow but, horror of horrors, my parachute had gone! It should have been in the stowage just forward of the cockpit on the starboard side, but I quickly realised that one of the others had taken it in the confusion. I went back along the fuselage – it's amazing how quickly one can move in an emergency – to see if I could find the missing one. The glare was still with me and now a great deal of smoke. I looked in the navigator's and wireless operator's stowages and the rear stowage above the bed – nothing – and all I could do was to return to my seat.

At first I could not think of anything to do – I'm sure this was due to a state of numb fear. Then I had an 'inspiration' – if I could get to the ground very quickly I might be able to crash-land the aircraft before it broke up. So, throttling back, I did the classic 'Action to be taken in the event of fire in the air' – sideslipping viciously from side to side. I was down to about 800 feet when suddenly the glare went out. The burning bit of flare caught in the bomb bay had broken off, though I didn't know that until later.

After all the glare my eyes weren't much use to me and it took quite a while before I could see the instruments properly, but I still had control. It seemed pretty hopeless to try to get back home alone, but then I hadn't a lot of alternatives except to try. Climbing to 5,000 feet, I left the controls and went back to the navigator's position to see what I could find. I found a map but most of the nav's stuff was lying about all over the floor. His log would have been useful, but I couldn't find it (it was found next morning on the floor). Popping back from the controls again to the nav's position, and using his protractor, I marked out a course and drew a line to England. I didn't really know where I was until I hit the French

T2835, AA–C, 75(NZ) Squadron, which later served on 12 OTU.

75(NZ) Squadron crew, Feltwell, 1941. L–R: Sgt Ted McSherry; Plt Off 'Artie' Ashworth; Plt Off Wilson (an Englishman, despite the RAAF uniform); Sgt Broad.

coast. There was some flak and searchlights to mark the position of Dieppe – recognisable by the angle of the coast to North. From here on it was plain sailing. From a quarter of an hour before the French coast there was nothing showing on the petrol gauges, so I had the engines running as economically as possible. I didn't care what part of England I hit and when I was about halfway across the Channel I switched the IFF to the 'Distress' position – it was very dark.

I had just sighted the English coast when both engines cut. I ran back down the fuselage to turn on one of the nacelle tanks. Normally, this was done by simply pulling a piece of wire in the side of the fuselage, but in this aircraft a trap for young players had been incorporated so that in order to pull the wire it was first necessary to slide a ring on the end of the wire to that it would slip through a slot in the aircraft's side. Using a strength born of a wild desperation index, I pulled the angle-poise light from the wireless operator's position round a strut to find out this fact, then pulled the wire which started the engine, then raced forward desperately to the cockpit. Here I could pull up the cross-feed cock and start the other engine.

After a few minutes I was over England and was guided to West Malling in Kent by searchlights – for which I was *very* grateful. After landing I was directed to a parking spot on the edge of the airfield. The engines now wouldn't stop, so I left them running and opened the bomb doors. After climbing down the ladder I moved aft to the bomb bay and there I found a parachute caught up in one of the bomb racks. Pulling the cords of the parachute, I could see that there was a round object at the end. At first I was distressed when I imagined that it was part of the crew, but it turned out to be the broken flare which had caused all the trouble. I rang Wyton to get someone to reassure my brother that I was OK. The 'missing' parachute I eventually found on the bed below the rear stowage. Next day I went back to base – by train!

One knotty point about flying Wellingtons was whether a Wimpy would (or could) continue flying with one engine defunct – an argument which has continued to the present day among Wellington men. John L. Whitworth, DFC, knew Wellingtons well, having been trained on them at 21 OTU initially, then completing a 37-sorties' tour of operations with No 37 Squadron in North Africa, and on return to the UK, instructing on Wimpys at 26 OTU, Wing until mid-1944, when he volunteered for the PFF and returned to the 'sharp end' flying Mosquitos with 142 and 162 Squadrons. His personal views on the one-motor debate are succinct:

> The whole matter resolves on which engines you had in your Wimpy. Most OTUs and many squadrons, until late 1942, had Pegasus-engined aircraft (Mk Is and Ics). Those with Merlins (Mk IIs) and Hercules engines (Mk IIIs & Xs) had approximately 25% and 50% more BHP respectively *and* feathering airscrews, which made maintaining height on one much more possible. The Pegasus was a wonderfully tough engine but had two major flaws – a non-feathering airscrew, and a high oil consumption and leakage problem. Ask any 2nd Dicky about this! He or the wireless operator will remember the oil reserve tank in the fuselage and so many pumps to each engine per hour! And the poor Erks who had to clean the nacelles and wings with best 100-Octane! When leaks and consumption got bad, down went the oil pressure and up oil and cylinder head temperatures. More pumps until the oil ran out! Eventually the engine would seize – you couldn't feather so had to flog along on minimum power and a windmilling prop until that happened. The airscrew would then churn itself off and drop away. Fire would break out but usually blew itself out helped by the extinguisher. I was never sure whether you were better off without the prop or not, but this happened to me twice on ops, and to two of my fellow Wimpy 'drivers'.
>
> The first time – my third op, as second dicky, was over the desert on 29 July 1942 in Wimpy Ic, DV429 of 37 Squadron. We flew for about two hours from 10,000 feet and just got back over the battle lines to the edge of the Qattara Depression before literally, deliberately flying into the ground – every mile mattered. A terrific impact in the dark but it didn't break up and we all walked out. A wonderful bit of flying by our Aussie skipper, Flying officer 'Mick' Moran – so sadly killed a few days later. The second time I flew back after about 1½ hours from 8,000 feet and made base with wheels down on 6 November 1942 in Z8908. Got a 'Mention', and the aircraft was repaired, re-engined, and flew again in a few days. We reckoned a good Mk Ic in the Middle East lost about 100 feet per minute 'on one', provided you had no load and could dump some petrol but couldn't maintain height. A great aircraft, the old Wimpy.

A.V. Rippengal, DFC, DFM – 'Tony' – had a fairly extended

acquaintance with a variety of Wellingtons. Starting with Mk Ics at 15 OTU, he ferried a Mk X to North Africa, then joined No 40 Squadron and completed two operational tours flying Mks I, III, and Xs. Returning to the UK in April 1945, he next added a Mk XIV to his log book and finally reverted to Mk Xs on a refresher course at Finningley in 1949. His experiences with the various Marks are therefore of particular interest.

I first met the Wellington at 15 OTU, Harwell on 19 January 1943. I was a fairly new Sergeant pilot* with some 280 flying hours to my credit on nothing much bigger than an Oxford. Moreover, I'd done my flying training in the USA under ideal conditions and on quite modern aircraft (for those days). Since November 1942 I'd been rehabilitated to English weather conditions and got to grips with the rather basic equipment of an Oxford. I was very impressed with the sheer size of the Wellington, an impression reinforced by the fact that I thought the airfield was really too small for it. The undercarriage was almost as wide as the taxy-ways and the least deviation invariably led to disaster. My first efforts to taxy the beast inevitably led to such chaos! As soon as any sort of wind caught that big tail, the aircraft demonstrated that it was completely in control. My efforts to resume command via the brakes were usually thwarted. The aircraft at the OTU were all Mark Ics and the air compressor supplying the brakes was woefully inadequate. About two good applications of brake were enough to exhaust the system and it then took 15-20 minutes of high rpm to restore the pressure – which was a bit tricky with no brakes!

My relations with my instructor were a little cool during the early stages but eventually I came to terms with the problem. Once airborne, however, I felt a lot happier. The Wimpy did not suffer from any vices that I can recall and was even quite tolerant of some mishandling. It did not even complain when operational 'exigencies' forced one to explore the limits of its powers. Happily, the Mk III onwards enjoyed some better equipment and a much-improved brake compressor obviated the early problems. I do, however, remember one or two shortcomings, though I suspect these were probably common to most of our aircraft of that era. Foremost was the heating which was variable, to say the least. The

*Later, Flight Lieutenant, DFC, DFM.

rear gunner usually had to rely on his Irvin jacket – and this was in Africa and Italy, so I felt sorry for those who operated over Europe in winter. The other problem was the auto-pilot which was also variable in performance and liable to give some nasty surprises. However, in view of our conditions of sand and dust in the desert, I think it's surprising that so much worked as well as it did. I cannot remember ever missing an op because my aircraft was unserviceable, nor did one ever let me down in the air. That I think must be my principal tribute not only to the Wellington, but also to our splendid servicing ground crews.

Lastly, I must mention the engine. The Pegasus as fitted to the Mk Ic were no doubt adequate in themselves but left the aircraft badly underpowered when it came to a full load. This was brought home to me in the heat of North Africa. We had a load of rodded bombs and a 4000 ft-high range of mountains to cross. Having climbed to about 3500 feet the aircraft refused to go any higher, while the engines were on their top temperature limits. It became necessary to divert to an emergency landing ground – complete with rodded bombs! The Mk III onwards, fitted with the various Hercules engines of 1750hp upwards, completely tranformed the Wellington and enabled it to do everything that was asked of it. These Marks I remember with great affection. In retrospect, I think the Wellington was a splendid aircraft – but I do wish those propeller tips hadn't been right outside my windows!

One of many Wimpy skippers who can testify to the ability of the aircraft to 'bring 'em back alive' on one engine is John R. Sutton, DFC. John flew operations in Wellingtons with Nos 99 and 215 Squadrons in the Far East theatre, and then ended his war as an instructor at 76 OTU, Aqir in Palestine. On the night of 25 October 1943 he piloted Wellington LB141, 'F' of 215 Squadron on a bombing raid against the enemy-occupied railway station at Sagaing. Leaving Jessore at 1606 hrs, he reached the target and released his load accurately on the station, starting some fires, but as he completed his bombing run his starboard engine failed completely. At that moment the Wellington was at 9000 ft and Sutton set off for a return flight to Chittagong – a journey of almost 300 miles which meant 'negotiating' mountains rising to 10,000 ft en route. His skill and determination paid off and he landed safely at Chittagong at 2230 hrs.

'Missing' engines were by no means the only problems for operational Wellington pilots, and the design's universal reputation

Rear fuselage of Wellington HE158, NA–L, 428 Squadron RCAF on its return from Duisburg, 9 April 1943. Its pilot, Sgt L.F. Williamson, received a CGM.

for sheer toughness in construction was justified on myriad occasions as Wimpy skippers and their crews struggled with aircraft with chunks of airframe and large areas of fabric shot away or burned off, and yet contrived to 'arrive' back safely.

One outstanding example occurred on the night of 8/9 April 1943 when a force of 392 bombers left UK bases to attack Duisburg. Among that force were 97 Wellingtons, including HE158, NA-L, of No 428 ('Ghost') Squadron RCAF, based at Dalton, and skippered that night by Sergeant Leonard F. Williamson, RCAF. Over the target 'L-for-Leather' received a direct hit in the rear fuselage from flak and shuddered violently. Williamson felt his rudder controls go slack, but continued with his bombing run-in, released his bomb load, then swung out of the danger zone. As Williamson set course for home he checked around for damage and casualties. The Wellington was obviously in bad shape – its hydraulics had been ruptured, leaving the undercarriage sagging down and the bomb doors remained open – so Williamson gave an order to his crew to be prepared to bale out. Each crew member acknowledged except the rear gunner, so Williamson sent his navigator back to see what was wrong.

The nav's report came as a shock – the rear turret and its occupant had been sliced away by the flak, while half the rudder fabric and yards of rear fuselage skinning had been ripped away, leaving the geodetic skeleton framework exposed. With minimal control, Williamson determined to bring his remaining crew home and finally succeeded. His courage and skill were officially acknowledged by the award of a Conspicuous Gallantry Medal (CGM) shortly after. Williamson was no exception to a host of Wellington captains who found themselves in charge of 'half a Wimpy' with hundreds of miles between themselves and a 'friendly' airfield. On the night of 6/7 July 1944, for example, Warrant Officer Custance was at the helm of Wellington LP130, 'D' of No 70 Squadron attacking the city of Budapest when another aircraft appeared from nowhere and collided. On recovering control of his aircraft Custance found that ten feet had been sheared off his Wellington's port mainplane – yet he brought 'D' back to the squadron base, Tortorella in Italy.

Yet another Wellington crew member who can testify to the strength of the aircraft is Flight Lieutenant C.L. Jones, an Air Observer who flew with Nos 9, 75 (NZ), 214 and 215 Squadrons and, later, at No 11 OTU – all in Wimpys, between September 1939 and November 1942 – during which period he survived several serious crashes:

To illustrate the strength and resilience of the Wimpy, on the night of 15/16 July 1940 we were in Wellington P9231, 'A' of 9 Squadron returning from a raid on Bottrop in the Ruhr Valley, and soon after leaving the target we ran into thick cloud which developed into severe electrical storms out over the North Sea. Suddenly came a loud explosion and thick smoke from the radio cabin. The wireless operator was unconscious on the floor – it appeared that he'd not wound up the trailing aerial and we'd been struck by lightning. A report from the rear gunner said that the aircraft was on fire, but when I climbed up into the astro-dome I could see that the whole aircraft was shrouded in a thick blanket of green light caused by St Elmo's fire, which persisted for a long time. Then the skipper reported that his magnetic compass was playing tricks, its needle oscillating badly, as was my own compass. So we decided to rely on the directional gyro compass, resetting this five degrees at 15-minute intervals.

Some ten minutes after ETA Base we were still in thick cloud even at 500 feet, with the whole crew on look-out. Lights were seen briefly and we circled and picked up what proved to be a gooseneck flarepath. This put doubts in our mind as to what sort of airfield it might be, but the skipper decided that he'd seen enough to convince him that it was an authentic airfield and decided to land without further ado, despite still only catching brief glimpses of the flares. The approach was anything but normal as we were not seeing the flares continuously – then we hit the ground with an almighty crash and bounced back into the cloud layer, but eventually hit the ground again and came to rest. In the silence which followed voices were heard outside and when we all got out we were promptly arrested by some soldiers! We had landed on a dummy airfield at Nazing Common, near North Weald. There were no injuries to the crew except for bruises and when daylight came it became obvious why we had bounced so high. Deep trenches had been dug and the earth banked up on the leading side, so we had hit one such banking and cleaned the undercarriage completely off. P9231 seemed to me a complete write-off* yet none of us had suffered injuries.

A second occasion was the first 1,000-raid against Cologne on 30/31 May 1942 when I was at 11 OTU, Bassingbourn. We were

*In fact, P9231 was repaired, re-issued and flown to India on 22 June 1944, where it was finally struck-off RAF charge on 1 January 1947. Author.

'allocated Wellington W5705, an aircraft with a bad reputation which had been confined to just circuits and bumps for a long time. The first air test revealed the aircraft's idiosyncrasies. On landing approach with 15-degrees of flap, when the engine revs were reduced, the aircraft tended to yaw and sink to a dangerous degree. The aircraft was declared u/s (*unserviceable*) and after a long series of tests over the next six days it was decided to 'recruit' a high level team to fly in the aircraft to see whether the problems were due to pilots or the aircraft. This 'crew' comprised the CTO (Chief Technical Officer), the Assistant CTO, two Flying Officer engineers, and three senior NCO fitters – it was so crowded on board that the Assistant CTO was back behind me sitting on the main spar. On the approach, with engines throttled back, there was a scream from the Assistant CTO – the trouble had been found! The fish-plates' holes – the plates joining the port and starboard sections of the main spar – had worn and elongated, allowing the section to 'float and pinch'; taking a large slice off the Assistant CTO's bottom! The rest of the day was spent in rectifying this with spacers and washers!

We were briefed for a 2230 hrs' take-off but I didn't get access to the aircraft until 1800 hrs and still had to swing the compass and loop aerial. We duly took off and bombed the target, but on the return we had severe engine trouble on the port side. It appeared to indicate lack of oil so I went to the pump abaft the main spar and pumped some oil through but this did no good. Eventually the port airscrew fell off and control of the aircraft was lost. It took both the pilot and myself to regain control – this all happening just short of the Dutch coast. We continued on our way, gradually losing height and soon down to 6,000 feet. After discussing all possibilities, it seemed quite obvious we wouldn't make land so it was decided to land in the sea near a rescue buoy if at all possible. We found such a buoy on our track and dropped a smoke float in preparation for ditching, when the rear gunner reported lights. These turned out to be Very lights, the colours of the day, being fired up on our crossing the English coast. These seemed so close that we decided to land and crossed the coast at a bare 600 feet. We were bound to run out of air space soon so I went back to the astro-dome to free this as an extra exit just in case.

Before I could free it, however, we ploughed through a line of poplar trees and hit the ground. I was knocked out and when I came to found myself up under the front turret! The rest of the crew were shouting for me to get out, thinking the aircraft was going to burn, so I forced myself into the pilot's seat and through the cockpit canopy. I was wearing the one-piece harness/Mae West with a CO_2 bottle – this last being activated by a metal trigger. As I was halfway out I could feel myself being crushed and began to struggle. The more I struggled, the greater the pressure – until I realised that while getting through the hatch I'd triggered the CO_2 bottle and was blowing up like a Michelin man. Again, the aircraft looked a complete write-off*, but no one had been injured – indeed, the rear gunner had remained in his turret the whole time.

For S.D. 'Darkie' Simpson, an air gunner, the Wellington played a major part in his wartime career, having flown in Mk Ics with 214 Squadron from November 1940 to August 1941, and later Mk Xs with 142 Squadron in North Africa from May to October 1943 – a total of 65 operational sorties apart from a long spell at 21 OTU in between his tours of operations. His memories of the aircraft are nostalgic, even to a degree sentimental, but when an aeroplace has borne a man safely through hundreds of hours of mortal peril who can blame him for feeling pure affection for his 'kite':

The first operational aircraft I flew in as rear gunner was 'Q-for-Queenie', 214 Squadron from Stradishall, with Sergeant Chapman as skipper. We did six trips in her. She was a scruffy old thing with a mind of her own. She took her time to reach 14,000 ft and any effort to get her above that height was not on – she knew her limits and started to 'fall off' – so we had to be content to level off at 14,000. She waddled rather than flew, squeaking and groaning her way along, and seeming to know when the navigator wanted a drift sight by flying straight and level immediately – though once the sighting was over she resumed her old ways. She tolerated 'George' very well, flying a straight and level course in 'his' clutches, and she seemed to know the flak-free zones – we didn't have a moment's trouble in that respect, but perhaps I'm not giving the Nav and skipper their due credit here! In those early days we were briefed as to target and time on target (anything up to an hour . . . .) and that was it – no designated heights, courses, or what-have-you.

*W5705 was completely refurbished and saw further service with Nos 21 and 25 OTUs, crashing at the latter unit on 30 January 1943. Author.

The sky was ours. Yet old 'Queenie' took it all in her stride, with no mechanical faults even in the coldest of weather with very little history of icing up.

I know we had a bit of engine overheating on occasion but pumping a gallon or two of oil in soon restored the pressure. She 'ponged' quite a bit, I might add – hydraulic oil and fluids, high octane, Elsan 'fluid', spilt coffee, leaky oxygen tubes and pipes, fabric dope – all combining to produce her own peculiar 'air' – but for all that was a true lady. Mind you, in saying what a marvellous aircraft 'Queenie' was, one mustn't forget the efforts of the ground crew who did a wonderful job. I cannot sing their praises too highly – always there at dispersal on our return, NCOs, Erks, and not forgetting the WAAFs.

Not every man who flew in Wellingtons looked at it through rose-tinted spectacles, however. J.A. Atkins, a Wop/AG, who eventually flew operations on Stirlings with No 149 Squadron, first met a Wimpy at 11 OTU, Westcott in April 1943:

Arriving from Gunnery School as a 'fully fledged air crew member', I climbed aboard my first Wimpy – without doubt the oldest, smelliest, dilapidated flying machine I'd seen in my life! In fairness, the serviceable Wellingtons were still being used on ops, so the throwouts and rejects were crashed into the air by sprog crews at training stations – those who flew Wellingtons on ops swore there were no better kites. For myself, I thought everything was so cramped. I was jammed so tight in the Wop's seat that any ideas of baling out in any emergency seemed not on. The outer covering was a joke – even the rain came in! On one such rainy night we were due for a cross-country training flip of about the three-hours' mark. Everything was going according to plan – navigation spot on, wireless working OK; the gremlins were having a night off – when suddenly the rear gunner started complaining, 'Who's throwing rubbish out of the window?' Even after trying to convince him that all the windows were shut he still insisted that rubbish was flying past his turret, so the skipper said, 'You're nearest, Jack. Go and see what he's on about.'

I took off my headphones, stood up, and turned to go back and sort out Curly's troubles. I thought I was floating on a cloud – there wasn't three square yards of fabric between myself and the rear turret; just lots of spars and wires! The whole lot had torn off and blown away!

I went forward and told the skipper who didn't believe a word of it, but the navigator quickly confirmed my stuttering and we cut out the final leg of our trip, getting to base as quickly as possible. We didn't mention all this to Curly in case he baled out! Patched up, this Wimpy was airborne again a couple of days later, but every Wimpy take-off and landing at OTU was an adventure. I think the WAAFs in the parachute section summed it up very well – they gave each crew member a heart-shaped perspex 'medal' which was inscribed WESTCOTT OTU – THE WORST OF YOUR TOUR IS OVER.

Another Wop/AG with good reason to remember the Wellington is Les Gore who totted up a full 600 hours in Wimpys; first at 11 OTU, Bassingbourn in February–March 1941, then an ops tour with No 75 (NZ) Squadron at Feltwell from March to July 1941, followed by a year as an instructor at 23 OTU, Pershore from where he added five more ops to his log book, including the first three 1000-bomber raids in 1942. Les survived a number of 'dicey' trips – staggering back to the UK with badly damaged Wellingtons – yet the Wimpy brought him and his crew home each time – as he describes the aircraft 'A very reliable and trusty friend'. Just two particular trips will illustrate Les Gore's reason for recalling the Wellington with gratitude in this context:

On 24 September 1941, at 23 OTU, I was in Wellington N2858, 'C3', as as W/T instructor with Sergeant Dowdswell as pilot. We were out on a routine cross-country and practice-bombing exercise with pupil navigator, wireless operator, and air gunner. I'd set my pupil an exercise to carry out and then joined the pilot at the dual control while we carried out the practice-bombing on Seagull island, Cardington Bay. Having completed a couple of runs at 10,000 feet, the pilot banked hard to starboard for a third run. There came a hard bump and within seconds we were diving hell for leather for the 'drink'! I glanced at the pilot who was pulling hard on his control column and he indicated that I should do the same on the dual control. Our joint effort couldn't move it fore and aft. The airspeed indicator showed about 300 mph with the altimeter going round like a broken clock.

The skipper had a brainwave and tried elevator trim, which did the trick, and we levelled off just below 1000 feet with the wings flapping like a swan. After we'd stopped shaking and the colour returned to our cheeks, he asked me to go back and check things out. I returned to the astro-dome to discover a gaping hole behind the starboard engine where the dinghy should have been stowed. It had inflated, broken loose, and wrapped itself around the starboard tailplane, dislodging the elevators from their runners and jamming them.

I reported our problem to base who gave us a diversion to a small airfield in North Wales, but Sergeant Dowdswell refused this because he knew that the airfield's runway ended up on a cliff edge, just short of the sea. He figured we had a better chance by returning to Pershore, using elevator trim for climb and decent aileron control.

With my help on the dual control we arrived over base, made one dummy run, then he made a perfect touchdown with the fire tender and blood-wagon (ambulance) in hot pursuit. The damage to the Wimpy was a bent main spar, starboard tail plane torn away from the fuselage with about a four-inch gap between it and the fuselage. The cause had been a panel which stove in during our turn, pressing on the release cable for the dinghy. I personally felt that Sergeant Dowdswell should have got a gong for his airmanship. Instead I got a 'rocket' for not staying with my pupil! Well, we were only a couple of mere Sergeants . . .

The other example of Wellington reliability came on the night of the third 1000-bomber raid, against Bremen on 25/26 June 1942. Les Gore was flying in Wimpy DV511, 'Z2', from 23 OTU, Pershore:

This time the target was Bremen which was hidden by cloud, but the main force had lit it up well. We were attacked by a Junkers Ju88 on our way home across Holland. One burst from him hit our hydraulics and port tanks, and we could smell the petrol leaking away. The gauges soon read zero so we thought we only had the two nacelle tanks left to get home on – or at least halfway across the North Sea at worst. We flew in on an SOS priority with a cone of lights put up by RAF Coltishall, and the faithful old Wimpy kept plugging away until – due to loss of hydraulics – we crashlanded at Coltishall. Inspection showed that in fact our tanks had resealed the damage but the gauge wires had been cut by bullets. We had no casualties though.

'Clarry' Hughes was a wartime navigator Flight Lieutenant, DFC, who flew in Wellingtons at 20 OTU, Lossiemouth, then with No 427 ('Lion') Squadron RCAF from Croft in County Durham. Starting its career with Wellington Mk IIIs in November 1942, the 'Lion' squadron began receiving Mk Xs from February 1943, operating these until the unit's eventual re-equipment with Halifax B.Vs from May 1943:

> The Wellington III and X were great aircraft to operate, having a higher operational ceiling than the Halifax. I think I'm right in saying that a Wimpy X could reach 21,000 ft, whereas the Halifax V tended to 'stick' at 19,000 ft. The trouble (from my personal point of view) with Wellingtons was the cold and draught. I normally had to stick the heating pipe into my boots to thaw out my feet, and the face microphones became iced up at altitude and only worked after stopping work to break the ice. Draught was always a problem, especially when our Wellingtons were adapted to carry a 4000lb 'Cookie' bomb. For this, on our unit, the bomb doors were removed, leaving the bomb partly outside the bomb bay and successfully deflecting a stream of icy air into the cabin. When the bomb was dropped the aircraft bounced with relief, but the back of the bomb bay then ventilated the cabin even more. Take-off was always impressive on the squadron because the CO* required 30-seconds' intervals, and one learned to move as soon as the wheels were lifted on the preceding aircraft off the runway. When we had to convert to Halifaxes no one wanted the change – which shows how the Wellington affected us.

The ability of a Wellington to continue flying in spite of seeming odds was demonstrated on myriad occasions – even when *both* engines were out . . . Bob Pearce, a Wop/AG, was serving with No 142 Squadron in the summer of 1941, and recalls:

> The night of 2 August 1941 proved rather more exciting than most for the crew of W5359,QT-B. Our skipper was Flying Sergeant Rich, second pilot Sergeant Brown, with the navigator Sergeant Green, Wop myself, Sergeant Pearce, and the front and rear gunners Sergeants Pringle and Probert respectively, while the target was Berlin. Our bomb load comprised two 1000lb and two 500lb bombs plus two containers of incendiaries and this was duly

*Wing Commander D.H. Burnside, DFC, RAF.

dropped on a searchlight battery in the centre of Berlin from a height of 20,000 ft. It was decided to maintain this altitude for the journey back until the Dutch coast was reached, then make tracks for Binbrook. The enemy coast was crossed at 14,000 ft and height continued to be gently reduced as we headed home. We'd become aware of low readings on the fuel gauges and decided to stay up at 14,000 ft. Then, some ten miles from the Lincolnshire coast, first one then the other engine just stopped. The props were feathered and an eerie silence prevailed. I was ordered to send an SOS signal and a position report, and in addition I sent out a 'Mayday' call on the R/T.

Dawn was barely breaking when we silently crossed the coast. We'd decided to make for Waltham aerodrome, a few miles from Cleethorpes, though this airfield was not yet in use and was littered with substantial obstructions. With no chance of going round again, a first-time touchdown was made, wheels up, with a landing speed of about 90 knots, and the Wellington skidded to a halt in showers of sparks after a run of about half a mile. We didn't hurry to leave the aircraft since we knew there was no risk of fire with the fuel having been exhausted (we *thought*) so we all collected in the cockpit, lit cigarettes, and discussed our next move. I was deputed along with the navigator to go to a distant Nissen hut which had a light on, which appeared to be some sort of guard room. A knock on the door, a long wait, then the arrival of a very sleepy soldier. 'Are you from that big glider?' he asked!

He made us very welcome, telephoned Binbrook to arrange transport, and organised welcome cups of tea. When we got back to camp there were two sequels. First, I got a rocket from the CO for sending out an SOS – 'It wasn't a true emergency,' he said! The second was that a modification to the fuel supply to hold in reserve the fuel in nacelle tanks had *not* been recorded in the Form 700. The aircraft had been equipped with a system of cables attached to the petrol cocks in the nacelle tanks, which, when pulled by the use of a curtain ring in the cockpit, released the fuel direct to the engines. We had landed with 135 gallons of petrol in each tank!!

A footnote to this incident should be added. Wellington W5359 was repaired and re-issued to No 305 Squadron on 10 October 1941, saw further service with No 1443 Flight, went to No 204 Squadron in Egypt, and finally crashed at Kabrit on 23 October 1942.

For the late Colin Williams the Wellington always remained his favourite aircraft. Trained on Tiger Moths and Oxfords, then Wellingtons, he flew 23 ops in Wimpys before a crash on return to base made him unfit for further air crew duties and he remustered to flying control staff:

My ops were basically no different to hundreds of other air crews. Like most blokes I was young, excited, frightened while actually operating over Germany, particularly hating flak and those bloody searchlights which seemed to sniff us out just as they wished. Night fighters? No, we only ever had one brush with a Jerry fighter and that only lasted a minute or two because my gunners were red-hot and ready for him, so I figure he decided to go find some poor unsuspecting kite instead. But the flak *always* bothered us, especially me – I almost needed a change of underpants after most sorties!

Yet the good old Wimpy never failed me – even the crash which took me off flying wasn't really her fault. We'd been badly hit by flak and I had no hydraulics for the landing, while my undercart was swinging loose all the way home. There was *something* about the Wimpy – call it sentiment if you like, but I always felt safe in her, no matter what punishment she took.

My main memory of the Wimpy was looking out through my side windows at those damn great props churning only inches away, and beyond them the wings gently waving up and down at me. In fact the whole airframe seemed to wander about in flight, but maybe I was imagining too much. This didn't bother me on ops – I'd got used to it at OTU – and in a way seemed to reassure me how strong the old girl really was. In fact the only crew member ever to complain about it was my rear gunner. In his office way back at the blunt end he suffered more than the rest of us when I had to take any violent manoeuvre to avoid lights or flak, because the tail end flexed fairly heftily.

The Wimpy had a well-deserved reputation for its strength, as I can testify. Several of my ops saw us coming home with torn fabric flapping like streamers from various parts of the wings or fuselage, yet apart from my last trip the airframe got away almost scot-free from any serious damage. One trip cost us about six feet off one wing tip, yet I had no problem bringing her back. Only the engines, Pegasus, ever worried me – not because they weren't good engines but because they never really gave me sufficient urge to climb to a decent height to get away from the flak. Still, you can't 'have everything. I once 'tested' the contemporary opinion that a Wimpy couldn't stay up long on just one Pegasus, deliberately cutting back on one engine during an NFT Night Flying Test. She dropped pretty rapidly and I quickly restored power – we had no feathering controls then – and landed quickly. I've heard other Wimpy crews complain that she was noisy and permanently smelly, but the noise never bothered me, while the internal smell – a combination of oil, petrol, and especially that fabric dope 'peardrops' aroma – was almost comforting; a familiar smell which made me feel at home. I rarely got the chance of flying in other types of bomber after I was medically grounded, but one trip, just a local stooge, in a Lancaster I found cramped and nowhere as pleasant as in the Wimpy. For me the Wellington was one of the truly great bombers of the war.

CHAPTER THIRTEEN

Ubendum, Wemendum

Air crews may come, and air crews may go, but the rock foundation of *every* RAF squadron or other unit were (and for that matter, still are . . .) the Erks – the universal, affectionate soubriquet applied to the RAF's unpublicised, seldom honoured, and even more rarely rewarded ground crew airmen and airwomen. Not for them the rakishly-tilted, crumpled peaked cap, top tunic-button carefully left undone, glamour of a pair of 'silver wings', or rows of bright medal ribbons offering public display of prowess. Living too often in accommodation which could only be termed primitive, working in conditions which would give a modern trades union official grey hairs and apoplexy, and paid a pittance, the Erks' life on any wartime operational unit was hardly a sinecure.

Yet the Erks gave unfailing support and loyalty at all times – the prime incentive was always to 'keep 'em flying'. Rigid parameters for working hours were non-existent up at the sharp end – all that mattered was finishing the job, even if it meant (as so often it did) working on through the night to ensure a flyable kite ready for its crew next day. Leave, weekend passes, or other perks were classified as privileges, granted only when Service 'exigencies' permitted. Whether at work or off-duty the keynote to an Erk's existence then was improvisation and self-help. Technical staff publications may have appeared to be the 'bible' for all matters connected with the servicing and preparations needed to get an aircraft airborne, but seasoned Erks soon discovered that many snags occurring had no solution printed in any handbook – only ingrained instinctive experience provided the answer.

As far as particular aircraft were concerned, the Erks had their specific likes and dislikes, just as air crews came to regard certain designs as dogs or great kites. The Wellington found favour with both air and ground crews, in itself a tribute to Barnes Wallis's brain-child. As one ex-Flight Sergeant fitter has put it:

There was just *something* about the Wimpy which put it in a class of its own; a sort of combination of tough old warhorse and mother-hen. I can't really define it, but I always looked on the Wimpy as almost a friend, whereas all other aircraft I worked on were simply aeroplanes.

The 'Chiefy's' sentiments were echoed by myriad Erks. But let them speak for themselves. Derek Pinches was an engine fitter who was stationed for a time at No 77 OTU, Qastina in Palestine, and recalled*:

Various aspects spring to mind even after all these years. Of having to wear plimsolls at *all* times, whatever the weather, whilst clambering over the aircraft . . . how easy for accessibility and maintenance the engines were . . . the 'do-it-yourself' atmosphere that prevailed to get jobs done, for example, we made a type of gantry mounted on the back of a very old lorry to enable us to remove the propellers when required . . . the hours I spent working with a rigger sewing patches of fabric to repair damaged sections . . . the perpetual smell of dope and the Elsan whenever entering the fuselage . . . my constant amazement at the amount of damage its type of construction could absorb and still fly . . . sitting on the wing filling up with petrol when the aircraft returned, seeming to take hours with the tractor and petrol bowser in front of the aircraft chugging away . . . how easy it was to change damaged cylinders . . . the faint smear of oil leaking from an engine that you never seemed to be able to find or cure! . . . the 'hand-crank' loading of bombs, usually done by the rigger and fitter supervised by an armourer who did all the 'grunting and groaning' for you . . . the 'pleasure and concern' expressed by the Flight Sergeant when the flotation bags in the bomb bays were accidentally inflated by some member of the ground crew . . . and not least, the extreme discomfort of working on top of the aircraft's fabric in the strong sunshine.

L.H. Jordan served on Wellingtons with No 38 Squadron during 1939-42, and describes some of the early problems – and solutions – during those initial years of Wimpy operations:

The squadron that I served with, No 38, was stationed at Marham, Norfolk with (initially) Mk I Wellingtons which had the double

*Letters to author, 1981

Erks of 420 Squadron RCAF. Standing: A.R. Meadows; K.R. Paul; Cpl M.E. Costello; B. Pullen; Cpl G.A. Deverall; M.L. Mounk; Cpl R.J. McMillan; Cpl M.J. Jackson; Cpl J.G. Edwards; J.C. Collins. Kneeling: Sgts J.G. Bradley & W. McCullough.

'Dress Informal'. Armourers of 38 Squadron, Libya, 1942.

'aerial pole atop the fuselage (before the introduction of the D/F cone type fitted aft of the existing front aerial), and the fixed perspex nose (fore and aft') 'turret' with single guns limited in movement. Midway along the fuselage, aft of the main spar, was a 'dustbin' turret which was hydraulically lowered in flight, but so much drag was experienced in flight that these were removed. To do this meant disconnecting the hydraulic pipe lines and electrics, then towing the aircraft over a prepared hole in front of the maintenance hangar on the grass. Here the turret holding bolts were taken out and the turret allowed to drop into the hole. The aircraft was then towed back into the hangar where a fabric and wood circular frame was fitted to the fuselage hole.

Another modification carried out in those early days was to the bomb bays. After bombing operations, aircraft were returning often with bomb 'hang-ups', and I've seen ground crews about to do their after-flight inspections open the bomb doors and having an anti-personnel bomb which had failed to release in the air drop out, exploding, killing ground crews, and setting fire to the aircraft. The modification was a simple idea. Aft of the main spar in the fuselage there was a drop-down area of about 18 inches at the rear of the three bomb bays where there was a plywood section. Here three half-inch holes were drilled and then duralumin cover plates fitted over the holes, so that any crew member, after a bombing run, could slide aside the small panel, shine a torch through each hole down the length of the bomb bays and thereby check for bombs 'hung-up'. Other modifications then included windscreen de-icers, which simply consisted of one-eighth inch copper piping running from the cockpit to the outside where de-icer fluid was sprayed on to the windscreen, fed from a small header tank, pumped out by a hand-operated force-pump. Another snag experienced by the flying crew concerned icing-up at altitude along the leading edges of the main planes and empennage areas. So a gooey, thick solution was issued, rather like brown figs all mashed up, in drums and this was smeared over all affected areas – it was not a great success. Speaking of wings, all main planes had to be taken off for the fitting of self-sealing fuel tanks – a major undertaking which entailed work going on day and night due to the shortage of aircraft.

During my time at Marham – I'm speaking of the early days of 1939-40 – quite a lot of air crew were 'rankers', such as AC2, AC1, and LAC, with LAC pilots occasionally flying Wimpys, and when

Wellington Ic,T2508,LF–O, 37 Squadron, January 1941 (Pilot, Flt Lt 'Cheese' Lemon, DFC) being 'prepped' for a sortie. The insigne motto read *'Defaecamus Luces Purpuras'* (Latin scholars may translate freely . . . . !)

'V-Victory' of 108 Squadron getting a wash-down at Fayid, 1941.

Z1091, 'A' of 419 Squadron RCAF being given an early winter morning Daily Inspection (DI). It eventually failed to return from an operational sortie on 12 February 1942.

Engine fitter relying on 'blind touch' servicing a Wimpy's Pegasus XVIII.

we went on operations we took our tool boxes with us so that immediately on return we could carry out our respective after-flight inspections at the dispersal sites, in my case as a rigger. One raid I flew on was to Wilhelmshaven when I stood by the flare chute sliding out bundles of 1000 propaganda leaflets. On another raid over some German forests I again stood by the flare chute, chucking out some wet phosphorous 'squares' which were *supposed* to set fire to anything they contacted on landing – another unsuccessful idea of those days. By the mid-1940 period volunteers for air crews were coming in at a fast rate, and to us 'Ground Staff' – to which we now reverted as these people took our places as flying crews – thought it somewhat strange that they were all wearing Sergeant's tapes on their arms!!

In October 1940 the bomb beams were taken out of the bomb bays of 38 Squadron's Wellingtons and in their places were fitted long, round, overload fuel tanks to enable the aircraft to fly to Malta on route to the Middle East as part of the build-up of General Wavell's forces. We left Marham in November 1940 and on arrival in Egypt became the first Wellington squadron to operate from RAF Fayid, though after a few operations from there the squadron was moved south to Shallufa, some eight miles from Port Suez. From here we operated at night against such targets as Derna, Tobruk, and Benghazi, apart from shipping and enemy airfields. Usually our aircraft would fly in daylight to some Advanced Landing Ground (ALG), such as LG09, near Fuka, outside Mersa Matruh, where they would be topped up with fuel, and the same again for the return flight.

With the appearance of Rommel and his forces, an attempt had to be made to cut his supply sea routes across the Mediterranean from Italy, and therefore it was decided to convert the old Wimpy into a torpedo-dropper. This conversion entailed quite a lot of work for the ground crews. Once again, bomb beams had to be removed in order to accommodate two torpedoes, while all the flotation bags were disconnected and taken out (despite the fact that the aircraft would be operating over the sea . . !). The front gun turret was removed and a fabric and wood fairing was put in its place, though the rear turret was retained. These torpedo-Wimpys then operated from Shallufa and Malta, with some telling results against enemy shipping. These sort of operations began in early 1942 and by the end of that year 38 Squadron Wellingtons were operating from Berka, near Benghazi, against shipping in and out of Tripoli, still torpedo-dropping, and that is where I left them on a posting to Spitfires and Hurricanes.

'Bert' Hands joined the RAF at the start of the war, and from March 1940 was trained as an electrician at RAF Henlow, from where he was posted in mid-June to No 15 OTU, Harwell to service the training unit's Wellingtons and Ansons. His memories of the Wimpy are pragmatic but affectionate:

For me the Wimpy was the finest twin-engined aircraft built for war; its only rivals being the Mosquito and the Junkers Ju88. I never knew anyone who worked on or flew in a Wimpy ever speak about their 'kite' without affection, even love. The sheer elegance of its lines, on the ground or in the air, was a great sight to behold, and far superior to a Whitley or Hampden. Of course, it had snags in all aspects initially but these were soon ironed out, and every one I ever flew in was grand. Being of geodetic construction, the electrical bonding was essential. Accurate and searching checks had to be made to ensure no difference of potential was caused – should such a difference occur it could cause sparking which, with the presence of petrol vapour, would lead to an explosion and fire. Earthing faults could prove a hazard, especially in the bomb gear. Insulation tests were required on 80-hour inspections officially, though many electricians carried these out before that specified stage. Many a ground crew has a story of 'the bomb that dropped off' through an earth fault . . .

Our electrical daily inspection (DI) was really quite straight-forward. Engines were the most important item, obviously. Our first check was on the condition of the battery. The battery housing was poor because of battery gassing which could cause corrosion to the metal. After many suggestions to overcome this, it was decided best to paint the battery area with anti-acid paint and have special heavy metal bases for the housing. Following the battery check, we checked all lighting inside and out, then had an engine run-up to test the generator, plus a charging, voltage, and controls check. Next test the pilot head, gunsights, electrical heaters, and change any burned-out light/lamp bulbs for navigation, identification, and landing. These lights could be quite a job, due to their locations, the hardest being the Ident Light high on the tail rudder – not the best job in a high wind. Disconnecting and re-connecting the starter motors and the generator could prove no easy task, though the subsequent use of loom wiring and plug/socket connections made these jobs so much easier.

Petrol and oil were real menaces to rubber insulation of electrical wiring, especially in the nacelles, where rubber was soon reduced to a pulp and therefore creating a constant requirement for re-wiring. Then plastic sheathing was introduced which prevented a good deal of deterioration to cables etc. The petrol gauge instrument was always at risk because of contact with petrol, whereby damaged and broken wiring gave inaccurate readings. Undercarriage indicator contacts usually suffered deterioration through oil contact, and needed *very* thorough checking.

In late 1941, while Harwell airfield was not in use temporarily, I worked on our Wellingtons at the Mount Farm satellite field, which were then being used for assimilated night flying by day. This amounted to flying in daylight with special goggles with filters to assimilate either full moonlight, part-moonlight, or no moon. Sodium lighting in the aircraft cockpit to illuminate the instrument panel, allied to sodium lamps in special containers laid out alongside the runway, added to the 'illusion'. However, the limited vision of the goggles never inspired confidence, and on those many occasions I had to fly in order to check out these various sodium lights etc, these flights proved more fearsome than any actual night flying. Sufficient to say this scheme was never really successful.

For many airmen recruited during the war into a technical trade the attitude encountered from pre-war 'regulars' occasionally created a certain amount of disharmony on any dispersal site, though this was only a situation met mainly in the early years of the war and even then was not common to all units by any means. One particular irritation to members of certain aircraft technical trades was the assumed 'superiority' of the engine and airframe tradesmen over all others, i.e. wireless, instrument, electrical, and armament tradesmen – these latter being referred to as 'ancillary trades'. It was, in effect, a hangover from the RAF in the 1920s and early 1930s when one engine and one airframe tradesmen – a 'fitter and a rigger' – were allocated a specific 'ground crew' for one biplane. To members of the armament trade the 'tag' of 'ancillary' was particularly annoying; after all, *without* armament, there would be no reason *for* an air force!

Such, at least, was the view of Jack Taylor – usually nicknamed 'Spud' – who served throughout the war as an armament mechanic,

Bombing-up.

214 Squadron air and ground crews examining flak damage at Stradishall, 1941.

rising to the rank of Sergeant before his final demobilisation in 1945. Jack, the son of a gamekeeper prior to the war, had been teethed on guns of the sporting variety from childhood, so it seemed only logical to plump for armourer as his trade on voluntarily enlisting in 1939 in the RAF. 'Actually', Taylor says:

> the recruiting officer asked me if I wanted to become an air gunner, but I declined, saying I'd rather live to see the end of the war . . . which didn't increase my popularity with a Warrant Officer in the same office who wore pilot's wings, though he was too old to be active air crew by then.

> After basic square-bashing and recruit school bullshit, I was sent on an armourer-guns' course for trade training, and duly passed out as an LAC, top of my class, with overall 84% pass marks. From what I could gather, the rest of my class had never handled any gun in their lives, so I obviously started out with an advantage there. My first posting was to the Station Armoury on the same camp! My duties were solely concerned with counting out training weapons to the trainees in the morning, then counting them back again at tea-time, day in and day out. In between these counting sessions, there was nothing else to do except guzzle tea, eat NAAFI wads, read papers, or dust the rifle racks once a week for the Stationmaster's inspection.* It didn't take long before I got utterly browned off with the boredom, and I kept banging in applications for a posting to a frontline squadron, *any* squadron, *any*where, as long as it was away from that bloody rifle-store. In the end it was six months, and a change of Armament Officer, before my latest application was approved, forwarded, and actioned, with a posting to a Wellington squadron. By then the spring of 1940 had 'sprung' in contrast to the awful winter just past, and my arrival at Marham, in the heart of Norfolk, was on a very pleasant sunny day, with the surrounding countryside alight with blooming nature – a good start, further enhanced when I found I was billeted in a peacetime barrack block with all mod cons on tap, so to speak, and a marvellous contrast to the muddied, cold, draughty wooden huts I'd endured at the armament training camp up north. Marham then had two Wimpy units, Nos 38 and 115 Squadrons, both fully operational and engaged in night raids over Germany. I was posted internally to the Station Armoury, but spent all my

*Stationmaster – contemporary RAF slang for any RAF Station Commander.

The Gentle Touch. WAAF mechanics servicing a Wellington.

R1598, KX–C, 311 (Czech) Squadron which crashed at East Wretham, 23 Oct 1941, but served later with 3 OTU.

time out on the dispersals, servicing the Wellingtons of both squadrons because we were short of armourers in general for the squadrons themselves.

At first, being a guns armourer, I was expected only to service the gun turret Browning machine guns, but as time went by I was gradually 'converted' to all forms of ironmongery, including bombs and pyrotechnics, bomb carriers, and even the electrical bombing gear set-up – all what is now termed 'on-the-job' learning under supervision of a regular-serving Sergeant and Corporal, both of them ex-Halton 'Brats' with a few years' service under their belts. Being so short of trained armourers then, I wasn't the only one to be made a jack-of-all-sorts because when the squadrons were on any reasonably strong operation, everybody within reach was roped in for bombing-up, or any other pure labouring job. The legendary RAF call for all available hands to help – i.e. 'Two-Six!' – could be heard almost every day around the aircraft dispersal sites, and every bod within hearing range was automatically roped in to help. Actual bombing up of a Wellington was no great problem, except the long narrow bomb cells didn't leave you much elbow room inside for checking bomb hooks, safety wires, or whatever, while the belly of a Wimpy, especially with the bomb doors down, was very close to the deck. A common joke at the time was that the ideal Wellington armourer should be three feet tall with arms fifteen feet long!

Despite the number of what might be called 'unskilled labourers' usually 'volunteered' for helping with bombing up, there were remarkably few accidents on my own dispersals. The Sergeant armourer was obviously a genius at his trade, and moreover had the God-given gift of being able to explain anything complicated in a way even *I* could understand – which was no mean feat! The only near-accident I saw was when some sprog electrician inside the cockpit pressed the wrong tit on the bomb gear and coolly jettisoned the whole bomb load back onto the grass. One poor airman happened to have his feet in the way – and a 250lb GP bomb on your foot doesn't make for a bright future as a ballroom dancer . . . I heard on the grapevine later that said airman needed one foot amputated.

Talking of feet, I remembered too a rather beefy Erk – he must have weighed about 16 stone – who calmly started walking along a Wellington fuselage top *in hobnail boots*! Each step produced a popping, tearing sound – he was breaking the fabric covering with each step he took. The language of the aircraft's Corporal rigger literally blued the air for a mile around! My stay at Marham was fairly short, because in October 1940 I was put on an overseas draft, given 14 days' embarkation leave, then took a troopship to Egypt, where I was to spend the next three years at various units in the Suez Canal area.

W.E. Wilkinson was an LAC fitter when he first worked on Wellington aircraft of No 142 Squadron at Binbrook in 1940:

The squadron was then equipped with Wellington Mk IIs with Rolls-Royce Merlin engines fitted with De Havilland hydromatic airscrews, and during the working-up period – the unit began converting from Fairey Battles in November 1940* – I became a fitter on the crew of Wimpy W5359,QT-B, of 'A' Flight. By the time we were declared operational I'd been promoted to Corporal and was NCO in charge of three aircraft on one dispersal, including W5359. Possibly the biggest snag with the Mk II was its tendency to drop its nose in a dive, caused by the thrust-line of the Merlin being higher and the airscrew being further forward of the CG than an Pegasus and Mercury engines of the Mk Is. This meant a pilot had to trim the elevator back to fly straight and level. Unfortunately, the trim tabs were interconnected with the flaps in such a way that when flaps were lowered the elevators were also lowered to keep the aircraft on an even keel. No harm was done until the flaps were fully lowered after touch-down. If the pilot hadn't centralised the trim tabs before using the flaps he had quite an appreciable amount of trim on, so that when the flaps were fully lowered the hydraulic pressure of the flaps ripped the whole trimming box off the fuselage – even experienced crews were guilty of this, especially after a long op.

Anybody who ever worked with Merlin engines will remember how easily they started, and the Mk II was, in my opinion, the easiest-started Wellington of them all; indeed, I *think* it was the only one which could be started by just one man. During 1941, however, we were re-equipped with Mk IVs with Pratt & Whitney Twin Wasp engines, and after our easy life with Merlins we were rudely awakened with the Wasps. The first snag encountered was a tendency for the bottom cylinders to fill up with oil. We had to

*First Wellington, W5356, received on 8/11/40, and eleven more by 22/2/41.

(Above) 149 Squadron
Wellington at Mildenhall
being refuelled and awai[ting]
its bomb load of 250lb G[...]

(Left) Erks with WS–Z, '[...]
of 9 Squadron, 1941. 'Zo[la]
was named from the girl
friend of Buck Ryan, a *Da[ily]
Mirror* cartoon hero of the[...]

'hand-turn the propeller four complete revolutions before attempting to start, to be sure we had not got an hydraulic lock in the cylinders. All too often we had, which meant removing cowlings and plugs to drain the bottom cylinders and then changing the plugs. Once this was accomplished starting was not too bad, at least until damp and cold weather started. As the Twin Wasp had petrol injection, we needed a crew man on the wobble pump to give us petrol pressure. As soon as the engine fired on engagement of the starter, the mixture control was moved from cut-out to auto-rich. This caused a jet of petrol at 5lb/sq. inch to be injected into the centre of the supercharger. However, if the engine didn't catch first time it became so hopelessly flooded that there was no chance of starting. This bad starting business was such a problem that both Nos 12 and 142 Squadrons were equipped with special Commer vans. These had a large petrol blowpipe in the van which led, via flame traps, to four large-diameter flexible pipes. These pipes were wrapped around the engine and the blowpipe lit. Once it had been warmed up to normal running temperature it would start up.

By the time 142 Squadron was equipped with Mk IVs it had moved to Waltham in November 1941, leaving 12 Squadron at Binbrook – Waltham being Binbrook's satellite airfield, just outside Grimsby. One very bad mistake made in respect of Mk IVs was underestimating their fuel consumption. So badly, in fact, that on the first Mk IV operations Nos 12 and 142 Squadrons had only 25 per cent of their Wimpys get back to Binbrook. Several landed in the North Sea, some at North Coates – a Flight Lieutenant Campling belly-landed at North Coates having run out of petrol before he could even get the undercart down. One Wimpy landed on married quarters at Binbrook, while two others landed at Binbrook with dead engines. Where Merlins had consumed about 85 gallons per hour, Twin Wasps were gulping down some 145 gallons per hour. Two other big snags we experienced with Twin Wasps were sludge in the oil preventing the two-stage supercharger changing speed, and the secondary windings in the magnetos breaking at the soldered joint due to the soldering flux not being removed during manufacture. Yet despite all my foregoing apparent 'prejudice' against the Wasp, I would emphasise that the Twin Wasp was in fact a very good engine, but it was certainly not designed to operate in English winter conditions.

'Jim' Murphy – eventually Squadron Leader J.H.F. Murphy, RAF Retd – was a Flight Sergeant in charge of first-line servicing with No 14 Squadron from October 1944 to June 1945 at Chivenor, having only recently returned from a four year tour of duties in the Middle East theatre. 14 Squadron had also just returned from the Mediterranean zone where it had been operating Martin Marauders in an anti-shipping torpedo-strike role, but on becoming based at Chivenor from 24 October 1944, it was re-equipped with Wellington GRXIVs fitted with Leigh Lights to operate over the Bay of Biscay and the Western Approaches in an anti-shipping role. The squadron's air crews were first given on-the-job conversion training on Leigh Light Wimpys with occasional near-comic results:

> Since the squadron's previous aircraft, Marauders, had tricycle undercarriages, there were, perhaps naturally, a few problems in getting used to aeroplanes with conventional tail-wheels. Our air crews were quite a mixed crowd, mostly British but including an assortment of Australians and at least one member of the South African Air Force (SAAF). Very early on in the conversion period one of our Aussie skippers pushed the stick forward when he was about half-way through his landing run, only to remember just too late that he didn't have a nose-wheel, and therefore too late to prevent his propeller's tips coming into contact with the runway. He taxied in with about three inches missing from each prop blade. He wasn't very popular with the squadron commander, Wing Commander E. Donovan, or the technical staff, myself included, because it meant that the aircraft had to go back to second-line servicing for shock load testing of both engines, and replacement of both propellers etc.
>
> As I recall, this conversion period lasted about three months, but was not without its share of dramas. The same Aussie who had 'cropped' his props was out on a Leigh Light exercise, trying to locate a simulated submarine, when for no known reason he flew straight into the sea. Rumour had it that he flew into a patch of thick mist and became disorientated or blinded by the reflection glare from the searchlight beam. Most of the crew were lost, though the skipper and (I think) one crew member were picked up and recovered in hospital.
>
> Then there was the evening when Flight Lieutenant 'Jock' Stewart was detailed for a normal night bombing exercise with practice flash bombs. He started down the runway under full

Flt Lt F.G. Holloway and his crew boarding T2984, 'B' of 99 Squadron on 9 April 1941, bound for Berlin and recalling Shakespeare's phrase 'Gentlemen of the shade, minions of the Moon' *(Henry IV, Pt 1).*

'power and on reaching apparent take-off speed duly selected his undercarriage 'Up'. Unfortunately, 'M-for-Mike' wasn't *quite* ready to get airborne – by about 10kph – and she sank back towards the runway with the propeller tips taking the first impact, then the bomb bay amidst a shower of sparks. Careering on down the runway to a final halt, the sparks increased to a blazing mass. I didn't think it was possible for anyone to survive as I watched it all happen from the Flight office, standing beside the Flight commander. I said, 'Let's get down there' but he said, 'No, Flight. You have to stay by the 'phone. I'll go.'

The next 10-15 minutes seemed the longest of my life as I watched the practice bombs and ammunition exploding – then the 'phone rang and a voice said, 'That you, Chiefy? This is Jock. We all got out.' They had each gone down to the rear turret and, one by one, climbed in, rotated 180 degrees and exited, repeating the process until all were out. The only casualty was the last man out, with singed hair and eyebrows.

Another occasion was a late afternoon when my six ops aircraft were being prepared for a night take-off, each being loaded with six depth charges etc. All the pre-flight inspections had been done by all trades except the armourers who always did their checks last. I was standing just outside the Flight office, waiting rather impatiently for those final signatures in the Form 700s, and watching my two intrepid armourers enter and leave each aircraft in turn. They climbed the ladder under the nose of No 4 on the line, directly facing me across the dispersal area, then – an awful moment – one after the other six depth charges fell out of the bomb bay onto the hardstanding! I don't think I waited for Nos 5 and 6 to fall, but was off like a whippet, yet before I'd gone 20 yards I was *passed* by the two armourers who were trying to break the sound barrier! When nothing happened – no almighty explosion as anticipated – I returned to my office, only to be met by the Sergeant armourer asking why I'd run? 'They wouldn't go off anyway, Flight.' He was quite probably right – but I'd have done the same again, given the same circumstances!

H.R.W. Kidney was a Corporal armourer serving on 38 Squadron at Shallufa, Egypt in 1942, at the period when Rommel's Afrika Korps had driven eastwards almost to the border of Egypt, and was poised for a final advance to Cairo and the Suez Canal area. As the Allied armies dug-in around El Alamein, a number of 'contingency' measures were prepared for the possibility of a Rommel occupation of Egypt etc.

One day our armament Warrant Officer sent for me and told me to report to a particular Wimpy with my 'bombing-up gear' and to be prepared to fly 'somewhere'. The Wimpy crew was a skeleton one i.e. just pilot, bomb-aimer, and myself, (and possibly a Wireless Operator). We flew up to Ismailia but on landing did not taxy to the hangars, but instead went to the furthest part of the airfield. There we were met by a Flight Sergeant, all alone, standing near a cluster of ancient 112lb RL dummy bombs. He briefed us about these bombs then left us to it. With the help of the air crew I bombed up the Wimpy with these dummies, and we then took off again, with myself in the front turret totally puzzled as to the object of this exercise, not having been briefed at all about this.

Once airborne we didn't gain altitude but *descended* to a few feet above the Suez Canal itself – I can recall looking *up* at some Arabs with their camels proceeding along the canal banks! Subsequently, 'the bomb aimer who had taken up his position began dropping the bombs at intervals in the canal between Ismailia and Port Suez, after which we flew back to Shallufa. Here I was immediately instructed *not* to discuss the 'exercise' with *any*one. Though it is merely a guess on my part, I can only assume it was literally a dummy run for a real bombing effort had Rommel actually reached the Canal – fortunately Alemein stopped him.

About that same time, due to the closeness of the front line in the Western Desert, it was considered prudent to move our Wimpy base to El Arish, towards the Palestine border. The ground crews were told to load as much of their technical equipment as possible into the Wimpys along with themselves, including myself. After flying for some time over the featureless desert we landed at an airfield which we assumed was to be our new base, but immediately on touchdown the Wimpys ran into stretches of soft sand. Our navigators had dropped a clanger – apparently we'd landed at a deserted World War One emergency strip miles from anywhere which had long ago succumbed to shifting desert sand!

It was impossible for the Wimpys to take off again in their heavily laden condition, some having to be dug out. So every piece of moveable equipment had to be off-loaded, including *all* ground crews, after which the kites just managed to get off, leaving the Erks and all their equipment stranded in the desert. Our location was several hundred yards from the coastline, and during our three days' wait to be rescued – we had all the emergency water and rations from the aircraft – we were twice invaded by night. As we slept some Arabic characters apparently decided to 'relieve' us of anything they could lay their grubby hands on, including three of our Lee Enfield rifles. They came and went completely undetected. The second invasion was by night too – a host of fairly hefty scavenging crabs who were most persistent in their assault and took some driving off. We were eventually 'retrieved' and taken to El Arish, only to be loaded soon after onto open railway wagons with all our gear and sent on to Haifa. After two days living in Haifa railyard, we were taken by road to St Jeans airfield, some 20 miles north of Haifa. Ironically, after only a few days at St Jeans I was flown back to Shallufa and remained there until the time of the battle of Alamein, after which we all began the long trek back to Libya by stages.

APPENDICES

The following list is a selection of the prime user-units of Wellingtons and does not include at least 150-plus known other squadrons/units which at some period operated a few Wellingtons on (mainly) second-line or non-operational duties. Additionally, Wellingtons were supplied to the French and Greek air services, while 'civilianised' versions were at one period operated during the 1939-45 war by British Overseas Airways Corporation (BOAC).

Squadrons: Nos 8, 9, 12, 14, 15, 24, 26 SAAF, 36, 37, 38, 40, 57, 69, 70, 75, 75 (NZ), 93, 99, 101, 103, 104, 108, 109, 115, 142, 148, 149, 150, 156, 158, 162, 166, 172, 179, 192, 196, 199, 203, 214, 215, 218, 221, 232, 242, 244, 281, 294, 300, 301, 304, 305, 311, 344, 405 RCAF, 407 RCAF, 415 RCAF, 419 RCAF, 420 RCAF, 424 RCAF, 425 RCAF, 426 RCAF, 427 RCAF, 428 RCAF, 429 RCAF, 431 RCAF, 432 RCAF, 458 RAAF, 460 RAAF, 466 RAAF, 524, 527, 544, 547, 612 AAF, 621, 716 FAA, 728 FAA, 758 FAA, 762 FAA, 765 FAA, 783 FAA.

Flights: Nos 1417, 1418, 1429, 1443, 1446, 1473, 1474, 1481, 1483, 1485, 1680, 1689; Nos 3, 4, 5, 9, 10, 1502, 1503, 1504, 1505 Beam Approach Training Flts (BATFs); Nos 1, 3, 92 Group Training Flts; Aden Flt; Malta Flt; 205 Group Comm Flt.

Operational Training Units (OTUs):
Nos 1(C), 3(C), 5(C), 6(C), 7(C), 9, 10, 11, 12, 14, 15, 16, 17, 18 (Polish), 19, 20, 21, 22, 23, 24, 25, 26, 27, 28, 29, 30, 32, 51, 54, 61, 62, 63, 76, 77, 78, 81, 82, 83, 84, 85, 86, 104, 105, 111.

Misc Units: Nos 1380, 1381, 1383 Transport Conversion Units; No 2 Flying Trng Conversion Unit; Nos 1651, 1665

Misc Units: conversion Units; Nos 1, 2, 3 General Reconnaissance
(cont)   Units; No 1 Torpedo Training Unit; No 1 ASV Training
                  Centre; Nos 301, 303, 304, 310, 311 Ferry Trng Units;
                  Aircraft Delivery Unit; Coastal Command Development
                  Unit; Air-Sea Warfare Development Unit; Central
                  Navigation School; Empire Air Navigation School;
                  Central Navigation & Control School; Nos 1, 2, 5, 6, 7,
                  10 Air Navigation Schools; Central Gunnery School;
                  Nos 1, 2, 3, 10, 11, 12 Air Gunnery Schools; No 1 Air
                  Armament School; Bomber Command Instructional
                  School; No 2 School of General Reconnaissance;
                  Central Flying School; Nos 2, 5 Middle East Training
                  Schools; Nos 101, 104 Flying Refresher Schools; Nos
                  201, 202 Advanced Flying Schools; No 228 Operational
                  Conversion Unit; No 9 Ferry Pilots Pool; Marine
                  Aircraft Experimental Establishment; Aeroplane &
                  Armament Experimental Establishment; Royal Air-
                  craft Establishment; Air Fighting Development Unit;
                  Signals Flying Unit; No 1 Radar Training School,
                  Chivenor.

Wellington squadron & OTU bases (excluding detachments)

Squadrons

8	. . . .	Khormaksar
9	. . . .	Stradishall, Honington
12	. . . .	Binbrook, Wickenby
14	. . . .	Chivenor
15	. . . .	Wyton
24	. . . .	Hendon
36	. . . .	Tanjore, Dhubalia, Blida, Reghaia, Alghero, Tarquinia, Thorney Island, Chivenor, Benbecula
37	. . . .	Feltwell, Malta, Fayid, Shallufa, LG09, LG224, Abu Sueir LG224, LG106, LG140, Benina, El Magrun, Gardabia E & W, Kairouan, Djedeida, Cerignola, Tortorella
38	. . . .	Marham, Ismailia, Fayid, Shallufa, Gambut, Shallufa, Kalamaki, Grottaglie, Foggia, Falconara, Luqa
40	. . . .	Wyton, Alconbury, Malta, Shallufa, Kabrit, LG222A, LG104, LG237, Heliopolis, LG237, Gardabia E & S.
57	. . . .	Feltwell
69	. . . .	Luqa, Northolt, Amiens-Glisy, Melsbroek, Eindhoven
70	. . . .	Kabrit, LG75, Kabrit, LG224, Abu Sueir, LG224, LG106, LG140, Benina, El Magrun, Gardabia E & W, Kairouan, Djedeida, Cerignola, Tortorella
75	. . . .	Honington, Stradishall, Harwell
75(NZ)	. . . .	Feltwell, Mildenhall, Newmarket
93	. . . .	Middle Wallop
99	. . . .	Mildenhall, Newmarket, Waterbeach, Pandaveswar, Digri, Chaklala, Jessore

101	....	West Raynham, Oakington, Bourn, Stradishall, Holme-on-Spalding Moor
103	....	Newton, Elsham Wolds
104	....	Driffield, Luqa, Kabrit, LG224, LG104, LG237, Soluch, Gardabia Main, Kairouan Cheria, Hani W, Oudna, Cerignola, Foggia
108	....	Kabrit, Fayid, LG105, Kabrit, LG237, LG09, LG237
109	....	Stradishall, Wyton
115	....	Marham, Kinloss, Mildenhall, East Wretham
142	....	Binbrook, Waltham, Kirmington, Blida, Fontaine Chaude, Kairouan, Oudna, Cerignola, Amendola, Regina
148	....	Stradishall, Harwell, Stradishall, Luqa, Kabrit, LG237, LG09, LG167
149	....	Mildenhall
150	....	Newton, Snaith, Kirmington, Blida, Fontaine Chaude, Kairouan W, Oudna LG2, Cerignola LG3, Amendola, Regina.
156	....	Alconbury, Warboys
158	....	Driffield
162	....	Shallufa, Bilbeis, Benina, LG91, Idku
166	....	Kirmington
172	....	Chivenor, Limavady
179	....	Wick, Gibraltar, Aqadir, Lagens, Predannack Chivenor, Benbecula, Chivenor.
192	....	Gransden Lodge, Feltwell, Foulaham
196	....	Driffield, Leconfield, Witchford, Leicester East
199	....	Blyton, Ingham, Lakenheath
203	....	Santa Cruz
214	....	Feltwell, Methwold, Stradishall, Honington, Stradishall
215	....	Honington, Bramcote, Bassingbourn, Asansol Pandaveswar, St Thomas Mt (Madras), Chaklala, Jessore
218	....	Marham
221	....	Bircham Newton, Limavady, Reykjavik, Bircham Newton, LG87, LG89, Shandur, Shallufa, Gambut, Berka 2, Grottaglie, Kalamaki, Edku

232	. . . .	Stoney Cross
242	. . . .	Stoney Cross
244	. . . .	Masirah
281	. . . .	Ballykelly
294	. . . .	Berka, Amriya S, Idku, Basra
300	. . . .	Swinderby, Hemswell, Ingham, Hemswell, Ingham
301	. . . .	Swinderby, Hemswell
304	. . . .	Bramcote, Syerston, Lindholme, Tiree, Dale, Talbenny, Dale, Docking, Davidstow Moor, Chivenor, Benbecula/Limavady
305	. . . .	Bramcote, Syerston, Lindholme, Hemswell, Ingham
311	. . . .	Honington, East Wretham, Aldergrove, Talbenny, Beaulieu
344	. . . .	Dakar
405	. . . .	Driffield, Pocklington, Topcliffe
407	. . . .	Docking, Skitten, Chivenor, St Eval, Chivenor Limavady, Wick, Chivenor
415	. . . .	Thorney Island, Bircham Newton, East Moor
419	. . . .	Mildenhall, Leeming, Topcliffe, Croft
420	. . . .	Skipton-onSwale, Middleton St George, Beaufarik, Kairouan/Zina, Hani E.LG.
424	. . . .	Topcliffe, Leeming, Dalton, Beaufarik, Kairouan/Zina, Hani E.LG, Skipton-on-Swale
425	. . . .	Dishforth, Beaufarik, Kairouan/Zina, Hani E.LG.
426	. . . .	Dishforth
427	. . . .	Croft
428	. . . .	Dalton
429	. . . .	East Moor
431	. . . .	Burn
432	. . . .	Skipton-on-Swale
458	. . . .	Holme-on-Spalding Moor, Shallufa, LG91, Blida, Protville, Bone, Alghero, Foggia, Gibraltar
460	. . . .	Molesworth, Breighton
466	. . . .	Driffield, Leconfield
524	. . . .	Davidstow Moor, Docking, Bircham Newton, Langham

527	. . . .	Digby, Watton
544	. . . .	Benson
547	. . . .	Holmesley South, Chivenor, Tain, Chivenor, Davidstow Moor, Thorney Island
612	. . . .	Wick, Davidstow Moor, Chivenor, St Eval, Chivenor, Limavady, Chivenor, Limavady, Langham
621	. . . .	Port Reitz, Mogadishu, Khormaksar, Mersa Matruh

OTUs

1(C)	. . . .	Silloth
3(C)	. . . .	Cranwell, Haverford West
5(C)	. . . .	Turnberry
6(C)	. . . .	Silloth, Kinloss
7(C)	. . . .	Limavady, Haverford West
10	. . . .	Abingdon
11	. . . .	Bassingbourn, Westcott
12	. . . .	Benson, Chipping Warden
14	. . . .	Cottesmore, Market Harborough
15	. . . .	Harwell, Mount Farm
16	. . . .	Upper Heyford
17	. . . .	Upwood, Silverstone
18	. . . .	Bramcote, Finningley
19	. . . .	Kinloss
20	. . . .	Lossiemouth
21	. . . .	Moreton-in-Marsh
22	. . . .	Wellesbourne Mountford
23	. . . .	Pershore
24	. . . .	Honeybourne
25	. . . .	Finningley
26	. . . .	Wing
27	. . . .	Lichfield
28	. . . .	Wymeswold
29	. . . .	North Luffenham, Bruntingthorpe
30	. . . .	Hixon, Gamston
51	. . . .	Cranfield
54	. . . .	Charterhall
62	. . . .	Ouston
63	. . . .	Honiley
76	. . . .	Aqir

77	....	Qastina
78	....	Ein Shemer
81	....	Ashbourne, Whitchurch Heath (i.e. Tilstock)
82	....	Ossington
83	....	Childs Ercall (i.e. Peplow)
84	....	Desborough
85	....	Husbands Bosworth
86	....	Gamston
104	....	Nutts Corner
105	....	Bramcote
111	....	Nassau

MISCELLANEOUS STATISTICS

*Production**

By Mark:		By Factory:	
Mk I	181	Blackpool	5540
Mk Ia	187	Chester	3406
Mk Ic	2685	Weybridge	2515
Mk II	401		†11461
Mk III	1519		
Mk IV	220		
Mk V	3	*	
Mk VI	64	As originally *built*.	
Mk VIII	394	Many were converted to	
Mk X	3803	other Mks while still on	
Mk XI	180	production lines; others were	
Mk XII	58	converted later in RAF use.	
Mk XIII	844	†Includes one prototype	
Mk XIV	841	B9/32 machine.	
Mk XVIII	80		
	11460		

*Comparative total productions of
RAF bombers*

Wellington	11,461
Lancaster	7,377
Halifax	6,176
Blenheim (all Mks)	5,371
Stirling	2,381
Whitley	1,814
Hampden (inc Hereford)	1,584

RAF squadrons equipped by 3/9/39

Sqn	1st aircraft received	Remarks
99	10 Oct 38	L4215. Fully equipped by 3 Jan 39
38	24 Nov 38	L430. Fully equipped by 30 Mar 30
149	20 Jan 39	L4249, L4252, L4253, L4254 – all this date
9	31 Jan 39	L4260, L4261 – both on this date
148	4 Mar 39	L4280, L4281, L4282 – all on this date
115	30 Mar 39	L4299
37	6 May 39	L4325. Fully equipped by 15 June 39
214	26 May 39	L4341, L4342, L4343 – all on this date. Fully equipped by 28 June 39
75*	29 June 39	L4366. Seven more added by 11 July 39
215	12 July 39	L4375. Fully equipped by 1 Aug 39

*NB: See main text for origination of No 75(NZ) Squadron

RAF Wellington strength as at 3 Sept 1939

On squadrons	160
On training units	1
On misc other units	2
In store	1
At makers etc	11
	175

Bomber Command, 1939-45

Following figures should be regarded as *confirmed minimums* only, due to lack of documentation and/or co-relation of statistics in existing RAF/Bomber Command unit records in certain areas.

Total individual sorties flown	47,409 (inc OTU/HCUs)
Total aircraft lost on operations	1386
Total aircraft written-off, accidents	377 (all causes)
Approx total bomb tonnage known dropped	42,000 †

†Actual figure impossible to confirm due to lack of evidence on disposal of bombs aboard 'missing' aircraft.

Comparative totals operational sorties flown by OTU/HCU crews

Wellington	6022
Mosquito	....1359 (1409 Met Flt only)
Halifax	1066
Lancaster	 736
Whitley	 690
Stirling	 467
Hampden	 252

Total individual sorties flown from UK, 1939-45 (all Commands)	63,976
Total operational flying hrs flown from UK, (all Commands)	346,440
Total flying hrs (training), post 1945	355,660

Coastal Command, 1939-45

Following figures, confirmed by postwar evidence, relate to all U-boats
confirmed as sunk or severely damaged by Wellingtons, either alone
or in conjunction with other aircraft types and/or RN vessels.

Squadron	Sunk	Damaged
172	U-126; U-231; U-268; U-364; U-376; U-502; U-575 (shared); U-614; U-665.	*Luigi Torelli*; U-66; U-159; U-270; U-332; U-415 (shared); U-437 (shared); U-459 (later scuttled); U-525; U-566.
179	U-134; U-211; U-412; U-435; U-542; U-566; U-618 (shared).	U-340 (shared/scuttled); U-343 (shared); U-415; U-667 (shared); U-760; U-1061.
407 RCAF	U-283; U-669; U-772; U-846	U-971; U-989.
612	U-193; U-545.	U-373 (shared); U-629; U-736.
304 (Polish)	U-321; U-441	*Reginaldo Guiliano*; U-629
311 (Czech)	U-578	U-106
621	U-852 (scuttled)	–
547	–	U-218

APPENDIX 4

Squadrons equipped

No.	Periods			Codes
8	Dec '43	–	May '45	A
9	Jan '39	–	Aug '42	KA : WS
12	Nov '40	–	Nov '42	PH
14	Oct '44	–	Jun '45	CX
15	Nov '40	–	Apr '41	LS
24	Aug '40	–	Dec '43	NQ
36	Dec '42	–	Jun '45	RW
37	May '39	–	Oct '44	FJ : LF
38	Nov '38	–	Jul '46	NH : HD
40	Nov '40	–	Mar '45	BL
57	Nov '40	–	Sep '42	DX
69	Aug '42	–	Feb '43	?
	May '44	–	Aug '45	
70	Sep '40	–	Jan '45	?
75 (NZ)	Apr '40	–	Oct '42	AA
75	Jun '39	–	Apr '40	FO
93	Dec '40	–	Apr '41	HN
99	Oct '38	–	Sep '44	VF : LN
101	Apr '41	–	Oct '42	SR
103	Oct '40	–	Jul '42	PM
104	Mar '41	–	Feb '45	EP
108	Aug '41	–	Nov '42	LD
109	Dec '40	–	Aug '42	HS
115	Mar '39	–	Mar '43	BK : KO
142	Nov '40	–	Oct '44	QT
148	Mar '39	–	Dec '42*	BS : FS(?)
149	Jan '39	–	Dec '41	LY : OJ
150	Oct '40	–	Oct '44	JN

*From 4/4/40 – 29/4/40 was 15OTU; reformed 30/4/40 & disbanded 23/5/40; reformed Luqa, Malta, 14/12/40.

No.	Periods			Codes
156	Feb '42	–	Jan '43	GT
158	Feb '42	–	Jun '42	NP
162	Jan '42	–	Sep '44	?
166	Jan '43	–	Sep '43	AS
172	Apr '42	–	Jun '45	WN : 1 : OG
179	Sep '42	–	Nov '44	OZ
192	Jan '43	–	Jan '45	DT
196	Dec '42	–	Jul '43	ZO
199	Nov '42	–	Jul '43	EX
203	Oct '43	–	Nov '44	?
214	May '39	–	Apr '42	UX : BU
215	Jul '39	–	Apr '40	BH : LG
	Feb '42	–	Aug '44	
218	Nov '40	–	Jan '42	HA
221	Nov '40	–	Aug '45	DF
232	Nov '44	–	Feb '45	?
242	Nov '44	–	Feb '45	KY
244	Feb '44	–	May '45	?
281	Sep '45	–	Oct '45	?
294	Sep '43	–	Apr '46	?
300	Dec '40	–	Apr '44	BH
301	Oct '40	–	Apr '43	GR
304	Nov '40	–	Jun '45	NZ
305	Nov '40	–	Aug '43	SM
311	Aug '40	–	Aug '43	KX
344	Nov '43	–	Nov '45	?
405	May '41	–	Apr '42	LQ
407	Jan '43	–	Jun '45	RR
415	Sep '43	–	Jul '44	NH
419	Jan '42	–	Nov '42	VR
420	Aug '42	–	Oct '43	PT
424	Oct '42	–	Nov '43	QB
425	Jul '42	–	Oct '43	KW
426	Oct '42	–	Jun '43	OW
427	Nov '42	–	May '43	ZL
428	Nov '42	–	Jun '43	NA
429	Nov '42	–	Aug '43	AL
431	Dec '42	–	Jul '43	SE
432	May '43	–	Oct '43	QO

No.	Periods			Codes
458	Aug '41	–	Jun '45	MD : FU*
460	Nov '41	–	Aug '42	UV
466	Oct '42	–	Sep '43	HD
524	Apr '44	–	May '45	7R
527	May '45	–	Apr '46	WN
544	Oct '42	–	Apr '43	?
547	Oct '42	–	Nov '43	?
612	Dec '42	–	Jul '45†	WL : 8W
621	Sep '43	–	Dec '45	?

*According to 458 Sqn history.
†612 Sqn had no Wellingtons Feb '43 to Apr '43.

Fleet Air Arm

716	Jul '44	–	Aug '45
728	1946		
758	Sep '43	–	Dec '43
762	Aug '44	–	Apr '45
765	Feb '44	–	Apr '46
783	Feb '44	–	Sep '44

NB: Where codes are marked ?, full confirmation of actual codes used (*if* at all) is lacking.

Wimpy Songs & Verse

Traditionally, members of the RAF (and any other armed Service) have always found an outlet for their complaints, views, and opinions in song and/or verse; usually composing fresh lyrics for well-known tunes of the contemporary period and, curiously (ironically??) often selecting hymns as the basis for such semi-plagiarisms. The Wellington became the subject for many such expressions of affection by individual squadrons during the 1939-45 war and a few of these musical (?) tributes have now established themselves as integral parts of RAF folklore. The following examples include probably the best-known such esoteric eulogies. The first here was composed by Flg Off 'Taffy' Evans, navigator, who was serving with No 75 (NZ) Squadron at Feltwell in 1940, and was titled *Wimpy Feltwell*.

As we go zooming through the skyways
You'll hear the people say
There goes Wimpy Feltwell
Just you watch her sway
Her engines are so noisy
They make a fearful crack
And you no sooner see her going
Than she is coming back.

Her name is Wimpy Feltwell
And you may ask me why;
But I really cannot tell you
So don't ask me to try
She rattles in the front part
And squeaks along the back
But when we're over Berlin
Good old Wimpy will bring us back.

Now Wimpy never grumbles
No, Wimpy never cries
For she is a perfect lady
With two great sparkling eyes
She's got a voice like Cyrus *1
And a face like Good Old Buck †2
Yes, she's the girl for me
Because she'll always bring me luck.

One night across the Wilhelmshaven
Our Wimpy made her way
'Mein Gott', said dirty Hitler
'Here's Feltwell. Let us pray'.
So down upon their knees they sank
And prayed with all their might
But Feltwell dropped their load of bombs
And blew them out of sight.

And now you have heard the story
Of our Wimpy, brave and bold
For she is the greatest Wellington
That Vickers ever sold.
In time we'll go to Heaven, – we hope!
With happiness to spare
But Heaven won't be nothing unless
Our Wimpy is also there.

*1–Wg Cdr (later AVM) C.E. Kay, DFC, OC 75(NZ) Sqn
†2–Grp Capt Maurice Buckley, CO, RAF Feltwell

Undoubtedly, the most famous tribute (?) in song to the Wellington was *The Benghazi Mail Run*, composed by members of No 70 Squadron in North Africa in 1941 to vent their views on the constant sorties mounted against the vital port of Benghazi, Libya. Sung to the tune *Clementine*.

Take off for the Western Desert
Fuka, 60 or 09*
Same old Wimpy, same old target,
Same old air crew, same old time.

Chorus:

Seventy Squadron, Seventy Squadron
Though we say it with a sigh
Must we do this bloody mail run
Every night till we die?

Navigator, have you lost us?
Come up here and have a look
Somebody's shot our starboard wing off
That's alright then, that's Tobruk.

Chorus: . . .

Forty Wimpys on the target
Two were ditched down in the drink
Then three others crashed on landing
Bloody Hell! It makes you think.

Chorus: . . .

Stooging round the Western Desert
With the gravy running low
How I wish I could see Fuka
Through the sandstorm down below.

Chorus: . . .

First it's Derna, then it's Barce
Even I.O. isn't sure
They've changed the bomb loads twice already
It's a proper Cook's Tour.

Chorus: . . .

All this flapping can't fool us
We know just where we'll have to be
Rumour's heard of a new target
But after all it's just B.G.

Chorus: . . .

To Benghazi is the slogan
We'll take the load right through once more
So start your engines, let's get cracking
The mail run's going as before.

Chorus: . . .

Intelligence tell us from his photos
We never hit a single flea
Sees no bomb holes in the rooftops
Only craters in the sea.

Chorus: . . .

He asks us if we're 'sure we pranged it?'
Must have been some other spot
Suggests we bombed a dummy target
Never heard such utter rot!

Chorus: . . .

Try to get your tour of ops in
Without your Wimpy being hit
If you do you'll go to Blighty
If you don't you're in the shit.

Chorus: . . .

Oh to be in Piccadilly
Selling matches by the score
Though we'd feel a bit chilly
There'd be no mail run anymore.

Chorus: . . .

*Fuka, LG60 & LG09 were all forward landing grounds used by the unit.

Another ditty, said to have originated in 70 Squadron but really an up-dated version of a very old RAF song applied to other aircraft dating back to the first world war, was sung to the tune *That Old-Fashioned Mother of Mine*.

There's an old-fashioned Wimpy
With old-fashioned wings,
With a fuselage tattered and torn.
She's got old-fashioned engines
All tied up with strings,
It's a wonder she's ever airborne.
Still she's quite safe and sound
'Cos she won't leave the ground
And there's something that makes her divine,
For the Huns up above are all taught to love
By that old-fashioned Wimpy of mine.

ASSOCIATED LITERATURE

The following past-published titles are of direct relevance to the Wellington story.

Vickers aircraft since 1908 .... C. Andrews; Putnam, 1969
Wellington Special .... A. Lumsden; Ian Allan, 1974
Wellington at War .... C. Bowyer; Ian Allan, 1982
Book of the Wellington .... RP Warplanes No.5, 1944
Wellington I & II .... C. Andrew; PROFILE No.125
Vickers Wellington Crash Log,
    1939-42 .... D.J. Smith; Private, n/d.
Wellington, Pilots Notes,
    APs 1578C/2068C/E .... HMSO, 1944-45
Famous bombers of WW2 .... W. Green; Macdonald, 1959
RAF Bomber Command & its   Moyes/Goulding; Ian Allan,
    aircraft, 2 Vols 1975-78
Aircraft of the RAF since 1918........ O. Thetford; Putnam, 1976
The British Bomber since 1914....... P. Lewis; Putnam, 1967
Bomber Squadrons of the RAF .... P. Moyes; Macdonald, 1964
Coastal & Support Squadrons
    of the RAF............................... J. Rawlings; Macdonald, 1982
9 Squadron .... T. Mason; Beaumont, 1965
Leads the Field (12 Sqn) .... T. Mason; Private, 1960
History of 15/XV Squadron .... N. Roberson; Private, 1975
History of 38 Squadron .... 38 Sqn, 1964
Special Operations (101 Sqn) .... R. Alexander; Private, 1979
Bomber Squadron at War
    (101 Sqn) .... A. Brookes; Ian Allan, 1983
Despite the Elements (115 sqn) ...... Private, 1983
In Brave Company (158 Sqn)......... Chorley/Benwell; Private, 1977
The Sky in our Ocean (311 Sqn) ..... Rijnhout/Rennison;
                                                          Private, 1980
We Find and Destroy (458 Sqn) ..... P. Alexander; 458 Sqn Council,
                                                          1959
Strike and Return (460 Sqn)........... P. Firkins; P. Brokensha, n/d
Barnes Wallis.............................. J. Morpurgo; Longman, 1972

Wellington Wings .... F. Chappell; Wm Kimber,
                                         1980

Pathfinder Cranswick.................... M. Cumming; Wm Kimber,
                                         1962

Wings of Night .... A. Hamilton; Wm Kimber,
                                         1977

Only Owls and Bloody Fools
  Fly at Night .... T. Sawyer; Wm Kimber, 1982
Aircraft versus Submarine .... A. Price; Wm Kimber, 1973
Men of Coastal Command, 1939-45.. C. Bowyer; Wm Kimber, 1985
The Strategic Air Offensive,   Webster/Frankland; HMSO,
  4 Vols 1961
RAF 1939-45, 3 Vols .... Richards/Saunders; HMSO,
                                         1953-4

RCAF Overseas, 3 Vols .... OUP, Toronto, 1944-49
RAAF Official History, 4 Vols .... AWM, 1954-63
New Zealand with the RAF, 3 Vols .. WHB (NZ), 1953-59
Bomber Command War Diaries ..... Middlebrook/Everitt;
                                         Macdonald, 1985

RCAF Squadrons & Aircraft.......... Kostenuk/Griffin; RCAF, 1977
Squadrons of the Fleet Air Arm ...... R. Sturtivant; Air Britain, 1984
Confound and Destroy (100 Group) . M. Streetly; Macdonald, 1978
Blida's Bombers .... Sqn Ldr E.M. Summers, MM;
                                         Private

The Desert Air Force .... R. Owen; Hutchinson, 1948
RAF Middle East Review,   HMSO
  1942-45 ....
RAF Middle East .... HMSO, 1945
Briefed to Attack .... H. Lloyd; Hodder &
                                         Stoughton, 1949

Night Strike from Malta................. K. Poolman; Jane's, 1980
Desert Air Force at War .... Bowyer/Shores; Ian Allan,
                                         1981

Spitfire Saga .... R. White; Kimber, 1981
Air War over Europe, 1939-45 .... C. Bowyer; Kimber, 1981
Guns in the Sky .... C. Bowyer; Dent, 1979
Bomber Barons .... C. Bowyer; Kimber, 1983
Tales from the Bombers.................. C. Bowyer; Kimber, 1985
For Valour – The Air VCs............... C. Bowyer; Kimber, 1978
The Thousand Plan....................... R. Barker; Chatto & Windus,
                                         1965

INDEX

Index

Place names

Wellington squadrons

Miscellaneous Units

`420 Flt	90	21 OTU	237, 244, 252
1417 Flt	192	23 OTU	254, 255
1443 Flt	257	26 OTU	244
1474 Flt	127	30 OTU	47
1 GRU	187, 188	55 OTU	131
2 GRU	188 f/n.	76 OTU	247
3 GRU	188 f/n.	77 OTU	261
11 OTU	249, 250, 253, 254	228 OCU	52
13 OTU	103	201 AFS	53
15 OTU	60, 222, 246, 267	1 ANS	37
20 OTU	256